Corporate Finance for Business

Ronny Manos · Keith Parker ·
D. R. Myddelton

Corporate Finance for Business

The Essential Concepts

Second Edition

palgrave
macmillan

Ronny Manos
The Faculty of Business
The College of Management Academic Studies
Rishon Lezion, Israel

Keith Parker
Cranfield University
Cranfield, UK

D. R. Myddelton
Cranfield School of Management
Cranfield University
Cranfield, UK

ISBN 978-3-030-92418-8 ISBN 978-3-030-92419-5 (eBook)
https://doi.org/10.1007/978-3-030-92419-5

Cover credit: Vanilllla/Shutterstock

This Palgrave Macmillan imprint is published by the registered company Springer Nature Switzerland AG
The registered company address is: Gewerbestrasse 11, 6330 Cham, Switzerland

Contents

List of Figures

List of Tables

Part I
Introduction

An Overview of Corporate Finance and the Structure of This Book

Corporate finance is concerned with the various decisions relating to sources and uses of finance in the corporation. The goal of these decisions is to create financial value for the owners of the firm, i.e. shareholders. This goal is called shareholder value maximization. It is achieved by making investment and financing decisions that result in the generation of returns to providers of capital over and above the minimum return they were expecting as compensation for giving the firm the use of their capital.

In order to maximize value to shareholders, the investment and financing decisions, that together make up corporate finance, aim to maximize profits, both in the long and short term. Figure 1 summarizes the corporate finance function and the structure of this book.

The book provides coverage of core concepts and techniques in the field of corporate finance. However, it is written at a point in time where corporate finance is evolving with social, economic and technological developments which have important implications for businesses.

For example, the 2008 global financial crisis has stimulated shifts in how we perceive finance, business and corporate citizenship. Such shifts in thinking contributed to the rise of the Social Business which aims to create social and/or environmental change while at the same time maintaining financial returns. Likewise, disappointment with avaricious bankers following the 2008 crisis added to the emergence of the Sharing-Economy company (e.g. Uber, Airbnb, and their likes), the business model of which is based on cutting intermediation, providing more choice to consumers, and sharing excess capacity. Certainly these innovative business models have great implications for the investments modern firms undertake. Moreover, some Social-Business and Sharing-Economy companies are also reshaping the finance industry and thus the way firms can raise finance (e.g. impact investment, peer-to-peer lending, crowdfunding).

Likewise, advances in technology have great implications for the way business is done and for the corporate finance function. Thus, using Business Intelligence means that data for decision making is readily available, while blockchain technology facilitates collaboration across the supply chain. Cloud computing allows companies to shift from capital-intensive investment to subscription-based cloud technology in the software as a service model.

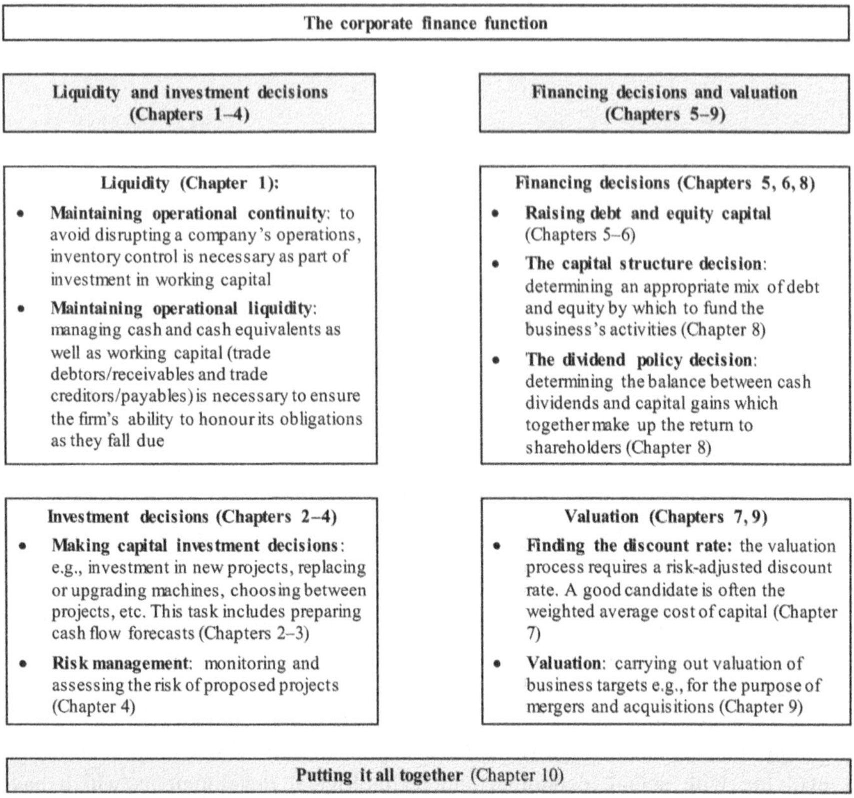

Fig. 1 The corporate finance function and the structure of the book

Indeed, as we were writing this book, the COVID-19 outbreak continued to disrupt small and large businesses, customers, markets and economies the world over. The pandemic has changed how businesses operate and people work. It has enhanced the rate of adoption of new technologies, finessed remote working and virtual interface and has consequently accelerated the challenges faced by the corporate finance function.

It is our argument, however, that despite those changes, the basic principles on which corporate finance is based, such as the time value of money or value creation, still apply. Take the dot.com bubble in the 1990s as one of many examples. In the early 1990s, the Internet created euphoria and high expectations with relation to technology companies and the future of online commerce. Investors' funds were poured into internet-based companies (offering, for example, online shopping, communication services and news) in the belief that they would be worth vast sums. Managers, owners and investors based their performance analysis on innovative metrics such as website traffic. It took the bursting of the bubble at the beginning of the 2000s, and the economic pain it caused to many, to remind us of the fundamental concepts in corporate finance. It turned out that cash flow forecasts, careful project appraisal and well thought-through financing decisions are as important in the internet era as they were before its advent. It is those fundamental concepts and techniques that are the topics of this textbook.[1]

[1] This book is a fully revised and updated edition of '*Managing Business Finance*' by D. R. Myddelton.

1 Cash and Working Capital

1.1 Introduction

In 2020, against the backdrop of the COVID-19 pandemic, an International Labour Organization survey of more than 4500 enterprises in 45 countries worldwide found that the greatest challenge businesses were facing had been cash management.[1] Indeed, over 60 per cent of surveyed enterprises reported that they did not have enough cash flow to pay salaries and maintain business operations and around a quarter anticipated losing more than 40 per cent of their staff. Micro and small enterprises as well as businesses in the tourism and hospitality sector were worst affected.

Even a profitable business, one whose revenues are higher than the costs borne in generating those revenues, can fail because of bad cash management—that is, not having enough cash to meet its liabilities as they fall due. Indeed, many of the businesses which went bankrupt during the COVID-19 and other crises were profitable when they collapsed. Another aspect of bad cash management is when the firm has lots of cash sitting idle, rather than being invested in profitable projects.

Thus, cash management—the way by which a company collects and invests its cash and cash-like items (cash equivalents)—is crucial to its survival. Cash flows in the firm arise from its operations, investment and financing activities, and the aim of cash management is to balance two needs. On the one hand, the firm needs to maintain liquidity—that is, the ability to quickly convert assets into cash without affecting their values. On the other hand, the firm needs to utilise resources effectively so that assets continuously generate sufficient returns to ensure the firm is profitable.

[1] *International Labour Organization* report entitled: '*A global survey of enterprises: Managing the business disruptions of COVID-19*' was published in Geneva and is available at https://www.ilo.org/global/about-the-ilo/newsroom/news/WCMS_762136/lang--en/index.htm.

R. Manos et al., *Corporate Finance for Business*,
https://doi.org/10.1007/978-3-030-92419-5_1

This chapter reviews cash and cash management. The next Sect. (1.2) discusses the meanings of cash and cash flows while Sect. 1.3 focuses on the differences between cash and profit. This is followed by Sect. 1.4 which is devoted to the issue of cash flow forecasting. To understand liquidity, we define and discuss working capital in Sect. 1.5. Working capital is the difference between the firm's current assets and current liabilities, the topic of the last three sections. In particular, Sect. 1.6 looks at inventory, Sect. 1.7 at receivables and Sect. 1.8 at payables. Section 1.9 concludes this chapter and is followed by some practice problems.

1.2 Cash

1.2.1 Why Do Firms Need Cash?

From a firm's point of view, 'cash' (sometimes 'liquid resources') is a current asset that comprises three items:

1. Cash in hand, which consists of notes and coins. Accountants call it 'petty cash', and in most businesses the amount is small.
2. Current accounts with banks (demand deposits), available to make payments by cheque or bank transfer or to draw out in cash. Such accounts don't usually earn interest.
3. Deposit accounts with banks (time deposits), which do earn interest; and can be converted into cash at short notice (often seven days).

Another current asset is 'marketable securities' which, for practical purposes, may be very similar to cash (cash equivalent).

Firms may need to have large sums of money available, for example, to pay wages or, from time to time, to pay for new equipment, to settle tax bills or to repay borrowing. Strictly speaking what one needs is not so much cash itself as the 'ability to pay'. Thus, most individuals now carry credit cards or various forms of digital money (e.g. PayPal, Google Pay, etc.) to let them make day-to-day purchases for which they might once have needed physical cash. In the same way, a firm which has arranged bank overdraft facilities may not need to hold any positive cash balance with its bank. It can simply instruct the bank to pay (e.g. using cheques/electronic cheques) or make transfers, up to the extent of its agreed borrowing limit.

1.2.2 Flows of Cash in Business

Cash flows are payments into the business and out of it. Cash inflows generally arise from three main sources, while outflows arise due to five types of uses. The sources of cash inflows include the following:

1. Owners (shareholders), who start the business with equity share capital (and sometimes contribute further share capital later).
2. Lenders (banks and others), who provide long-term or short-term funds.
3. Customers, in respect of goods or services sold to them.

Cash inflows from owners and lenders relate to financing activities while cash inflows from customers relate to operating activity. Moreover, funds deriving from sales to customers are sometimes referred to as internal finance, and funds directly from owners or lenders as external finance.

The five main activities that give rise to cash outflows in a business include the following uses:

1. Investing in long-term assets (also referred to as fixed assets, non-current assets or capital assets). Examples include buildings, property and equipment.
2. Investing in short-term ('current') assets, such as stocks of goods (inventory).
3. Paying wages, overheads and other current expenses.
4. Paying taxes to government.
5. Providing returns to investors, including paying interest to lenders and dividends to shareholders.

Cash outflows relating to long-term assets are part of the firm's capital investment activity. Thus, cash may be used to acquire assets with a useful economic life longer than a year, that are not intended for sale in the normal course of business but are expected to generate future cash inflows for the firm. In contrast, cash outflows relating to short-term assets are part of working capital investment (discussed later in this chapter). In this case, cash is used to ensure the firm can meet its short-term liabilities. Likewise, cash outflows relating to wages, overheads, taxes and other expenses are part of the firm's operating activity, while payments to owners and lenders are part of its financing activity.

Figure 1.1 shows the main sources of funds (which create cash inflows) and uses of funds (which create cash outflows) in business.

1.2.3 Free Cash Flow

'Free cash flow' represents the excess of net cash generated above the level of reinvestment needed to maintain the scale of the business in future. In practice, it is often difficult to measure precisely how much spending on fixed assets is for 'replacement' and how much represents 'expansion'; hence it is hard to determine the amount of 'free cash flow' accurately.

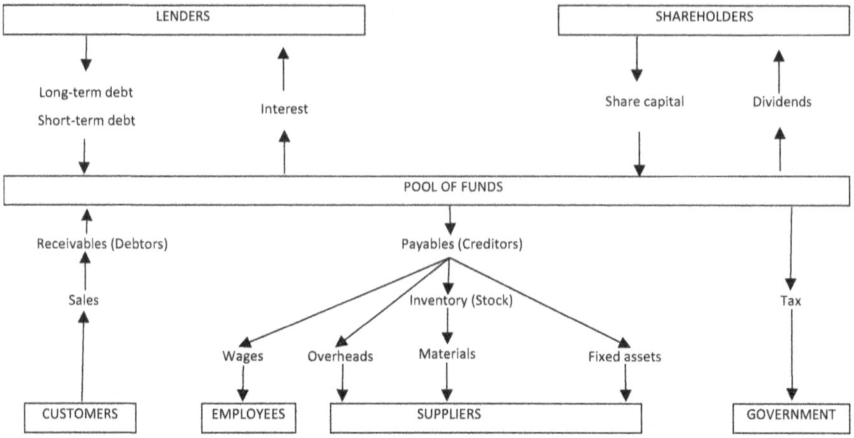

Fig. 1.1 Main flows of funds in business

1.3 Cash and Profit

1.3.1 Cash and Profit are Different

Cash and profit are two of the main concerns of the financial manager. Both are important, but they are different. Cash is a liquid asset owned by a business, a means of payment enabling it to buy goods or services. A firm's cash balance can be either too large (earning a low rate of return) or too small (risky). Profit is an accounting measure of improvement in well-being, the surplus earned after deducting all business expenses from sales revenues and other income for a period. In general, the larger the profit the better.

Table 1.1 lists and classifies some of the main differences between cash and profit. It shows that most of these differences disappear sooner or later. Most items relate to the short run (such as amounts owing for credit sales); some relate to the medium-term (depreciation of fixed assets and borrowing and repaying loans); and only a few items remain different through much of a company's life (non-depreciable fixed assets such as land, and new issues or buy-backs of share capital).

In 'accrual' accounting, the amount of expenses charged in a period will usually not equal the amount of cash paid out. The reason is that in accrual accounting revenues and expenses are recorded when the transaction occurs, which is not necessarily when payment is received or funds paid out. The idea of accrual accounting is that for reporting purposes, it makes sense to match revenues with the costs associated with generating them. For example, where a firm acquires tangible fixed assets for cash, it does not deduct the whole cost from profit in the same accounting period. Instead, the firm's accounts charge only a fraction of the cost as depreciation expense in each period of the asset's life.

If a firm sells goods for more than they have cost, it has made a profit. But until the customers have paid for the goods, it may have no cash. In contrast, when a

Table 1.1 Why profit and cash may differ

Items that appear in the Income Statement (P&L a/c) but are not cash flows	
Expense:	**Balance sheet effect:**
1. Purchase on credit	1. Accounts payable (creditors) up
2. Tax charge not yet paid	2. Tax liability up
3. Write off bad debt or stock/inventory	3. Accounts receivable (debtors) or inventory down
4. Depreciation of fixed assets	4. Net fixed assets down
Income:	**Balance sheet effect:**
1. Sale on credit	1. Accounts receivable (debtors) up
2. Reduce provision for expense	2. Provisions (liabilities) down
3. Share of subsidiary/associate profit	3. Fixed asset investment up
Items that are cash flows but do not appear in the Income Statement (P&L a/c)	
Payment:	**Balance sheet effect:**
1. Purchase of stock/inventory for cash	1. Inventory/stock up (offset by cash down)
2. Payment of account payable (creditor)	2. Accounts payable (creditors) down (offset by cash down)
3. Purchase of fixed asset for cash	3. Fixed assets up (offset by cash down)
4. Pay dividend, buy back shares	4. Equity down (offset by cash down)
Receipt:	**Balance sheet effect:**
1. Credit customers pay	1. Accounts receivable (debtors) down (offset by cash up)
2. Sale of fixed asset for cash	2. Fixed assets down (offset by cash up)
3. Borrow long term	3. Long-term liabilities up (offset by cash up)
4. Issue share capital for cash	4. Equity up (offset by cash up)

business borrows money, the immediate result is to increase its cash balance. But no company would dream of treating the amount borrowed as a profit! It will have to repay the loan in due course.

Are cash flows less open to 'creative accounting' than reported profits? Probably not: in the short run firms can manipulate cash flows even more easily than accrual accounting numbers by means of 'leads and lags'. For instance, they can delay many cash payments (or cash receipts) for a while. The accounting principle requiring consistency of treatment over time is an important safeguard for readers of accounts. In the long run, it can be much more difficult to affect cash flows, but the same is true of accounting profits.

1.3.2 Cash Flow and Depreciation

The financial press often uses the term 'cash flow' to mean 'retained profits plus depreciation' for a period. The point is that depreciation is merely an accounting entry in the period in which it appears as an expense. By spreading the cost of the asset as depreciation expense over the economic useful life of the asset, depreciation is merely the articulation of the matching principle of accounting (i.e. matching income with the expense incurred in generating it).

In contrast, the only cash payment involved in the purchase for cash of a fixed asset is the transaction at the start of its life. So, since the accounts have deducted depreciation expense from turnover in measuring profit, it needs to be 'added back' in order to translate the figure for profit into an estimate of 'cash flow' for the period. (Depreciation is not the only item in the Income Statement which may not represent cash—see Table 1.1—but it may often be the most important item.)

1.3.3 Cash or Profit: Which Matters More?

Both cash and profit matter, but people sometimes wonder whether one matters more than the other. A firm which discovers a profit opportunity *ought* to be able to raise enough money to finance the project if capital markets are working properly. From that viewpoint, profit matters more than cash.

And what about share prices? Is it profit (usually measured as earnings per share, i.e. the profit for the year divided by the number of shares in issue) or cash flow that drives share prices? Since profit and cash often tend to move together, it can be hard to tell. Some years ago, US tax rules allowed companies to switch from first in, first out (FIFO) to last in, first out (LIFO) in valuing inventory. This would reduce reported profits, but it would also reduce tax payable and thus *increase* cash. Shares in companies that made the change performed better than shares in companies which chose not to. Conclusion: where earnings per share and cash flow moved in opposite directions, cash seemed to matter more than profits.

Still, 'creative' accounting may sometimes fool readers of accounts into making wrong estimates of the future, which can then affect share prices. And managers may be very concerned about the amount of earnings their companies report if their pay partly depends on it.

1.4 Cash Flow Forecasting

1.4.1 Two Methods of Cash Flow Forecasting

No company wants to run out of cash. Creditors that a company was unable to pay might force it into liquidation; or at least it might have to raise funds at a very high cost, and subject to burdensome conditions. A company's cash balance should be high enough to protect against any serious chance of running out, but not so high as to tie up excess funds in low-yielding uses. Financial managers of a business must decide what cash levels to aim at. Then they need to forecast the amount and timing of likely future sources and uses of cash.

Cash flow forecasting is the process of preparing a detailed forecast of cash inflows and outflows over the coming period. It requires an estimation of the amount and timing of future cash receipts and payments and has the following benefits:

1. It tests in advance the financial results of plans, before making firm commitments.
2. It reveals possible future needs to raise more capital, which may take time to arrange.
3. It helps avoid piling up non-interest-bearing cash.

There are two key methods of forecasting cash flows, the 'receipts and disbursements' method and the 'projected (pro forma) balance sheet method'. We shall now discuss each method in turn.

1.4.2 'Receipts and Disbursements' Method of Cash Flow Forecasting

The 'receipts and disbursements' method involves preparing a future-looking schedule of the firm's cash inflows (receipts) and cash outflows (payments). This approach is useful for short-term forecasting when it is possible to identify cash flows with acceptable accuracy.

Under this method, a cash flow schedule is prepared for projected cash receipts and, separately, for cash payments (disbursements). The schedules are based on cash flows rather than on the accrual basis of accounting because the aim is not to estimate future earnings, but to anticipate the amounts and timing of future cash inflows and outflows.

Once ready, the two schedules are combined, to create a projected ending cash balance. In what follows we briefly discuss the preparation of the two schedules. It is important to note that we are dealing with a forecast where many items are not easy to predict with precision.

1.4.2.1 The Schedule of Cash Receipts

The schedule of cash receipts is based mainly on projected sales as this nearly always represents a firm's main source of cash receipts. Forecasting cash receipts from sales may be subject to a large margin of error, since it depends on three different estimates, each of which may vary:

1. The physical volume of sales.
2. The average selling price per unit.
3. The average delay in payment (credit period taken) by customers.

In addition, the cash receipts schedule will also include non-recurring cash inflows such as from the disposal of old equipment, as well as cash inflows from investments (i.e. interest or dividends). There may also be capital transactions that give rise to cash inflows, such as borrowing, or issuing new share capital.

Importantly, the schedule of cash receipts must also include the beginning cash balance (the ending cash balance from the previous period). Example 1.1 illustrates the preparation of the cash receipts schedule, the first part of the cash flow forecasting under the 'receipts and reimbursements' method. For simplicity, Example 1.1. assumes there were no non-recurring cash inflows nor any cash inflows from investments:

Example 1.1—Preparing the Cash Receipts Schedule

A financial manager is preparing a six-month cash forecast beginning in January. She decides to start by estimating cash receipts from sales, with the following basic assumptions:

- Sales revenue will be £200,000 a month for the first three months, rising to £250,000 for April and May, and to £300,000 in June.
- 10 per cent in value of the sales are expected to be for cash; the rest on credit terms resulting in the collection of cash on average one month after the date of the credit sale.
- At the beginning of the period receivables amount to £185,000.

Table 1.2 translates these assumptions into a schedule of month-by-month expected cash receipts from sales. Cash received in the period differs from the value of goods sold, due to credit.

Over the whole six months the totals are as follows:

	£'000
Opening receivables	185
Add: Total sales	1,400
	1,585
Less: Closing receivables	270
= Cash received in period	1,315

Table 1.2 Cash receipts schedule: January to June (£'000)

£'000	January	February	March	April	May	June	Total
(1) Total sales	200	200	200	250	250	300	**1,400**
(2) Credit sales (90% of sales)	180	180	180	225	225	**270**	1,260
(3) Cash sales (10% of sales)	20	20	20	25	25	30	140
(4) Accounts receivable paid up (1 month delay)	**185**	180	180	180	225	225	1,175
(5) Total cash inflow from sales (3 + 4)	205	200	200	205	250	255	**1,315**

As compared with total sales of £1,400,000, there is an £85,000 shortfall of cash received (at only £1,315,000). This results in an £85,000 increase in receivables between the start and end of the period (from £185,000 to £270,000).◄

1.4.2.2 The Schedule of Cash Disbursements

The schedule of cash disbursements will include cash payments relating to inventory purchases, as well as payments relating to other operating expenses such as payroll, rent, utility bills, etc. Other cash payments to appear on the disbursements schedule include those relating to taxes and to financing activity, such as debt repayments, interest, dividends and share repurchases.

Cash payments for operating expenses often relate fairly closely to sales volume, after allowing for time-lags. Though stocks of materials may vary for a number of reasons (see later in this chapter), purchases of materials normally vary more or less with expected future sales. Suppliers will probably allow a credit period, so payment of cash in respect of purchases may occur at about the same time as sales are made (though somewhat before they are paid for by the client).

Short-term sales fluctuations may not much affect some other expenses. The labour force, for example, may be fairly stable in the short term. And many overhead expenses, such as office rent, utilities, etc. may be more or less 'fixed' (both in amount and in timing) in the short term. It may be more difficult to forecast discretionary expenses, such as advertising and staff training. These can be subject to change at short notice.

1.4.3 Pro Forma Balance Sheets Method of Cash Flow Forecasting

An alternative to the 'receipts and disbursements' cash flow forecast method is the 'projected (pro forma) balance sheet' method of forecasting funds requirements. It involves a forecast of *all* balance sheet items (not just cash) at a definite future date, including four major steps:

1. Forecasting the net total amount for each of the assets.
2. Listing the liabilities:
   (a) that will occur without special negotiation (such as trade payables and taxation);
   (b) that have to be specifically arranged (such as bank overdrafts).
3. Estimating profits for the period, less dividend payments. Since profit is a residual between two much larger amounts (sales turnover, less total expenses), this may be subject to a wide margin of error.
4. Totalling the estimates of assets, liabilities and shareholders' funds, to reveal whether there remains a surplus or shortage of funds on the date chosen. Any surplus would somehow be invested, and a projected shortage might be covered

by raising more money, or in some other way (such as reducing one or more assets).

As stated, the pro forma balance sheet method forecasts all the balance sheet items, not just cash. It can help forecast certain financial ratios, such as return on net assets (RONA)[2] which enables the firm to assess how well it utilizes assets to generate profit (or, indeed, it may be based on the assumption that certain financial ratios remain constant). It can also make rough—but often helpful—forecasts where forward plans may not yet exist in sufficient detail to allow cash flow forecasting.

The method forecasts balance sheet amounts only at the end of the period, not during the interim. It will therefore reveal maximum needs for funds only if the balance sheet date represents a moment of maximum strain. (If there is doubt about the most suitable date to choose, one can always make several projections at different dates.) Moreover, it is often worth noting in writing the key assumptions which underlie the forecasts; and it can be useful to try to assess the rough margin of error in the key items. Use of spreadsheets makes it easy to prepare detailed forecasts and to test them by varying the assumptions (e.g. using sensitivity analysis—a method we discuss in Chapter 4).

Using the same assumptions, the 'projected (pro forma) balance sheet' method and the 'receipts and disbursements' method should (of course) produce the same estimate for the end-of-period cash balance. The pro forma balance sheet method forces an explicit assumption about fixed assets and the components of working capital. These may be very important; yet they can be surprisingly easy to overlook in a cash flow forecast.

1.5 Working Capital

As previously mentioned, a company may be profitable and endowed with assets, yet may find it difficult to honour its liabilities as they fall due; that is, may lack liquidity. The cash flow forecast may help the firm to ascertain its free cash flow which represents the excess of net cash inflow over the level of reinvestment needed to maintain the scale of the business in future (e.g. paying bills, wages and suppliers on time).

But even if the firm does not have sufficient cash to pay its debts, it may have sufficient current assets that can be easily converted into cash. The difference between the firm's current assets and current liabilities is its working capital,

[2] $RONA = \frac{Net\,profit}{Fixed\,assets + (Current\,assets - Current\,liabilities)}$. Note (see later in this chapter) that: $Current\,assets - Current\,liabilities = Working\,capital$.

as defined in Eq. 1.1:

$$\begin{aligned}
Working\,capital &= Current\,assets - Current\,liabilities \\
&= (Inventory + Receivables + Cash\,and\,cash\,equivalents) \\
&\quad - (Payables\,and\,accruals) \qquad (1.1)
\end{aligned}$$

[Note that some authors differentiate between Gross Working Capital, that is, just the firm's current assets, and Net Working Capital, which corresponds to Eq. 1.1, which deducts current liabilities from the current assets. Henceforth, when we refer simply to 'working capital', we strictly mean *net* working capital.]

There are a number of ratios that are based on the working capital. For example, the return on net assets ratio (which measures how well a firm utilizes its assets to generate income) uses the working capital figure as part of its denominator (see footnote 2 in this chapter). Likewise, the working capital ratio (sometimes referred to as the current ratio), which is the ratio of current assets to current liabilities, indicates whether the firm has sufficient current assets to cover its short-term liabilities, and is an indication of liquidity:

$$Working\,capital\,(or\,current)\,ratio = \frac{Current\,assets}{Current\,liabilities} \qquad (1.2)$$

In addition to the working capital ratio there is the acid-test ratio which compares the firm's current assets *excluding inventory* (i.e. its cash and accounts receivable) to its current liabilities.

The formula for calculating it is:

$$\text{Acid-test ratio} = \frac{Current\,assets - inventory}{Current\,liabilities} = \frac{Cash + accounts\,receivable}{Current\,liabilities} \qquad (1.3)$$

Like the working capital ratio, the acid-test ratio is also a measure of liquidity. It is, however, a stricter measure of short-term liquidity as it excludes inventory from current assets, presuming that inventory is a less liquid current asset compared to cash and accounts receivable (which are often referred to as 'quick assets'). Another popular ratio to measure the firm's liquidity is the working capital to sales ratio, calculated by taking working capital as a percentage of annual sales. The working capital to sales ratio (normally shown as a percentage) tells the firm what is the proportion of sales that go to finance working capital (i.e. for meeting liquidity):

$$Working\,capital\,to\,sales\,ratio = \frac{Working\,capital}{Sales} \times 100 \qquad (1.4)$$

Thus, working capital as well as the ratios that use it, provides useful tools to measure and manage liquidity.

1.5.1 Liquidity

We already discussed the importance of liquidity: the ease with which an owner can turn an asset into cash. Liquidity refers to both the speed and the certainty of turning assets into cash. In a perfect capital market, liquidity would not matter since an asset's owner would always be able to borrow its full value. But in the real world it may often be easier to turn cash into assets than assets into cash.

As usual, managers need to seek a balance. Having too little liquidity might lead to problems in paying bills; while having too much might result in a low rate of return. Managing working capital, in particular by controlling the *working capital cycle*, is crucial for maintaining liquidity.

1.5.2 The Working Capital Cycle

We have seen that working capital is the excess of current assets over current liabilities. It is defined as inventory plus receivables plus cash, minus trade payables and accruals. The two largest items that normally make up working capital are inventory and receivables (see Eq. 1.1). These two items represent a firm's investment in goods which are unfinished, unsold or unpaid for. In some countries these together can amount to nearly half the total of all assets of listed companies. Thus, in view of its size, working capital is clearly important to many firms, large and small, and a useful tool with which to manage it is the working capital cycle.

The working capital cycle (sometimes referred to as the cash conversion cycle) is defined as the time it takes (in days) to convert current assets into cash:

$$Working\,capital\,cycle = Inventory\,days + Receivables\,days - Payables\,days \tag{1.5}$$

where:

1. $Inventory\,days = \frac{Inventory}{Cost\,of\,goods\,sold} \times 365$. How long it takes the firm to convert its inventory into sales (to sell its inventory). The shorter, the better.
2. $Receivables\,days = \frac{Accounts\,receivable}{Sales} \times 365$. How long it takes the firm to collect cash after the sale of goods/services (or how long it takes debtors to pay you).
3. $Payables\,days = \frac{Accounts\,payable}{Cost\,of\,goods\,sold} \times 365$. How long it takes the firm to pay its trade creditors.
4. Cost of goods sold = the direct cost of producing the goods or services the firm provides.

The cost of goods sold includes the costs of labour and materials directly used in the production process (although note that some of these costs are not paid for on credit, such that the payables days figure as calculated in 3. above is often not very accurate). It is sometimes expressed as a proportion of sales:

$Cost\ of\ goods\ sold\ ratio = \frac{Cost\ of\ goods\ sold}{sales} \times 100$. (Also called the cost of sales to revenue ratio).[3]

As shown in Equation 1.5, the working capital cycle measures how long the firm's cash is tied up as inventory. A short working capital cycle indicates efficient working capital management. As an illustration, if inventory days is 60, receivables days is 30 and payables days is 40, then the working capital cycle is $(60 + 30 - 40) = 50$. It means the firm has to wait 50 days from buying the raw material to produce a product until it receives payment for the final good.

Later in this chapter (see Example 1.2 in Sect. 1.7) we illustrate how to calculate one of the three components of the working capital cycle of Eq. 1.5 (receivables days). Before that, a more practical illustration of the working capital cycle is the significant impact that the COVID-19 pandemic had on it during 2020. In their annual Working Capital Report 2020, PwC UK[4] found that between the second quarter of 2019 and the second quarter of 2020, business revenue had decreased by 16 per cent, leading to a 5 day increase in the working capital cycle. According to the report, the most significant change was in inventory days, which increased by eight days.

One way for a firm to shorten its working capital cycle is to increase the length of time it takes to pay its payables (see Eq. 1.5). However, although this may be a quick fix to improve the working capital cycle in the short term, it is not a sustainable solution for the long term.

Indeed, in its *Working Capital Report for 2019/20*, PwC[5] reports that payables days had *decreased* for the second successive year, demonstrating that increasing payables days is not a practical ongoing working capital management strategy.

A firm needs to determine a suitable level of investment in working capital—and then carry out the policy. Managers may 'decide', for example, that receivables should average no more than one month's credit sales; but someone still needs to make sure that the customers owe no more than that. In other words, working capital does need to be 'managed'.

Figure 1.2 shows the working capital cycle of a manufacturing business. The business first buys raw materials on credit (creating accounts payable), then uses labour and capital equipment (in various proportions in different industries) to

---

[3] Note that gross profit is the difference between *sales* and *cost of goods sold*, and the *gross profit margin* (or *gross margin ratio*) is the ratio of gross profit to sales:

$$Gross\ margin\ ratio = \frac{Gross\ profit}{Sales} \times 100 = \frac{Sales - Cost\ of\ goods\ sold}{Sales} \times 100$$

As you can see, the relationship between *cost of goods sold ratio* and the *gross margin ratio* is as follows:

$$Gross\ margin\ ratio + Cost\ of\ goods\ sold\ ratio = 100\%$$

[4] PwC UK, Working Capital Study 20/21 "Act Now to Recover" available at: https://www.pwc.co.uk/services/business-restructuring/insights/working-capital-study.html.

[5] PwC, Working Capital Report 2019/20: "Creating value through working capital—Unlocking cash in a digital age" available at: https://www.pwc.com/gx/en/services/deals/business-recovery-restructuring/working-capital-opportunity.html.

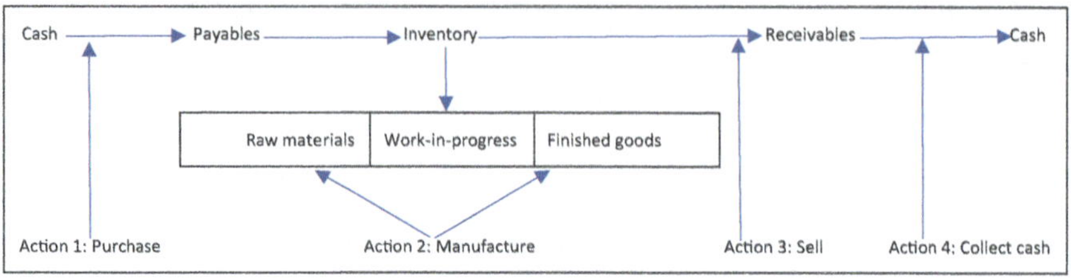

Fig. 1.2 The working capital cycle

convert them into finished goods. Often there are intermediate stages of partly-completed goods, known as work-in-progress.

On the sale of the finished goods, legal title passes to the customer (creating accounts receivable); and it is at this point that Accounts recognize the sale and the profit thereon. The customer either pays cash or buys on credit. If the latter, when the debtor finally pays cash to settle their account, they complete the transaction (the firm collects the cash). Where the customer orders goods which then have to be made, the sale is recognized when manufacture is completed, and the goods are delivered.

Thus, the working capital cycle involves using cash to acquire raw materials, to pay for overheads and to pay labour wages to convert materials over time into finished goods, which the firm then sells to customers who finally pay for them. A profitable business should receive more cash at the end than it pays out ('invests') during the working capital cycle. This is in order to pay at least the following: (a) taxes on profits; (b) interest on borrowing; (c) dividends to shareholders and (d) the replacement cost of capital assets.

In times of inflation, merely increasing the money amount of assets may not represent 'real' growth. This serious accounting problem affects both planning cash flows and measuring profit or loss. It is a worrying sign if a company can only maintain its existing level of business by raising more long-term capital. A healthy firm ought to be able at least to maintain its present real size out of internally generated cash flow, though it may have to raise new long-term capital in order to finance real expansion.

1.5.3 Financing Current Assets

A hotel may always be full even though no single person is permanently resident. In the same way, each item in working capital may be 'current' (since individual items of inventory and receivables are continually turning into cash), but the net total may in effect represent a long-term investment requiring long-term finance to support it.

Some companies' current assets may fluctuate during the year, perhaps because of seasonal sales or production patterns. For example, garden equipment sales may

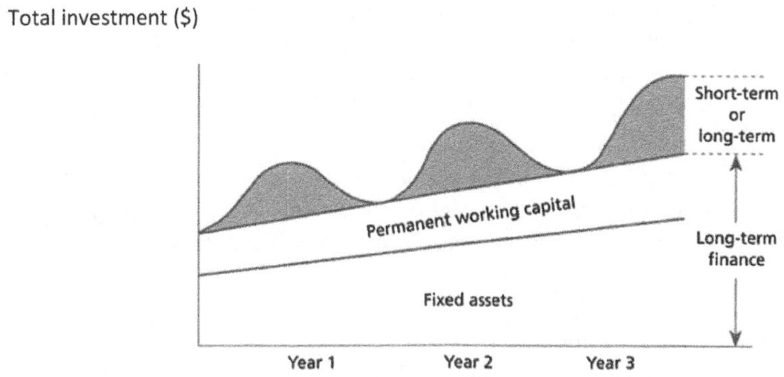

Fig. 1.3 Financing seasonal current assets

be highest during the spring and early summer, whereas toy sales may tend to peak towards Christmas. Figure 1.3 shows two approaches to financing short-term peaks.

A cautious company may aim to finance its maximum need by long-term funds. This low-risk policy will leave surplus cash to invest (at a fairly low rate of return) during the off-peak period. A more aggressive company, in contrast, may finance only its minimum level of net current assets with long-term funds. It will be in the riskier position of needing short-term finance during the seasonal peak; but by restricting its financing to what it needs it may hope for higher returns for shareholders. In either case, the net accounting total of 'working capital' may actually be fairly constant—since short-term surplus cash or short-term borrowing (negative cash) would both themselves count as part of the 'net working capital' amount.

As shown in Eq. 1.1, working capital is made up of inventory, receivables, cash and payables. We have discussed cash at some length, and it is now time to discuss the other three components of working capital.

1.6 Inventory

1.6.1 Types of Inventory

Money invested in inventory ties up financial resources which a firm could have used elsewhere. This represents a real *opportunity cost*. We shall discuss this term in Chapter 2, but in essence, an *opportunity cost* is the loss of potential gain from the next best alternative that is forgone when the course of action in question is chosen. For example, when purchasing inventory, it means that the money used cannot be deposited in the bank to earn interest. Thus, the interest lost is the opportunity cost of money being tied up in inventory.

As shown in Figure 1.2, a manufacturing company holds three main types of inventory: (1) raw materials; (2) work-in-progress and (3) finished goods. Most firms also hold stationery and maintenance supplies for use in the course of business. (They are usually included with raw materials inventory.)

Inventory is normally stated in accounts 'at cost' (or net realisable value if lower). The 'cost' of bringing a product to its present location and condition includes production overheads, based on the normal level of activity.

What determines inventory levels? In general, the following could explain inventory levels:

1. the level of sales volume
2. the relationship between production and sales
3. the nature of the production process
4. the cost of holding inventory.

Service industries tend to have low inventory because they usually cannot 'store' their products in finished form. The same may be true of some 'manufacturing' companies, such as newspaper publishers.

The first component of inventory, namely **raw materials**, represents a buffer between outside suppliers and the demands of the production process. The level depends mainly on buying aspects including:

1. the nature of the goods, i.e. whether they are perishable, bulky, expensive
2. possible interruptions to supplies, e.g. from crop failures
3. opportunity for economies of bulk purchasing
4. expected changes in future prices and in sales volume
5. how quickly suppliers can deliver more supplies of components.

As an example, Toyota is believed to be the first organization to apply the '*just in time*' (JIT) approach of delivering components several times a day. The aim is to reduce the waiting time for components while simultaneously minimizing holding costs. Thus Toyota, other Japanese car manufacturers and other organizations that subsequently adopted the JIT system, used it as a means of meeting consumer demand with minimum delays.

Second in inventory components is **work-in-progress** which depends largely on the following:

1. method of production, such as batch versus flow
2. the importance of set-up costs
3. the length of the process. For example, bakeries will have lower work-in-progress than shipyards
4. whether subcontracting is possible.

Managing the process is likely to be important; for example, trying to eliminate bottlenecks.

Finally, **finished goods inventory** represents a buffer between customers' demand and possibly intermittent supply from the purchasing or manufacturing side of the business. The level depends mainly on selling aspects:

1. whether the firm is making goods to order
2. the reliability of sales forecasts
3. the number of product lines and the range of choice for customers
4. policy on the risk of stock-outs
5. expected changes in sales volume.

Costs of holding inventory will vary for different industries, and may include such items as handling costs, storage costs, insurance and obsolescence, as well as interest on the money amount tied up. Average inventory holding costs may total as much as 25 per cent of book value a year, hence there is a clear need to balance the benefits from holding inventory at any given time against the costs. Too little inventory may delay the production process or fail to satisfy customers; too much may be very expensive and risk decay or obsolescence.

1.6.2 Managing Inventory

Forecasting whether a change in sales volume is temporary or more permanent can be crucial in deciding whether to change the rate of production or of purchasing. A wrong decision could mean either piling up unwanted inventory or else running out of inventory and thus losing potential sales. Either could be very expensive. The essence of business is judging the direction, extent and timing of changes in market conditions in an uncertain future. Box 1.1 illustrates how disruptions to supply chains could be triggered by unexpected conditions in the market.

Box 1.1: Nando's Chicken's Disruptions To Supply Chains That Were Triggered By The COVID-19 Crisis Highlight The Complexities Of Managing Inventories[a]

Peri-peri chicken fans were disappointed and frustrated when Nando's announced the temporary closure of nearly 50 restaurants. A chicken shortage has been blamed, presenting a serious challenge for the company. Hungry customers will no doubt be asking whether the supply could have been better managed. Similar questions were more widely raised at the beginning of the pandemic when supermarkets ran out of toilet roll and flour.

The current shortages of chicken at Nando's are due to disruptions in supply, which could not necessarily have been expected. Inventory control systems usually base their stock calculations on a regular lead time (the length of time from placing an order to when the product arrives and is ready for the customer). If there are occasional minor variations in the lead time, the calculations can be adjusted accordingly. But, such an approach breaks down if there is a sudden major problem unlike any others that have gone before.

In this situation, we should have some sympathy for Nando's. It would be incredibly wasteful of them to carry large stocks of raw chicken in anticipation of a possible major disruption. If they were to do this in normal times, a significant proportion of meat would be unused and go off. Clearly, this is not a viable solution.

Instead, the problem of major disruptions calls for a different approach to forecasting, known as scenario planning. The problem at Nando's seems to have been caused by labour shortages at their suppliers. And while the timing of labour shortages could not have been anticipated, their occurrence—at some point—could have been foreseen. In a scenario planning exercise, managers imagine major causes of disruption that could happen in the future. This sort of exercise will never be perfect, and some events will remain uncovered, but this should not deter progress being made by thinking through potential supply chain problems and the company's response.

For example, if an organization is reliant on a single supplier for a product, then they may consider introducing a second supplier, who will also receive regular orders and can flex to respond to higher order volumes if there are problems with the first supplier. This can also help to address responses to unexpected spikes in demand. And if a problem affects all suppliers, then plans can be put in place to order larger quantities of substitute products.

[a] Extracts from Boylan, J., 'From Nando's Chicken to microchips: why pandemic shortages are hard to predict', The Week, 23.8.21, available at: https://www.theweek.co.uk/news/uk-news/953900/from-nandos-chicken-to-microchips-why-pandemic-shortages-are-hard-to-predict.

The scenario planning methods suggested by the writer in Box 1.1 will be discussed in detail in Chapter 4 (there, we shall refer to it as scenario analysis). An alternative method for controlling inventory levels is 'ABC analysis' presented in Fig. 1.4. This method assumes that a small proportion (say 20 per cent) of the total *number* of items will usually account for a large proportion (say 80 per cent) of the total *value* of all items. (It is sometimes called the '80/20' rule.)

The implication for management is fairly obvious. Rather than pay equal attention to all items, it may make better commercial sense to look first at the few Class A items which account for most of the value, then at Class B items, and only at the end consider the many small Class C items.

Another useful tool is to calculate the rate of inventory turnover in a period, by dividing the cost of goods sold in a period by the amount of inventory held.

Fig. 1.4 ABC analysis

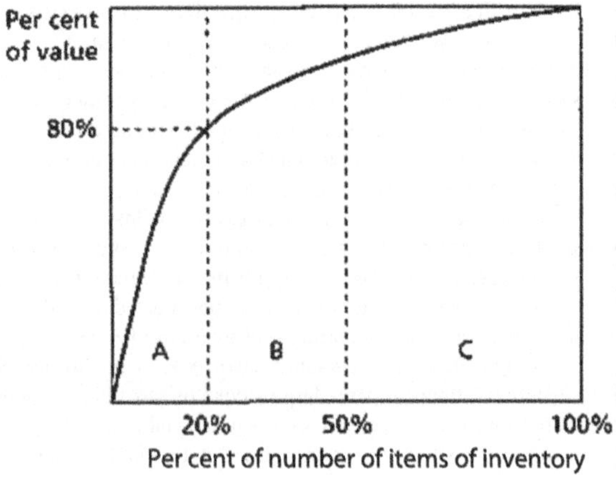

From a financial point of view, both production managers and sales managers may have reasons for preferring high levels of inventory (that is, low rates of inventory turnover). In practice, therefore, it is important to hold managers responsible for *all* the costs of holding inventory, including imputed interest.

In theory one can develop 'economic order quantity' (EOQ) models to determine the optimum pattern of re-ordering inventory. Such models attempt to balance the cost of holding inventory against the cost of reordering, in the context of annual usage. In practice there is often so much variation and uncertainty that commercial judgement is likely to be more important.

1.7 Receivables

1.7.1 Components of 'Receivables'

The current asset heading 'receivables' may include a number of items other than amounts due from trade customers (i.e. trade receivables), as listed in Table 1.3.

Table 1.3 Typical items included in 'receivables'

1. Trade receivables
Less provision for bad or doubtful debts
2. Proceeds due from disposal of fixed assets
3. Prepayments
4. Tax recoverable
5. Other receivables
6. Receivables due after one year

Trade receivables themselves are shown net of any provision for doubtful or bad debts. There may be proceeds due from the sale of fixed assets or of business units. Nearly always there will be some prepayments, for insurance, rent, etc. There may also be amounts due in respect of tax recoverable. Finally, often there are miscellaneous 'other' receivables.

1.7.2 Individual Customer Credit

Trade receivables may include individual or small business customers for whom the firm has provided credit. There are normally two decisions to make in advance about those customers: whether to extend credit at all; and, if so, up to what maximum amount. There are several ways to check the creditworthiness of potential new customers: credit bureau reports, past financial statements, bank references, trade references from other suppliers, and perhaps even the views of the selling firm's own sales people.

The credit control system should include a regular review of all customers, to ensure that they are not exceeding their maximum credit limits (either in amount or in time). But one must be realistic: people will tend to ignore unduly low credit limits.

Some customers ignore credit terms blatantly—either the total amount of credit or the period of credit taken. Ultimately there is an implied threat of legal action against customers who fail to pay amounts according to the credit terms agreed. But it is probably better to avoid this if possible: the supplier wants their money but dislikes the trouble and expense of taking formal legal action against the debtor.

One useful way to get money from overdue receivables can be simply to telephone and ask directly why they haven't paid. Some companies even telephone large customers *during* the credit period to confirm that they can expect to receive the amount owed on the due date. This also enables them to sort out any queries in good time. Such behaviour is not unreasonable; it is merely business-like.

In the end, however, a seller may prefer not to do business with a customer who takes too long to pay. The authors are aware of the tale of one of the UK's biggest book publishers which closed the credit account of a large book retailer 'because of persistent late payments over an extended period'. Publishers need retail outlets for their books; but the outlets also need suppliers.

1.7.3 Overall Credit Control

Regardless of the management of each individual credit customer, the firm also needs to manage its overall credit. A powerful simple tool for measuring receivables is to calculate '*Receivables days*', the average number of days' sales still owing at the end of a period. Receivables days is the second component of the working capital cycle (see Eq. 1.5), defined (see point 2, in the definitions for Eq. 1.5) as the ratio of accounts receivable to sales, multiplied by the number of days in the period, normally a year (365). Example 1.2 illustrates the calculation.

Example 1.2—Calculating Receivables Days

Sales for the past calendar year amounted to €180,000, and receivables at the end of December totalled €30,000. So, receivables days are 61 days:

$$Receivables\,days = \frac{Accounts\,receivable}{Sales} \times 365 = \frac{€30{,}000}{€180{,}000} \times 365 = 61\,days$$

Or we could do the sum in two stages:

1. $Daily\,sales = \frac{Sales}{365} = \frac{€\ 180{,}000}{365} = €493$
2. $Receivables\,days = \frac{Accounts\,receivable}{Daily\,sales} = \frac{€30{,}000}{€493} = 61\,days$

Let's assume that out of the €180,000 sales recorded last year, December sales accounted for €25,000 and November sales for €15,000. Assuming customers pay in date order, we could perform a more accurate estimate, relating to actual sales month by month rather than to averages.

Thus, using the sales information we have for the two months of November and December, and the end of December outstanding amount of €30,000, this would suggest:

1. all of December's €25,000 sales (=31 days)
2. plus €5,000 of November's €15,000 sales (= one-third of 30 days; about 10 days)

Thus, a total of (31 + 10)= 41 days.◀

The amount 'invested' in receivables (or 'accounts receivable') depends partly on the volume of credit sales. Since most firms want to increase sales volume, the main way of trying to control total credit outstanding is to limit the average period of credit taken by customers. This depends both on the credit terms offered and on the effectiveness of the seller's collection procedures.

Over four years, one major company reduced its average credit period from 137 days to 92 days. With sales of £600 million a month, the saving of 45 days' credit amounted to saving an investment in receivables of about £900 million! Even in times of low interest rates, the potential prize of the interest saved would certainly make the employment of a few competent credit controllers seem very worthwhile.

Good credit managers are quick to respond to changes in the overall pattern of receivables. They also tend to operate with specific targets, either in absolute money amounts or in terms of receivables days. Of course, proper management of receivables requires continual vigilance throughout the year.

If the average credit period which customers are taking is too high, or increasing beyond target, management must find out why. Has trade credit policy changed? Or the mix of customers changed (e.g. between domestic and export)? Is the company giving priority attention to the largest customers? Sending out invoices and statements promptly? Chasing up slow payers urgently enough?

1.7.4 Risk and Return from Receivables

Selling for cash avoids any need to 'invest' in receivables by (in effect) lending the debtors money. But most companies want to offer terms at least nearly as attractive as their competitors, as a marketing device. The two main risks in extending trade credit are that the customer will either take too long to pay, or else fail to pay at all (bad debts).

In practice opportunity losses[6] due to receivables taking too long to pay tend to be far more important than losses—although sometimes dramatic—due to bad debts. For example, some large companies or government departments are very bad debtors, in that they sometimes take a long time to pay, even though their accounts may be most unlikely to end up literally as 'bad debts'. Being 'important' customers (and knowing it), they often take much longer to pay than the official credit terms offered. Yet nobody doubts that they will pay all right *in the end.* In that sense they are 'good' debts, but often very slow. Time is money... The large company mentioned above, which succeeded in reducing by 1.5 months the average credit period taken by its customers, was notorious for taking a very long time to pay its own bills.

One way of viewing the opportunity cost of credit is to recognize the true cost of allowing a cash discount to customers who pay promptly. If customers on average take 45 days after invoice date before paying, then a 2 per cent discount for payment of cash within 10 days would cost 2 per cent for 35 days credit saved. This amounts to an annual rate of over 20 per cent a year ($2 \times 365/35 = 20.9$ per cent) which is likely to be far more than the company saves in interest by receiving the payment earlier. What matters here is the 45 days' credit which customers *actually* take on average, not the company's official credit terms of (say) 30 days.

There are two problems in practice with offering cash discounts for early payment, apart from the fact that they may need to amount to a high interest rate in order to be attractive. First, receivables/debtors who cannot pay soon enough to claim the cash discount may then choose to pay very late. Second, it can be tricky withdrawing the cash discount at a later date if the firm wants to change the policy.

Another possible approach would be to charge interest on overdue accounts, but this is not popular nor easy to implement (though threatening to charge interest may hurry some receivables up). Some countries have legitimized this by enshrining the right to charge interest on late payments in law, but with mixed success. Box 1.2. presents the UK government's instructions for charging interest on late commercial payments.

Box 1.2: Charging Interest on Late Commercial Payments: UK Government's Guidance[a]

"The interest you can charge if another business is late paying for goods or a service is 'statutory interest'—this is 8% plus the Bank of England base rate for business to business transactions. You cannot claim statutory interest if there's a different rate of interest in a contract.

[6] An opportunity loss refers to the value of a potential profit that was not realized because a course of action was taken that nullifies the chance to seize this opportunity. We referred to this earlier in the chapter by its alternative name, opportunity cost.

Example:
If your business were owed £1000 and the Bank of England base rate were 0.5%:

- the annual statutory interest on this would be £85 ($1{,}000 \times 0.085 = £85$)
- divide £85 by 365 to get the daily interest: 23p a day ($85 / 365 = 0.23$)
- after 50 days this would be £11.50 ($50 \times 0.23 = 11.50$).

Send a new invoice if you decide to add interest to the money you're owed.

[a] Late commercial payments: Charging interest and debt recovery, GOV.UK at https://www.gov.uk/late-commercial-payments-interest-debt-recovery/charging-interest-commercial-debt.

The 'return' from extending credit to customers consists of the marginal contribution to profit from the extra sales made (assuming that there would have been no sale without offering credit). Trade credit policy has to balance the possible return against the risk. Incurring *no* bad debts at all suggests that a firm is probably taking too few credit risks. In view of the likely returns foregone, it makes little sense to refrain from making sales on credit to 99 customers on the off-chance that the 100th customer may fail to pay the whole amount due.

1.7.5 Factoring

Factoring is another method of reducing the risk associated with receivables. It is a financing method by which a firm sells its accounts receivable for cash, but at a discount, to a third-party. It is a useful tool to increase the firm's liquidity by turning its accounts receivable into cash early.

Basically, and subject to variations, factoring works as follows:

1. Firm A selects a factoring company to which it sends invoices it has billed to its customers, due for payment sometime on a future date.
2. the factoring company pays firm A a percentage of the invoices and then handles the collection of the full payment from the customers of A.
3. the customers pay the invoices upon maturity, and the factoring company pays the remaining percentage of the invoices to firm A, less a factoring fee.

Thus, factoring is used to reduce the amount of working capital tied up in receivables. The factoring company buys some, or all, of the firm's debts, at full value less a factoring charge, and then undertakes to collect those debts. Sometimes any bad debts remain to be borne by the firm itself not by the factor (which affects the charges). Most factoring arrangements allow the factoring company to reject some customers, perhaps on grounds of poor creditworthiness. The factoring service may also include sales ledger administration (for an extra fee).

Reverse factoring (also known as supply chain finance) is an alternative method which also allows a company to improve its cash flow by reducing accounts receivable. Like factoring, reverse factoring allows the firm to receive early payment on its invoices, only this time the initiator is the buyer rather than the supplier as in traditional factoring. Sometimes the buyer allows suppliers early access to payment of their invoices in return for a discount.

Benefits for buyers from reverse factoring include:

1. strengthening relationships with their suppliers.
2. providing suppliers with early payment, thereby improving the suppliers' liquidity position. This reduces the risk that suppliers will encounter cash flow difficulties, causing disruption in supply chains.

Box 1.3 presents some challenges relating to factoring and reverse factoring (supply chain finance) that are likely to arise at any time, but particularly during periods of economic uncertainty when businesses, especially small ones, are exposed to risk and pressures.

Box 1.3: Factoring in Times of Crises[a]

In the current period of economic uncertainty, increasing pressure on businesses is making fraudulent activity an ever-present risk for lenders—a trend not only troubling for the affected company or companies, but also for the wider economy. In particular, corporate fraud has the potential to dissuade banks from lending—a dangerous outcome during a global crisis which has significantly constrained liquidity and limited funding for businesses.

Each year, fraud costs the global economy over US$5 trillion. However, fraud committed by companies accessing asset-based finance solutions, particularly those which rely on invoices, such as factoring and supply chain finance, can be especially difficult to catch. It is not uncommon for these instances of fraud to go undetected for years. It emerged last year, for example, that directors from a UK electrical goods wholesaler submitted £550,000 worth of false invoices from 44 false debtors to their factoring company over the span of 18 months before they were caught.

However, by implementing the correct processes and staff training, combined with sophisticated fraud prevention technology, factors can remain vigilant and detect the human and data related signs of fraud as they arise.

Circumstantial and premeditated fraud

Fraud in the factoring industry broadly falls into two categories: circumstantial and premeditated. The former generally happens when struggling businesses need cash urgently, but the necessary funding cannot be made available. As a result, opportunistic business-owners may produce an invoice slightly early and submit it to their factor for an advance payment.

This kind of fraudulent 'pre-invoicing' behaviour can be incredibly difficult for lenders to identify. And, while it may be committed by a borrower intending to legitimately raise the invoice, it can quickly evolve into a much greater problem of 'fresh air' invoicing, as the business-owner will likely continue to face the same underlying cash flow problem.

Unlike circumstantial fraud, premeditated fraud is a form of organised crime. Here, criminals target factors by creating fake businesses to represent the cash-limited supplier and its customer(s). To portray these businesses as legitimate, fraudsters create fake invoices to extract advances from the factor; they then use this money to 'pay off' the invoices, effectively recycling the factor's cash, generating the appearance of real cashflows and a growing business. This all seems fine until such time as the fraudsters go for 'the kill', take the money and disappear…..

[a] Extracts from a blog post by Kevin Day, CEO, HPD software, London. The blog post is entitled "How to prevent factoring and invoice finance fraud during the current COVID-19 crisis", published on 13 October 2020, by Finextra Research, and available at: https://www.finextra.com/blogposting/19408/how-to-prevent-factoring-and-invoice-finance-fraud-during-the-current-covid-19-crisis

1.8 Payables

1.8.1 Components of Payables

The amount of current liabilities (liabilities due to be paid within one year) to deduct from current assets determines the extent to which working capital needs long-term funds to finance it. Table 1.4 sets out a typical list of items of current liabilities, and they are discussed below.

First on the list of Table 1.4 is the item Trade payables. Suppliers tend to sell goods and services on credit rather than for cash, with a time lag of up to 3 months between supply and payment. Unlike bank overdrafts, trade credit usually needs little formal negotiation (except perhaps for new firms); yet for many companies it can be an important 'permanent' source of finance.

Purchasers should be aware of any cash discounts which suppliers are offering for prompt payment. The implied annual rate of interest can be high, so if financial resources permit it is often worthwhile taking advantage of them. Otherwise, at least purchasers should take the maximum credit period available. At the other end of the payment scale, it may seem almost cost-free to take extended credit from those suppliers that permit it. But the obvious risk is that the supply of goods or services may eventually stop, possibly at a most inconvenient time. Also, if supplies are ever short for some reason, good payers may well receive preferential treatment.

Table 1.4 Typical items included in 'current liabilities'

1. Trade payables
2. Accrued charges
3. Social security and other taxes
4. Corporation tax
5. Deferred income
6. Short-term borrowings

The average period of credit which a firm allows to customers is often similar to that which suppliers allow the firm itself, though the periods can vary in different industries. But the total *amount* of receivables may often be larger than the total for trade payables ('accounts payable'). Firms which add a lot of value will tend to have low trade payables, since a high proportion of their costs will comprise wages rather than raw materials or bought-in parts. Some other non-cash expenses, such as depreciation, will not appear in trade payables, which may, however, include amounts for purchases of fixed assets not yet paid for. Indeed, separate disclosure seems a good idea.

Second on the list is the item accrued charges. It consists of costs incurred for goods and services which suppliers have not yet invoiced. Typical examples might be utility charges, rent and business rates or audit fees. The total of accrued charges can be surprisingly large.

Social security and other taxes comes next, followed by corporation tax. Amounts owing for social security and other taxes include income tax and social security taxes deducted at source from employees' wages but not yet paid over to the authorities, as well as employers' social security 'contributions'. Amounts due for Value Added Tax or its equivalent are also included under this item. In contrast, corporation tax refers to tax payable on profits and it appears under a separate heading both in the Income Statement and in the Balance Sheet.

Deferred income follows. Some kinds of enterprise, for example, magazine publishers or schools, regularly receive significant amounts of income in advance of providing services. This is called 'income received in advance' or 'deferred income'. Any such amounts not yet fully earned by the end of a financial year obviously cannot be shown as revenue in that year's Income Statement. Instead, they appear as a separate item under current liabilities in the balance sheet. Strictly the current liability is to provide the service in future (normally within twelve months of the balance sheet date), not to pay money. But if, for some reason, the services were never provided, there would probably be a legal liability to repay at least a proportion of the amount received in advance.

Lastly, certain items of short-term finance, such as bank overdrafts and short-term loans, also form part of current liabilities. These short-term assets normally carry interest, and firms have to negotiate them specially.

1.9 A Concluding Note

If a company reports a profit of $500,000, it is not necessarily the case that it has this amount readily available. In other words, cash and profit are not the same.

Profit is the difference between revenues and the expenses incurred in generating it. The calculation of profit is based on the accruals principle, of recording revenue and expenses when a transaction occurs rather than when payment is received or made. In contrast, cash flow refers to money moving into and out of the business. With cash flows, the amount and timing of the payments are the determining factors, with no regard to matching between revenues and the expenses that generated them.

One key difference between profit and cash flows is the way that depreciation is treated. Depreciation is the spreading of the cost of an investment over its useful economic life. It is an application of the accounting principle of matching revenues with the costs of generating them. Thus, while depreciation is treated as an expense in calculating profit, it is not a cash flow item. The cost of the machine is recognized as a cash outflow when the payment is made.

Recording and forecasting cash flows is important for various reasons, an important one of which is to maintain operational liquidity—that is, the ability to honour obligations as they fall due. Indeed, failure to manage liquidity can have serious implications for the firm's ability to fund its day-to-day operations and to survive. This is true even for profitable firms!

Thus, to help maintain liquidity, the firm should also manage its working capital—the difference between current assets and current liabilities. The rationale here is that current assets, although not necessarily cash, can usually be converted into cash more easily and quickly than long-term assets such as property or machinery.

In this chapter we looked at cash, liquidity and working capital, and discussed cash flow forecasting. As previously noted, cash flow forecasting is helpful for liquidity management, but it is also a crucial step in the capital investment process, which is the topic of Chapters 2, 3 and, to some extent 4.

1.9.1 Problems

Problem 1.1 A company is set up with $200,000 cash; and during its first six months the following events and transactions occur:

- January: machinery is bought for $100,000 cash.
- February: goods are bought for $50,000 cash.
- March: the same goods are sold for $150,000 cash.
- April: further goods are bought for $200,000 cash.
- May: the goods are sold, on two months' credit, for $300,000.
- June: valuers reckon the machinery is now worth $80,000.

Calculate:

a) profit for the six-month period
b) cash flow from operations for the period
c) the end-of-June cash balance.

Problem 1.2 A firm buys a machine for £200,000, expecting it to last for ten years.

a) What depreciation would you suggest is charged each year as an expense against profits?
b) Assuming that annual pre-depreciation profits amount to £50,000, what would the annual post-depreciation profits be?
c) Would your answer to (a) change if annual pre-depreciation profits of only £15,000 were expected next year? Why or why not?
d) Soon after buying the machine, the firm decides it would be sensible to rely on only five years' useful life from the machine. Annual pre-depreciation profits were still expected to amount to £50,000 over ten years. What effect, if any, would this have on:
   i. the annual depreciation charge?
   ii. annual post-depreciation profits?
   iii. cash flow?

Problem 1.3 A company with current liabilities of £120,000 has the following current assets: inventory £80,000; receivables £60,000 and cash £40,000.

a) What is the current ratio?
b) What is the acid-test ratio?
c) What is the amount of working capital?

Problem 1.4 Centaur's accounts contain the following items:

- Annual sales: $5,000,000
- Cost of goods sold: $3,000,000
- Inventory: $400,000
- Receivables: $300,000
- Payables: $280,000.

Calculate:

a) (i) Working capital; (ii) Working capital cycle, and its components
b) (i) Cost of goods sold ratio; (ii) Gross profit; (iii) Gross profit margin ratio
c) (i) Current ratio; (ii) Acid-test ratio; (iii) Working capital to sales ratio.

Basic Capital Project Appraisal 2

2.1 Introduction

This chapter is one of the most important chapters of the book. Not only does it introduce key concepts in corporate finance, such as 'time value of money' and discounting, but it also illustrates the technicalities of discounting (e.g. how to discount 'annuities', perpetuities, etc.).

We start (Sect. 2.2) by introducing the underpinning rationale for the techniques we will be using throughout the rest of the book. This is followed (Sect. 2.3) with a discussion of the capital investment process. In Sect. 2.4 we introduce two simple methods that require little understanding of the concept of cash flow and the difference between cash flow and profit. We then have a section (Sect. 2.5) that provides the necessary background to using more sophisticated methods of project appraisal, namely the concept of the time value of money. The reader should then be ready for Sects. 2.6 and 2.7 where the principal tools for project appraisal are explained and illustrated. We end the chapter with a concluding note (Sect. 2.8), followed by some practice problems.

2.2 Shareholder Wealth Maximization

In a classic article dated September 1970 which was published in the *New York Times Magazine*, the American economist Milton Friedman argues that managers are the agents of shareholders. As such, their responsibility is to '*conduct the business in accordance with their desires, which will generally be to make as much money as possible while conforming to the basic rules of the society, both those embodied in law and those embodied in ethical custom*' (Friedman 1970).

By purchasing shares in a company, shareholders, who seek to earn high returns and to maximize the value of their investments, grant managers the right/responsibility to determine the projects in which their wealth is to be invested.

R. Manos et al., *Corporate Finance for Business*,
https://doi.org/10.1007/978-3-030-92419-5_2

In other words, shareholders delegate the investment decision to the managers of the company. Assuming that managers accept this responsibility and adopt the goal of shareholder wealth maximization, the techniques we describe in this chapter, and indeed, throughout the book, are based on achieving this goal.

As a caveat, it is important to note that due to *conflicts of interests*, which give rise to *agency costs* (see Chapter 8), it is sometimes argued that for various reasons managers do not always make decisions that are consistent with shareholder wealth maximization (e.g. they prefer to increase their personal corporate expense account instead of investing corporate money in high return projects). Others argue (most notably Edward Freeman in a 1984 book) that managers should not have only shareholder wealth maximization as their goal, but instead they should aim to maximize the wealth of all stakeholders (e.g. because by aiming to maximize wealth to shareholders, they fail to take account of the rights of other stakeholders such as employees or the community in which the firm operates) (Freeman 1984). However, bearing this caveat in mind, we continue under the assumption that corporate decisions are aimed at maximizing shareholder wealth.

2.3 The Capital Investment Process

2.3.1 An Overview of the Capital Investment Process

Capital investment means spending money (or resources) now in the hope of getting more back later. But this need not appear in the balance sheet as a fixed (non-current) asset: examples of 'revenue investments' might be research projects or promotion of brands. 'Investment' as such is not worthwhile: it needs to yield a profit. This applies even (perhaps especially) to so-called 'strategic' investments—though *measuring* profit can be very difficult.

There are several key stages in the investment process, as Table 2.1 shows. Probably the most important step is the first—finding worthwhile ideas for capital investments. They may stem from spotting opportunities or from responding to

Table 2.1 Key steps in the capital investment process

1. Generate ideas: opportunities and solutions to problems
2. Search out relevant information
3. Identify possible alternatives
4. Determine specific project details
5. Evaluate financial consequences
6. Assess 'non-financial' consequences
7. Make a decision
If to proceed:
1. Implement and control the project
2. Monitor results

problems in all areas of the business. This requires alertness, imagination and a commercial way of thinking.

Another aspect of finding worthwhile projects is to identify parts of the business that don't generate a profit. Then—if you can't find a way to make them profitable—simply *stop doing them.* Reducing losses is a good way to increase net profits; and there may sometimes also be cash receipts from disposing of assets.

To analyse a project may require data about customers, competitors, technology and so on. One must also explore alternative ways to achieve the aim of a project. Most companies try to screen some alternatives out before spending too much time on them.

Capital investment may encompass the whole range of strategy, R&D, marketing, production, as well as finance. There will be a need for detailed market forecasts, engineering estimates, political assessments and so on. Hence large projects involve groups of people from many parts of the business.

Later sections of this chapter and the next deal with the *financial* details of appraising capital projects. But other aspects may be more important. For example, sometimes projects contain 'strategic options' which can be difficult to quantify (see Chapter 4).

Even after the decision to commit funds to a project, it still remains to implement that decision. This vital process may take many months, and mistakes here can be very costly. Delays can easily lead to large cost over-runs or loss of market share to competitors. Where conditions have changed, the actual project may not be quite the same as the one that management approved. This may be revealed by post-project audits (see Chapter 3).

2.3.2 Estimating Net Benefits

It can be hard to estimate a project's net benefits in future. What consumers will want in a few years' time, what competitors will be up to, how production methods and technology may change—all are uncertain. Yet they may affect the project's duration, sales, selling prices, costs. And even in so-called market economies, firms must cope with extensive and often changing government interference—from regional government, national government, federal government or from the European Union.

Three main kinds of capital project are: replacing equipment, to reduce costs or improve quality; expanding productive capacity, to meet growing demand; and providing new facilities, to make new products. An expansion or new-product project may promise to increase sales revenue by more than operating costs and thus increase profits. A cost reduction project, in contrast, may not affect sales revenue at all: the net benefit of the project is lower future operating costs than would otherwise occur (see Fig. 2.1).

In projecting how much net improvement will result from a project, the forecast of sales revenue is often critical. For example, publishers may be able to calculate production costs quite closely, with a fixed selling price, but sales volume may

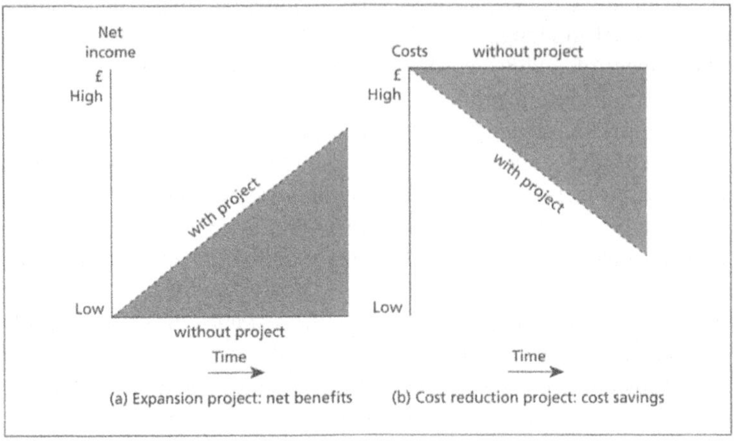

Fig. 2.1 Incremental benefits for different kinds of project

be very uncertain; or petrol companies may be fairly sure how much petrol they will sell, but not what the selling prices will be. On the other hand, shipbuilding on a fixed-price contract would provide almost certain sales revenue, but uncertain costs and timing.

Reaching a sensible answer may depend on asking the right questions. For example, for a capital project the choice may be:

1. Whether or not to buy machine H.
2. Whether to buy machine H or machine J.
3. Whether to buy machine H now or later.
4. How many machine Hs to buy.

We shall not deal in this chapter with how to *finance* capital projects (for example, whether to buy or lease machine H). As a rule, it is best to separate the question whether a project is worthwhile from the (usually less important) question of how to finance it. Often companies, in effect, have a pool of funds from which they can finance all worthwhile projects.

2.3.3 Another Look at Cash Flow Forecasting

A great deal of information, albeit estimated, is likely to be available to those examining a project to decide whether or not to go ahead with it. It will be necessary to sort out the relevant from the irrelevant—and this requires a very different approach to an accounting viewpoint. We have already introduced the concept of cash flow forecasting in Chapter 1, but here we expand on it further and in the context of project appraisal, as will be illustrated later in this and the next chapter.

Firstly, we are only interested in the future—anything that has already happened (usually expenses, such as a market survey) is a sunk cost and there is nothing we can do (presumably) to get it back if we don't go ahead with the project. Of course, such costs will be relevant when we do a post-project appraisal to see how successful the project actually was, but they are not relevant in deciding right now whether to go ahead. Similarly, items to which we are irrevocably committed, even if not paid yet, are not relevant.

Second, we want to know what difference a project will make, so we take into account only the *incremental* cash flows from capital costs, revenues and expenses. That is, cash flows that will occur if the project goes ahead but not otherwise. Indeed, sometimes cash flows do not arise because of the decision to undertake the project, and these are also incremental. For example, if we cannot sell an old machine because we now consider using it in the new project, this is a lost opportunity and the amount we would have sold it for should be included as a negative amount in the cash flow forecast (see Example 2.1).

Example 2.1 The treatment of lost opportunities in the cash flow forecast

If we go ahead with a project, we shall use some spare land we already own; but if not, we shall sell the land for £400,000. Then if the project goes ahead there is a 'failure to inflow' of £400,000—being the loss of the £400,000 cash inflow that would occur if the project did not go ahead. This is an opportunity cost, and, as such, it is a negative in our calculations.◀

Third, we are interested in the impact of the project on the whole business—we should not look at it entirely in isolation. In other words, all cash flows incremental to the project should be considered, even if they are incidental to it. For example, we might have a potential project for a new product which seems highly profitable at first sight—but what if it is a partial substitute for another product which we already make? We need to consider the lost revenues from that product as a negative in our calculations. But bear in mind also that we would certainly (one hopes!) not manufacture the items we are no longer likely to sell, so it is only the revenues less the variable costs of production—also referred to as the lost contribution—that need to be taken into account.

Fourth, let's develop the concept of relevancy a little further. As we saw above, incidental costs are relevant, even if they are not directly related to the project. Likewise, some amounts might be wrongly included in the project's cash flow forecast when they are not incremental and therefore not relevant. A good example is allocation of overheads (maybe Head Office expenses) to the project even when no additional expenses are incurred as a result of the project, but they merely represent a reallocation of existing expenses that would be incurred anyway. These should be ignored in preparing the cash flow forecast for appraising the project.

Fifth, timing is important. We shall discuss this issue in the context of the time value of money below, but the basic concept is that when preparing cash flow forecasts, the accruals concept of accounting is irrelevant. We discussed this in Chapter 1, giving the example of depreciation which is not a cash flow item (although it may have cash flow implications on tax payments). In contrast, the amount we paid for the machine (rather than the spreading of this cost over the useful economic life of the machine) should be included in the cash flow forecast at the point of time that it was actually paid out.

Lastly, we should remember that payments to providers of finance, such as interest paid to lenders or dividends paid to shareholders, are not included as cash flows in the cash flow forecast. We shall see later that including those financing costs in the cash flow forecast represents, in effect, double counting.

2.3.4 A Word About Layout

Spreadsheets are obviously the best tool to use for project appraisal, and one has to give some thought as to how best to lay them out. There are many ways this can be done, and the authors prefer to think of time moving from left to right—although top to bottom is an alternative. Each year of the project could be a column heading—years 1, 2, 3 and so on. If you are thinking to yourself, yes, but how many years into the future do we go, as very few projects simply stop at a moment in time—we will tackle this point later. Meanwhile, we need to introduce the concept of 'Year Zero'. You will soon see that mathematically we regard cash flows occurring in a particular year as happening at the *end* of the project year. This does not much matter with inflows and outflows such as sales and raw material costs that happen gradually throughout the year, but many projects have very substantial cash flows (usually negative) at the very *beginning* of the project. If they are put into year 1 they will be treated as having happened a whole year into the project—far better to put them into year 0. After all, the end of year 0 (EOY 0) is pretty well the equivalent of the beginning of year 1. We care about this because we will see in Sect. 2.5 that the timing of the cash flows is of great importance.

It may seem a strange question, but we also need to ask ourselves what we mean by a plus and a minus number in the spreadsheet. In project appraisal we are interested primarily in cash flows, and clearly a plus is a positive cash flow. However, we have to relax the cash flow rule slightly when it comes to projects such as investing in cost saving equipment. Here, there will be a substantial negative cash flow when, for example, the new machinery is purchased, but no actual inward cash flows to offset against it, so we would never make such an investment! What we have instead are what the authors like to call 'failures to outflow'—in other words, money that was going to flow out but now doesn't do so because of the savings from the investment in the cost saving equipment. This is not literally a cash inflow, but should be regarded as a plus in the spreadsheet—what you might call an opportunity benefit! Similarly, Example 2.1 looked at an opportunity cost, or 'failure to inflow'.

2.4 Simple Appraisal Methods

2.4.1 Average Accounting Return on Investment

Profitability is often expressed as an annual rate of return on investment (ROI).

Example 2.2

Table 2.2 shows two rival capital projects, each lasting for three years. Project A requires an initial investment of £9,000, Project B of £15,000. Project A will produce cash receipts of £3,000 in Year 1, £4,000 in Year 2 and £8,000 in Year 3; while Project B will produce cash receipts of £6,000 in Year 1, £8,000 in Year 2 and £10,000 in Year 3.◀

When we deduct the initial investment from total cash receipts (in effect charging depreciation), Project B yields a larger total profit (9 versus 6). The projects have the same life (three years), so Project B also yields a larger average annual profit than Project A (3 versus 2). But if we divide the average annual profit by the initial amount invested, Project A produces a higher annual rate of return on investment than Project B (22 versus 20 per cent); so using this method we would say that Project A is (slightly) better.

The average rate of return on investment (normally in terms of an annual percentage) does tell us something about a capital project's estimated profitability. But the averaging process cuts out relevant data about the *timing* of the returns.

Example 2.3

Suppose we now compare Project B (as before) with a new Project C which also requires £15,000 initial investment (see Table 2.3). Project B's expected profits (its cash inflows less £5,000 depreciation) are £1,000, £3,000, and £5,000 in Years 1, 2 and 3; while Project C's expected profits, let us suppose, are £5,000, £3,000, and £1,000 (in the reverse order to Project B).

Table 2.2 Project A versus Project B

£000	Project A				Project B			
Year	**0**	**1**	**2**	**3**	**0**	**1**	**2**	**3**
Investment outflow	-9				-15			
Cash receipts		+3	+4	+8		+6	+8	+10
Net profit		+6				+9		
Average Annual Profit (AAP)		+2				+3		
AAP/Investment		2/9				3/15		
Average Accounting Return on Investment		**22%**				**20%**		

Table 2.3 Cash flows for Project B and Project C

£000	**Project B**				**Project C**			
Year	**0**	**1**	**2**	**3**	**0**	**1**	**2**	**3**
Investment outflow	−15				−15			
Cash receipts		+6	+8	+10		+10	+8	+6
Net profit	+9				+9			
Average Annual Profit (AAP)	+3				+3			
AAP/Investment	3/15				3/15			
Average Accounting Return on Investment	**20%**				**20%**			

The average annual rate of return on investment is the same for the two projects: 20 per cent per year (£3,000/£15,000). The only difference is that Project C gives a profit £4,000 larger than Project B in Year 1, but £4,000 smaller in Year 3. (This is actually a cash inflow difference of £4,000 as well.) In total, over the whole three-year life of the projects, this difference balances out; but the larger cash inflow in Year 1 under Project C can be invested for two years to yield a positive extra return. In view of this, Project C is better than Project B; but the average rate of return on investment method, which ignores the timing of the returns, conceals this relevant point.◀

Where the returns happen to be the same in each year of a project's life (like an annuity—see later in this chapter), this timing objection matters less. But the use of the average accounting return on investment also raises some tricky questions. For example: What do we mean by 'return' and by 'investment'? How do we handle tax and inflation? How do we estimate the life of the project? What about capital recovery? How can we determine the minimum acceptable rate of return?

2.4.2 Payback

Even more widely used than the average accounting return on investment is the payback method. This shows how many years it will take before a capital project 'pays back' the amount invested (that is, before the total net cash receipts exceed the initial investment). The shorter the payback period the better. To calculate the payback period, we look at after-tax cash receipts from a project, rather than accounting profits. For example, we only deduct cash expenses from sales receipts, not depreciation.

Example 2.4

Let us now look again at Project B and Project C, each costing £15,000, assuming that they generate cash evenly throughout each year (see Table 2.3).

The payback period for Project B is easy to calculate. £6,000 is repaid in Year 1, £8,000 in Year 2 and £10,000 in Year 3. Thus Project B's payback period is 2.1 years (two years totalling £14,000 plus one-tenth of Year 3 @ £10,000 equals the initial investment of £15,000). In a similar way we can calculate Project C's payback period as being only 1.6 years (Year 1 £10,000 plus 5/8ths of Year 2's £8,000). Table 2.4 shows the payback period calculations while Fig. 2.2 presents a graphical picture of the payback periods.◀

The payback method of project appraisal has one clear advantage over the average rate of return on investment method: it takes timing into account, at least to some extent. It is also simple to calculate and easy to understand, which may explain why so many companies still use it. But the payback method has a serious disadvantage: it totally ignores cash receipts *after* payback. This is vital since there can be no profit unless we get back *more* than the original investment.

Table 2.4 Payback periods for Project B and Project C

£000	Project B				Project C			
Year	**0**	**1**	**2**	**3**	**0**	**1**	**2**	**3**
Investment outflow	−15				−15			
Cash receipts		+6	+8	+10		+10	+8	+6
Accumulated cash receipts		**+6**	**+14**	**+24**		**+10**	**+18**	**+24**
Payback period in years				+2.10			+1.63	
				2 yrs 1 month			1 yr 7 months	

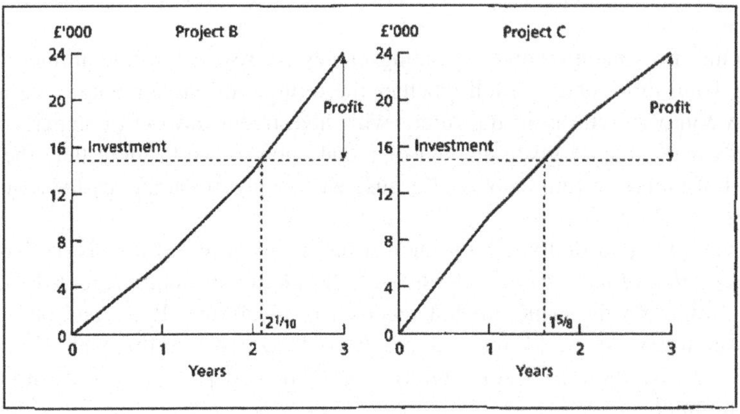

Fig. 2.2 Payback periods for Project B and Project C

Example 2.5

Suppose that in Year 4 Project B produces a cash inflow of £20,000 while Project C produces only £1,000. According to the payback method, that would not change the relative merits of the two projects: Project C would still be 'better' than Project B because of its shorter payback period. This clearly does not make business sense!◄

While it may be a useful relative measure of risk (faster payback means less risk), the payback method does not measure profit. Nor is it clear how to determine a suitable minimum payback period. After all, some very successful drugs have taken more than ten years to pay back all the investment in research and development. And you can get the best possible payback—instantaneous!—by not investing at all!

In practice, companies often use payback as a rough screening device, especially for simple projects at lower levels of the firm. And where the return happens to be the same in each year, then the payback method may rank projects in the same order as the more accurate methods of assessing whether capital projects will yield a profit—to which we now turn.

2.5 The 'Time Value' of Money

You may remember from Example 2.3 that both projects generated the same Average Accounting Return on Investment (AARoI) because their *total* cash flows were equal. However, we observed that Project C must be better than Project B because Project C had the higher cash flows *earlier* in its life cycle than Project B, which had the higher cash flows later. Those early high cash flows of Project C could be invested in other projects, or used to pay down borrowings—but the AARoI was unable to discriminate between the two. We are now going to address this problem.

Capital investment involves spending money (or resources) now in the hope of getting back more later. To tell whether the returns are large enough, we need a way to compare returns in the future with investment now—to compare money amounts over time. A given amount of money now is worth more than the same amount of money in future. Why? Because we can invest the money today to yield a return.

Hence, the opportunity to earn interest on money received now is the basis for the *time value of money* concept—that is, the idea that money received today is worth more than the same amount received in the future. If we had an amount of money today, we could, for example, have deposited it in the bank, lent it out, invested it elsewhere to yield a return—or used it to pay off a loan and hence saved on interest.

Note that if we were not promised a return for delaying access to our money, most of us would probably prefer to spend it today. So, the interest we are promised for giving someone else (the bank, a borrower) the use of our money is a form of compensation we demand for delaying consumption. The promise of receiving interest also compensates us (perhaps only partially, these days!) for the possibility that inflation between now and when the money is received would diminish the purchasing power of our money. Moreover, having the money today is certain while a promise for money in the future is uncertain. In other words, interest is also a compensation for risk. Lastly, as mentioned above, when we agree to delay the receipt of money, in effect we give up the opportunity to invest it elsewhere. For example, if we lend the money to someone else, we give up the opportunity to deposit it in the bank to receive interest. So, we ask that person to compensate us for this lost opportunity.

Example 2.6

Let us suppose that we can invest money today to yield 8 per cent a year. Then £1,000 invested today will grow (compounding once a year) to the following amounts:

In 1 year's time to £1,000 × 1.08 = £1,000 × 1.080 = £1,080
In 2 years' time to £1,000 × $(1.08)^2$ = £1,000 × 1.166 = £1,166
In 3 years' time to £1,000 × $(1.08)^3$ = £1,000 × 1.260 = £1,260

Thus, using an interest rate of 8 per cent a year, the future value of '£1,000 now' is £1,260 at the end of three years. Or, looking at it the other way round, the present value of '£1,260 that one expects to receive at the end of three years' is £1,000 now (see Table 2.5). All other things being equal, one should be indifferent between receiving the £1,260 in three years and £1,000 now.◀

What then is the present value of '£1,000 one expects to receive at the end of three years'? Clearly it must be £794, as follows:

$$£1,000 \times 1/(1.08)^3 = £794$$

Table 2.5 Future values of '£1,000 now' at 8 per cent a year

	End of Year 0 (now) £	End of Year 1 £	End of Year 2 £	End of Year 3 £
Future values →	1000 →	1080 →	1166 →	1260
Present values	1000 ←	1080		
	1000 ←		1166	
	1000 ←			1260

We can prove this by showing what would happen if we invested £794 today at 8 per cent a year. Each year the effect of compound interest is to add 8 per cent of the start-of-year cumulative amount invested, as follows:

After 1 year the amount becomes: £794 + £63 = £857
After 2 years the amount becomes: £857 + £69 = £926
After 3 years the amount becomes: £926 + £74 = £1,000

Thus, we can see the present value of £1,000 one expects to receive at any future date (see Table 2.6).

Assuming an interest rate of 8 per cent a year, the present value of any amount (call it 'a') one expects to receive at the end of three years is 0.794*a*. The 8 per cent here is the discount rate, and 0.794 is the discount factor (DF) for three years at 8 per cent a year: $1/(1.08)^3$. (We shall normally use discount factors correct to three decimal places. This is accurate enough for most practical purposes, though it can cause minor 'rounding' problems.)

The Appendix provides tables of discount factors for annual interest rates between 1 and 25 per cent and for 1–50 years hence. Table A1 shows the present value of $1 (or, of course, any other currency) to be received at a future date for a range of discount rates. Thus, looking across to the 8% column, and looking down to Year 3, we see the factor of 0.794, which we have been discussing.

So, we have found what we were looking for—a way to, as it were, discriminate more and more against cash flows the further into the future they occur. For example, picking the discount factor for 3 years at a discount rate of 8% from Table A1, we can calculate that £1,000 received at the end of year 3 has a present value of:

$$£1000 \times DF^{3yrs}_{8\%} = £1000 \times 0.794 = £794.$$

Table 2.6 Present values of '£1,000 in future' at 8 per cent a year

	End of Year 0 (now) £	End of Year 1 £	End of Year 2 £	End of Year 3 £
Future values	794 →	857 →	926 →	1000
Present values				
$= \frac{1000}{1080} \times 1000$	926 ←	1000		
$= \frac{1000}{1166} \times 1000$	857 ←		1000	
$= \frac{1000}{1260} \times 1000$	794 ←			1000

However, at the end of year 20, the same £1,000 had a value of just:

$$£1000 \times DF_{8\%}^{20yrs} = £1000 \times 0.215 = £215.$$

2.5.1 A Note on the Discount Rate

The discount rate is the interest rate used to determine the present value of future cash flows, to reflect the fact that an amount of money to be received in the future is worth less than the same amount received today. The process of transforming a future sum into its equivalent in terms of today by applying a discount rate is called discounting.

The discount rate represents the interest rate that we forego by not having the money today and missing out on the opportunity to invest it and earn a return. This is why we sometimes refer to the discount rate by the name 'the opportunity cost of capital'. Because it reflects the return we could have earned, had we not delayed the receipt of the money, the discount rate is also sometimes called 'the minimum required rate of return', 'the hurdle rate' or just 'the cost of capital'.

Moreover, as we mentioned above, by discounting future amounts of money we also account for the fact that money received today is certain while the promise of money in the future is uncertain. Thus, the discount rate can be viewed as compensation for risk, and the higher the uncertainty of a future amount of money, the higher the discount rate we use in discounting that future value into a present value. More on that in later chapters.

2.6 Net Present Value and Variants

2.6.1 Net Present Value (NPV)

Thus far, we have used as the discount rate the interest rate that we could receive on our money if we don't invest in the project. Most companies however use their overall cost of financing as the minimum required rate of return on a capital investment project. This is a mixture of their cost of borrowing and the cost of having money from shareholders. (Its calculation is dealt with in depth in Chapter 8.) Why would a company invest in a capital project expected to yield *less* than its financing costs? We need to get a higher return from capital projects for the investment to be worthwhile. (At this stage we ignore tax and possible differences in riskiness, and we will also add some complexities to the hurdle rate later on.)

The net present value (NPV) method of investment appraisal calculates a project's profit by comparing cash payments and cash receipts at the same point in time—the beginning of the project. It does so by discounting expected future cash flows back to the present (that is, back to the 'end of Year 0'). We know how to do this—we multiply the net cash flow for each year (including the initial investment) by the discount factor from Appendix Table A1 for each year at the appropriate discount rate—and then sum up all the resulting present values to give the Net Present Value. If the NPV is positive, we know the project is worthwhile—the owners of the business will be better off than if the project is not undertaken. Put differently, a positive NPV project creates value to shareholders, over and above their minimum required return.

Conversely, if the NPV is negative, the project is said to destroy value. It does not even provide the minimum return that finance providers required. *Thus, firms that seek to maximize value to shareholders should reject negative NPV projects, and accept positive NPV projects.*

Example 2.7

Nellam Inc is thinking of expanding its fleet of vehicles by one 20-ton truck costing $52,000. It would operate the truck for four years and then scrap it. The company expects net cash inflows from the extra business to be $12,000, $14,000, $16,000 and $18,000 in Years 1–4, which we assume to occur at the end of each year. (These amounts are cash flows: straight-line depreciation on the truck of $13,000 a year has not been deducted.) Its hurdle rate is 8%.

Should Nellam acquire the extra truck? We can compare the two choices as follows:

1. Invest $52,000 in buying the truck and receive the resulting cash inflows.
2. Do not buy the truck—in which case Nellam will merely potentially save the 8 per cent a year financing costs on the $52,000.

Table 2.7 sets out the expected financial results from the project.

We see that the project's net present value is negative. Hence the project is not worthwhile. The cost of investing in the project is £52,000 now, while the present value of the expected positive future cash flows in years 1–4 (discounted at 8 per cent a year) is only £49,044. That is hardly smart business: it represents a loss (in present value terms) of £2,956.◀

Note that if we revisit Projects B and C (Example 2.3), where you will remember the cash flows were the same in total, but the positive cash flows occurred

Table 2.7 Net present value for Nellam's new truck project

Line	End of year	0	1	2	3	4
1	Cash flow	-52,000	12,000	14,000	16,000	18,000
2	Discount factor @ 8% a year	1.000	0.926	0.857	0.794	0.735
3	Present value (line 1 * line 2)	-52,000	11,112	11,998	12,704	13,230
4	**Net Present Value (sum of line 3)**	**-2,956**				

Table 2.8 Net present values for Projects B and C (Figures in '£000)

		Project B				Project C			
Line	**Year**	**0**	**1**	**2**	**3**	**0**	**1**	**2**	**3**
1	Investment outflow	−15				−15			
2	Cash receipts		6	8	10		10	8	6
3	Discount factor @ 8% a year	1.000	0.926	0.857	0.794	1.000	0.926	0.857	0.794
4	Present value (line 1 or 2 * line 3)	−15	5.56	6.86	7.94	−15	9.26	6.86	4.76
5	**NPV (sum of line 4)**	**5.36**				**5.88**			

in the opposite order to one another, and apply the NPV technique to them, the following results (Table 2.8).

The average annual return on investment was 20% for both projects, even though we 'knew' intuitively that Project C was better because the larger cash inflows happened earlier and could be reinvested. But the *NPV* of project C (£5,880) is larger than that of Project B (£5,360), so we would always (correctly) choose C over B: the NPV approach is superior.

Remember that in computing the NPV we have been assuming that cash flows arise only at year ends. In practice they may occur more or less evenly throughout the year, but our assumption (which is common) is simpler and unlikely to change the decision. After all, nearly all the numbers we use are only estimates. (For obvious reasons, we do make a different assumption when calculating payback periods.) However, if, for example, there is likely to be the *substantial* expense of a major overhaul of the plant and machinery early in the fourth year of a project, it would be better to put it as a negative in year 3, as 'early in year 4' is closer to the end of year 3 than the end of year 4.

Notice that we round all numbers to the nearest currency unit. There is no advantage in spurious accuracy. Figures for cash flows are usually no more than estimates; their precise timing is often uncertain; and determining the 'correct' discount rate to use is not at all easy.

A great advantage of the NPV method is that it enables companies to compare different projects at the same point in time (EOY 0); if we have to choose between two different projects, in principle we should choose the one with the higher NPV (but see the section 'Profitability index' below for a caveat); if both have a positive NPV and we *don't* have to choose between them, we should do both. (For example, Projects B and C are both worth doing as they both have positive NPVs, but if we had to choose, we would do C with its *larger* NPV.)

The NPV method, as we have seen, compares cash receipts and payments expected to result from a capital project. It multiplies them by discounting factors to translate all expected future cash flows from a project into present values (that is, into EOY 0 money terms). Figure 2.3 pictures this approach.

Discounted cash flow (DCF) methods, which include both the NPV and the Internal Rate of Return (see Sect. 2.8), involve forecasting both the amount and the timing of incremental cash flows which will occur if a firm undertakes a

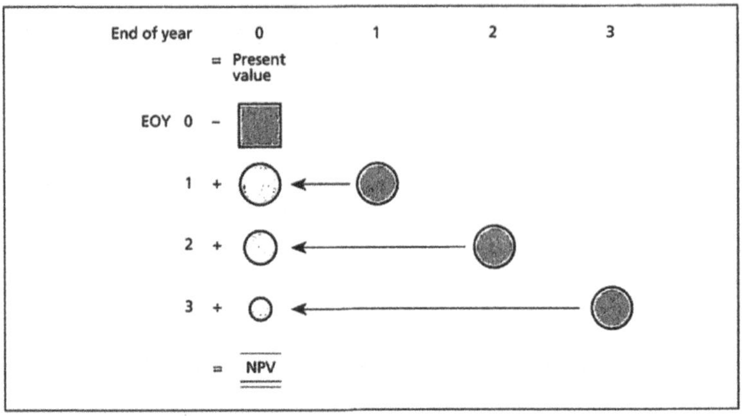

Fig. 2.3 The discounting process in net present value (NPV)

Fig. 2.4 Valuing a capital asset

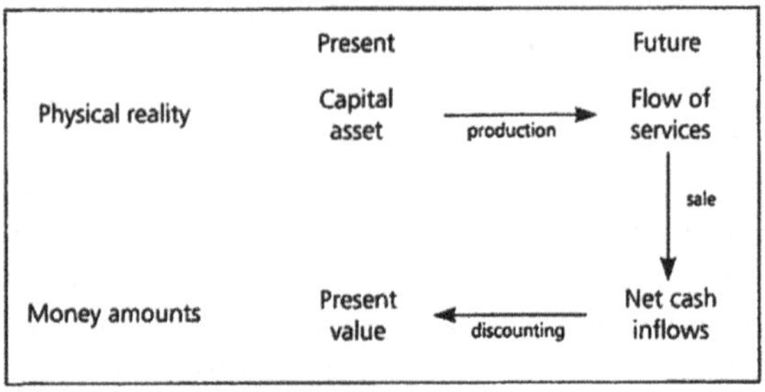

project, but not otherwise. Remember that DCF methods deal with cash flows and *not* with accounting profits, income and expenses. Hence in listing future cash flows we ignore non-cash items such as depreciation. To tell whether we expect a project to be worthwhile, we are, in effect, simply seeing whether or not the present value of the project's discounted net receipts exceeds the present value of the cash investment.

Figure 2.4 shows a way to picture this valuation process. The project's cost may simply be the amount of the initial cash investment, as in the Nellam truck project. But sometimes projects consist of several cash payments spread out over time, which themselves need to be discounted back to present value terms. It is not always easy to tell what discount rate to use for such 'deferred' investments—the same discount rate as for future cash receipts or some lower-risk discount rate.

The NPV method, in theory, will always give the correct answer if one assumes all three of the following:

1. One can correctly forecast the amounts and the timing of all the future cash flows.
2. One can correctly estimate the risk-adjusted cost of capital (to give the discount rate).
3. There are no relevant non-quantifiable aspects to a capital project.

The sweeping and unrealistic nature of these three points makes it clear that in practice no method, however theoretically satisfactory, can guarantee to give a precisely 'correct' answer. The business world is much too uncertain for that.

Should a company go ahead with a project which promises a sufficient positive NPV, but which may result in losses for accounting purposes in the first year or two of its life? In general the answer is 'Yes'. Unless the project is so large that it threatens to swamp the rest of the company's business, one can usually count on poor accounting results for one project being offset by good accounting results for others.

2.7 Annuities and Perpetuities

2.7.1 Annuities

If we are going to receive the same level of cash flows year by year from year 1 onwards, which is called an annuity, there is a shortcut we can take in working out the NPV of those cash flows. When might that happen, you may well be asking yourself? Well, in Chapter 5 we will be looking at how to value debt instruments—where the same amount of interest is paid or received every year for a period of time. Also, sometimes when we don't know how long a project will go on for, or how to value an acquisition's cash flows well into the future, we might assume net cash flows per year of a constant amount after some 'accurate' calculations of the early years. Hence we might calculate years 1–10 accurately (with each year giving a different net cash flow), then assume an annuity for years 11–20. Table A2 in the Appendix shows the present value of annuities, that is $1 per year to be received for a number of future years for a range of discount rates. Thus, again using the 8% column, when we look down to Year 3 we see an annuity factor of 2.577. This represents the present value of $1 received at the end of Year 1 (0.926) plus the present value of $1 received at the end of Year 2 (0.857) plus the present value of $1 received at the end of Year 3 (0.794). Thus Table A2 is a *cumulative* version of Table A1 (2.577 = 0.926 + 0.857 + 0.794).

Example 2.8 Valuing an annuity

An investment of €50,000 is expected to yield a net cash flow of €8,000 per year for 10 years from the end of year 1. What is its NPV at a discount rate of 8%? (Table 2.9).◄

2.7.1.1 Perpetuities

If you look carefully along the '20 years' row of Appendix Table A2, can you see a relationship between the discount rate and the number the annuity factor is heading towards? Try 17 and 20%. 17% has an annuity factor close to 6 (5.628), and 20% has an annuity factor close to 5 (4.870). That is, 1 divided by the discount

Table 2.9 Valuing an annuity (figures in €'000)

Years	**0**	**1–10**	
	−50	8	*(we are receiving €8k each year from 1–10)*
Annuity factor @ 8%	1	6.710	*(this is from the 8% column and 10 year row of Appendix Table A2)*
Present Value	−50	53.68	
NPV	**€3.68k**		

rate, if you think of the discount rate as a decimal. 1/0.17 = 5.882 and 1/0.20 = 5. In fact, the annuity factor to apply to equal cash flows coming in *forever*, known as a **perpetuity**, is simply 1/r, where *r* is the discount rate. So, for example, to find the NPV of $100 flowing in from the end of year 1 to infinity at a discount rate of 10%, you multiply the $100 by 1/0.10; that is, 100/0.10 = $1,000.

2.7.1.2 Annuities and Perpetuities Starting at a Point Other Than Year 1

Sometimes, as mentioned above, the 'annuity' (or perpetuity, if you think the cash flows will go on indefinitely) part of a project will start some way into the project, but the annuity factors table assumes cash flows from the end of year 1. The example we gave above was: accurate calculations for the first 10 years, then an annuity (of say, $100) for years 11–20:

Year 1–10	Years 11–20
Calculated accurately	100 per year

Assuming a 10 per cent discount rate, this can be dealt with in either of two ways:-

i. **Finding the annuity factor from the annuities table** ($r = 10\%$)

Years 1–20	8.514
Less years 1–10	6.145
Therefore Years 11–20	2.369

By subtracting the factor for years 1–10 from the factor for years 1–20, we get the appropriate factor for years 11–20. So, the NPV of the annuity element of the project is:

$$100 \times 2.369 = 236.9$$

ii. **Discounting twice**. Imagine yourself at the end of year 10. At that point, you will be receiving an annuity from, as you then see it, the end of year 1 until the end of year 10. From the table, the factor is 6.145. But that will give you the annuity's net present value at the end of Year 10, where you were imagining yourself. But we want its value *now*. So, we simply multiply that value by the ordinary discount factor for year 10 (from Appendix Table A1). At a discount rate of 10 per cent, this is 0.386. Multiplying, $6.145 \times 0.386 = 2.372$. Multiply this by the \$100 per annum annuity gives 237.2. Allowing for rounding, this is the same result as the first method.

If you do your calculations on a spreadsheet, the annuity factors table might be of little use to you because you can always construct a very wide spreadsheet covering each year independently (for example, \$500 in year 1, \$500 in year 2, \$500 in year 3 and so on). Nevertheless, it can save a lot of time and space if you are considering a very long annuity—and can save you an infinite amount of space if looking at a perpetuity!

2.7.2 Profitability Index

Companies may sometimes choose to 'ration' capital, for strategic or other reasons. A variant of the NPV method may then be useful, called the profitability index (PI). This method divides the present value of a project's cash inflows by the present value of the investment. In the Nellam truck project of Example 2.7, this is \$49,044/\$52,000 = 0.94 as shown in Table 2.10.

Clearly if the index exceeds 1.00, the signal from the numbers is 'go ahead'—just like a positive net present value. (Sometimes the index is multiplied by 100, which would give a figure of 94 here.)

Where there is capital rationing (see Chapter 3), companies may use the profitability index to rank projects. Where not all projects with a positive net present value can go ahead, a company may prefer those with higher PIs (rather than those with higher absolute NPVs).

Table 2.10 Profitability Index (PI) for Nellam's new Truck Project

	End of year	0	1	2	3	4
1	Cash flow	-52,000	12,000	14,000	16,000	18,000
2	Discount factor @ 8% a year	1.000	0.926	0.857	0.794	0.735
3	Present value (line 1 * line 2)	-52,000	11,112	11,998	12,704	13,230
4	Present value of cash inflows	49,044	*(Adding up the figures for years 1–4 in line 3)*			
5	**Profitability Index**	**0.94**	*(Present Value of cash inflows / Initial investment)*			

Table 2.11 Discounted payback period for Project B (figures in '£000)

Line	Year	0	1	2	3
1	Investment outflow	−15			
2	Cash receipts		6	8	10
3	Discount factor @ 8% a year	1.000	0.926	0.857	0.794
4	Present value (line 1 or 2 * line 3)	−15	5.56	6.86	7.94
5	**Net Present Value (sum of figures in line 4)**	**5.36**			
6	Accumulated discounted cash inflow		5.56	12.42	20.36
7	**Discounted payback period**				**2.32**
					2 yrs, 4 months

Another use for the profitability index may be to indicate the margin of safety for a project. If, for example, the PI is above 1.00 but not more than (say) 1.20, then the estimates of future cash flows don't have to be out by much before the PI may fall below 1.00. On the other hand, where the PI exceeds 1.50, there is quite a large margin of error before the project fails to seem worthwhile.

It should be noted that some textbooks recommend calculating the PI as the NPV of the project *including the initial investment*, divided by the initial investment. Thus projects with a negative NPV will have a negative PI (Nellam's is −2956/52000 = −0.057). Obviously the PI calculated this way can still be used to rank projects under capital rationing and indicate a margin of safety, but a PI of 1.20 calculated under the first method will be 0.2 calculated under the second.

2.7.3 Discounted Payback

The payback period which we discussed earlier can also use discounted cash flows, to give a discounted payback period. Table 2.8 showed the result of discounting Project B's cash inflows of £6,000, £8,000 and £10,000 in Years 1, 2 and 3 at 8 per cent a year to a net present value of £5.36k.

As presented in Table 2.11, the *discounted* payback period is 2.32 years. Given an initial investment of £15k, this is arrived at as follows. £12.42k present value received by the end of year 2, plus £2.58k/£7.94k = 0.32 of Year 3, and assuming for this purpose that cash is received evenly throughout the year.[1]

The discounted payback period of 2.32 years that we calculated for Project B can be compared with the simple payback period calculated in Table 2.4 of 2.10 years. It should be obvious why using *discounted* cash flows will always lengthen the payback period. This refinement, however, does not overcome the main drawback of the payback method (namely, that it does not measure profitability); though if there is a finite period within which discounted pay back is expected to be achieved, at least that implies that the NPV is positive.

[1] The figure of £2.58k is the £15k investment less the £12.42k accumulated discounted cash inflow at the end of year 2.

2.8 The Internal Rate of Return

Another widely-used method of discounting cash flows is the internal rate of return (IRR) method (also called the DCF yield method).

The NPV method lists the amount and the timing of all the expected incremental future cash flows from a project; and the IRR method does the same. The NPV method then applies a pre-selected discount rate to see whether the net total of all the discounted cash flows is positive or negative. If the NPV is positive, then the project is worthwhile (from a financial point of view); if the NPV is negative, it is not.

In contrast, the IRR method determines, by trial and error, what is the (unknown) discount rate which, when applied to the same cash flows, will produce a net present value of exactly zero. That discount rate is the project's 'internal rate of return'. To see whether or not a project is worthwhile, the firm must compare its IRR with the hurdle rate (or criterion rate)—which, of course, is the pre-selected discount rate used in the NPV method.

Example 2.9

In Table 2.7, using an 8 per cent discount rate, we found an NPV of −$2,956 for Nellam's new truck project. The project's IRR must therefore be less than 8 per cent, since in order to produce an NPV of zero, we need to discount the project's future cash inflows rather less. Unless you use a spreadsheet IRR function, the answer can only be found by trial and error. Thus, in Table 2.12 we calculate the NPV again, using discount rates of 6 and 4 per cent (note—these are just 'educated' guesses!). Since one result is positive and the other is negative, it is evident that the IRR must lie somewhere between 4 and 6 per cent (closer to 6 per cent, since that NPV was closer to zero).

We can estimate the approximate IRR as follows. By changing the discount rate from 4 to 6 per cent, the NPV changed from +2,108 to −528. In other words, a 2 percentage point change in the discount rate led to a 2,636 (that is, 2,108 minus −528) change in the NPV. So, a 1 percentage point change in the discount rate would lead to a 2,636/2 = 1,318 change in NPV. Remember that

Table 2.12 Calculating the IRR by trial and error: Nellam Truck Project

Line	End of year	0	1	2	3	4
1	Cash flow	-52,000	12,000	14,000	16,000	18,000
2	Discount factor @ 4% a year	1.000	0.962	0.925	0.889	0.855
3	Present value (line 1 * line 2)	-52,000	11,544	12,950	14,224	15,390
4	**NPV (sum of figures in line 3)**	**2,108**				

Line	End of year	0	1	2	3	4
1	Cash flow	-52,000	12,000	14,000	16,000	18,000
2	Discount factor @ 6% a year	1.000	0.943	0.890	0.840	0.792
3	Present value (line 1 * line 2)	-52,000	11,316	12,460	13,440	14,256
4	**NPV (sum of figures in line 3)**	**-528**				

we are looking for the discount rate that gives an NPV of zero. Trying 6% gave us a small negative NPV of −528, so we require a reduction in the discount rate of 528/1318:

$$IRR = 6\% - \left(\frac{528}{1{,}318}\right) = 6\% - 0.40\% = 5.60\%$$

Or we could start from the other end, with 4%, which gave us a positive NPV such that the discount rate needs to be increased, thus:-

$$IRR = 4\% + \left(\frac{2{,}108}{1{,}318}\right) = 4\% + 1.60\% = 5.60\%$$

We could check that using a discount rate of 5.6 per cent produces an NPV of very nearly zero (it is only very nearly zero rather than zero because we have rounded the numbers in our calculations). One could also use the Excel® function = irr to find a more accurate estimation of the project's IRR.

Once the IRR is found, Nellam would need to compare it with the required minimum hurdle rate. If that hurdle rate is 8 per cent and the IRR is 5.6 per cent, clearly the project is not acceptable as it provides an internal rate of return (5.6%) that is lower than the opportunity cost of capital (8%) which investors can get elsewhere on similar-risk projects.◄

Figure 2.5 shows what the truck project's net present value amounts to for a whole range of discount rates. Three values are worth noting:

1. Using a 0 per cent discount rate, the NPV is + \$8,000 (i.e. the same as summing all the undiscounted figures, including the initial investment).
2. The net present value is zero at a discount rate of 5.6 per cent; this is the internal rate of return.
3. Using an 8 per cent discount rate (the hurdle rate), the NPV is −\$2956.

A project with a higher internal rate of return may not always be 'better' than a project with a lower IRR, even on financial grounds. This is for two main reasons. First, the amount invested may be different. Is a 40 per cent IRR better than 15 per cent? Perhaps not, if one earns the 40 per cent return on an investment of £100, but the 15 per cent on an investment of £10,000. The *scale* of the investment may be relevant.

The second reason is that the IRR, in effect, assumes reinvestment (of cash inflows) at the project's own internal rate of return. But this is unlikely to be the actual cost of capital, which makes it hard to compare two different projects. In contrast, the NPV method always assumes that a firm can reinvest its cash inflows at the discount rate it uses for the project (i.e. the opportunity cost of capital).

The IRR method is also subject to certain other technical problems: for example, if there are negative net cash flows in years other than year zero of the project's

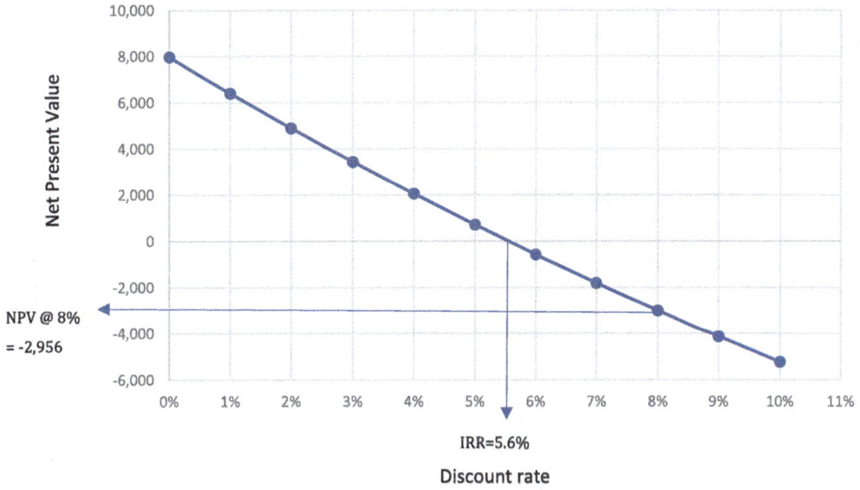

Fig. 2.5 NPV of Nellam's truck project at various discount rates

life, there will be more than one solution to the project's IRR. And it is not so versatile and robust as the NPV method in some respects: for instance, NPV can use different discount rates for different kinds of cash flows, or for different periods, which IRR cannot.

2.8.1 A Note on Using Excel®

We are assuming that most readers will be using spreadsheets to do their calculations, including the NPV and IRR, although we have described the NPV and IRR calculations from 'first principles' above. Naturally the use of the NPV and IRR functions in Excel® saves a great deal of time, but one point in particular needs to be borne in mind. The NPV function treats the first number in your list of values as having happened at the end of year *1*, not the end of year *0*. Consequently, if, when constructing your formula, you highlight the whole row of cash flows including year 0, you will get the wrong answer! The solution is as follows: if your net cash flows including year 0 are in cells A2 to E2, your NPV formula should be:

$$= \text{A2} + \text{NPV}(\textit{Discount rate}, \underline{\text{B2}} : \text{E2})$$

That way, you have not discounted the year 0 cash flow, and have correctly discounted the rest. *However*, to calculate the IRR you need to *include* year 0 as follows:

$$= \text{IRR}(\underline{\text{A2}} : \text{E2}, \textit{0.06})$$

Note that the formula asks for a guess at the answer (the 0.06, or 6 per cent, above, which is our guess), although it also works without. This is because Excel® is trying many different discount rates in a process of trial and error to reach an NPV of zero, and the process is quicker if a ball-park figure is suggested.

2.9 A Concluding Note

In this chapter we have looked at several discounted cash flow methods. The two most widely used are Net Present Value (NPV) and Internal Rate of Return (IRR). Even where one of the DCF methods appears to show that a project is worthwhile, it is still important for managers to satisfy themselves about the business case for it. In other words, *why* should a particular project make a profit? If there seems to be no specific reason, then the apparent result of the financial assessment must be open to doubt. All experienced managers know how easy it is for optimistic assumptions to make a project look good. That is why it is sensible to try to identify which are the key assumptions underpinning a project.

It cannot be too strongly stressed that financial estimates are nearly always just that—estimates—and often with a very large margin of error. It might not be going too far to call them guesses. In making good business decisions, judgement about the uncertain business future is likely to be far more important than technical expertise with discounted cash flows.

2.9.1 Problems

Problem 2.1

a. Calculate the *present value* of the following future cash flows at the given annual rate of interest (r) in each case:
   i. £550 1 year away, $r = 10\%$.
   ii. £1,728 3 years away, $r = 20\%$.
   iii. £251 2 years away, $r = 12\%$.
   iv. £2,000 9 years away, $r = 8\%$.
b. At 12 per cent a year, what is the present value of an annuity of €200:
   i. for 8 years?
   ii. for 20 years?
   iii. for 50 years?
   iv. for 30 years, between 21 and 50?
   v. for ever (a 'perpetuity')
c. Which would you rather have (starting at the end of year 1):
   i. £3,000 a year for the next 20 years, discounted at 20 per cent a year?
   ii. £2,000 a year for the next 20 years, discounted at 12 per cent a year?
   iii. £1,000 a year for the next 20 years, discounted at 3 per cent a year?

d. At 12 per cent a year, which would you prefer:
   i. $500 a year for seven years, or
   ii. $700 a year for five years?

Problem 2.2

a. A project is expected to yield €1 million at the end of Year 10. The initial outlay is €463,000. What is the internal rate of return (IRR) on the project?
b. A project requiring an initial outlay of £5,400 will yield returns of £1,000 a year for 10 years.
   i. What is the internal rate of return (IRR) on the project?
   ii. What annual money returns would be needed to yield a 20 per cent per year internal rate of return?
c. What is the present value of:
   i. $1,200 a year receivable from the end of Year 3 to the end of Year 7 at an interest rate of 20 per cent a year?
   ii. $4,000 a year payable from the end of Year 5 to the end of Year 10 at an interest rate of 15 per cent a year?
   iii. $800 a year receivable from the beginning of Year 4 to the end of Year 8 at an interest rate of 12 per cent a year?
   iv. A pension of $5,000 a year receivable from the end of Year 20 to the end of Year 40 at an interest rate of 15 per cent a year?
d. Three projects each requiring an initial investment of £4,200 each produce a net present value of zero after discounting at 6 per cent a year:
   1. a 5-year annuity of £997.
   2. a 10-year annuity of £571.
   3. a 20-year annuity of £366.

   What happens to the present value of *each* project if the discount rate:

   i. falls to 4 per cent a year?
   ii. increases to 8 per cent a year?

Problem 2.3 A firm is considering one of two projects, H and J:

End of year	0	1	2	3	4
H cash flows (€)	−1000	+500	+400	+350	+300
J cash flows (€)	−1000	+400	+400	+400	+400

a. Which of these two projects has the higher net present value at a discount rate of 15 per cent a year? By how much?
b. What is the payback period of each project?
c. What is the discounted payback period of each project?

Problem 2.4

a. Project T requires an initial investment of £200,000 (which is non-returnable), and is expected to produce cash inflows of £70,000 a year at the end of each of the next five years. Is it worth investing, if the opportunity cost of capital is 15 per cent a year? Calculate your answer using:
   i. Net Present Value method
   ii. Internal Rate of Return method.
b. A company expects to reduce labour costs by $20,000 a year if it invests $50,000 in new equipment which will last five years. Ignoring tax:
   i. What is the annual increase in accounting profit?
   ii. What is the average accounting return on investment?
   iii. What is the annual net cash inflow?
   iv. What is the payback period?
   v. What is the NPV at 15 per cent a year?
   vi. What is the IRR?

References

Friedman, M. (1970). The Social Responsibility of Business Is to Increase Its Profits. *New York Times Magazine*, 13 September 1970, 122–126.
Freeman, R. E. (1984). *Strategic Management: A Stakeholder Approach*. Boston: Pitman.

More on Capital Projects 3

3.1 Introduction

In the summer of 2021, the American *Keel News* radio station reported on a $200 million capital project by Amazon to build a warehouse in *Shreveport* in the US state of Louisiana.[1] According to all involved, the project was expected to create 800 construction jobs as well as 1,000 full-time jobs where workers would be paid at least double the minimum wage to work in a state-of-the-art technology environment. Louisiana Governor, John Bel Edwards, described the Amazon Shreveport project as *the most tremendous (project) anywhere in the United States of America* with expected impact across the economy of northwest Louisiana.

There is no doubt that deciding to go ahead with such a mega-project required Amazon to engage in a serious capital appraisal process as discussed in the previous chapter. However, while Chapter 2 introduced the basic concepts of capital project appraisal, there are always more complex issues that big projects such as the Amazon warehouse in Shreveport, as well as smaller projects, need to address. The aim of this chapter is to extend the discussion in Chapter 2 and, based on key concepts we introduced in Chapter 1 (e.g. *working capital*), to cover additional complications relating to project appraisal and management.

We begin in the next section (Sect. 3.2) by looking again at *working capital* which was introduced in Chapter 1 in relation to liquidity management, while here we look at it in relation to capital project appraisal. From there we move to discuss taxation (Sect. 3.3) and then to look at projects of unequal length (Sect. 3.4). Initiating a project is important but ending projects could sometimes be a complex matter too. Thus, in Sect. 3.5, we turn our attention to capital disinvestment. Section 3.6 deals with inflation while Sect. 3.7 briefly discusses various issues

[1] https://710keel.com/the-new-amazon-warehouse-in-shreveport-is-jaw-droppingly-huge/, 13 August 2021.

R. Manos et al., *Corporate Finance for Business*,
https://doi.org/10.1007/978-3-030-92419-5_3

relating to capital planning and budgeting. The last Sect. 3.8 provides concluding notes, followed by some practice problems.

3.2 Working Capital

Chapter 2 made it clear that discounted cash flow techniques unsurprisingly need to be applied to cash flows. So, if we have created our project spreadsheet based on cash flows, that is fine. But the chances are that we have used the sales figure for each of the years of our project, rather than the receipts from sales—and, of course, these will be different if we have granted a period of credit to our clients or customers; and probably we have used the purchases figure for each year rather than the amounts we have actually paid for each year. Also, inventory that we have purchased might be accounted for in the spreadsheet as a cost only when sold (as part of the cost of sales) rather than when actually purchased. Consequently, we will have to make a working capital adjustment as follows.

3.2.1 Receivables

Suppose a five-year manufacturing project will generate sales revenue of €220,000 a year; and that receivables of €56,000 will be outstanding at the end of each year. We could show cash receipts as follows: €164,000 in Year 1, €220,000 in each of Years 2–5 and €56,000 in Year 6. More usual, however, is to show sales revenues as if they were cash receipts of €220,000 for each of Years 1–5; in which case we also need to show an 'investment' in receivables of €56,000 at the end of Year 1, to be recovered at the end of Year 5. (The cash is likely to come in much nearer the end of Year 5 than the end of Year 6.)

3.2.2 Inventory Less Payables

If the project incurs cash expenses of €120,000 a year, that may involve inventory of materials, work-in-progress and finished goods. Those will only appear in the income statement as 'cost of sales' when matched later against sales. So, we might show an 'investment' in inventory of, say, €40,000 at the end of Year 0, in advance of making any sales. (We would assume that inventory is recovered in cash in full at the end of a project, in this case at the end of Year 5.)

Any investment in inventory may be partly offset by the extension of credit from suppliers. Suppose this amounts to €30,000 outstanding at the end of each year. The result would be a net cash investment in advance of only €10,000 (that is, €40,000 in inventory less €30,000 credit from suppliers). We would expect to clear this net amount, as a cash receipt, at the end of Year 5.

3.2.3 Overall Position

On the basis of these assumptions, Table 3.1 sets out (in € thousands) the cash flows in respect of working capital for the project. If the amounts involved were fairly small, it might be simpler to show the net outflow of €66,000 as a single amount arising at one point in time (the end of Year 0 or the end of Year 1).

We normally expect to recover the whole of the net amount invested in working capital at the end of a project. But of course, in a discounted cash flow analysis we have to allow for the time that it is invested. Thus, using a 10 per cent a year discount factor, Table 3.2 shows that the net present value of the amount invested in working capital in this case would be €19,918 (a negative, of course).

In order to simplify the working capital adjustment, some organizations calculate their working capital to sales ratio and apply it throughout. (Working capital is here defined as receivables plus inventory minus payables.) It is important to note that the working capital requirement each year is the *change* in working capital, not the absolute requirement. If in doubt you will see that the (new) project in Table 3.3 shows no change in sales between years 2 and 3. If there is no change in sales, why would there be any change in the working capital requirement? Moreover, it may well be best to assume the working capital requirement happens at the beginning of each year (i.e. the end of the previous year), so each number needs to be moved one year to the left. Bear in mind that an increasing working capital requirement is a negative cash flow and vice versa. Note that this method has the advantage of showing the working capital being recovered at the end of the project rather than a year later (there are no sales in year 5—the project effectively ended at the end of year 4).

Table 3.1 Investment in working capital (in € thousands)

End of Year	0	1	2	3	4	5
Inventory	-40					40
Payables	30					-30
Receivables		-56				56
	-10	-56				66

Table 3.2 Present value of investment in working capital

End of Year	0	1	2	3	4	5
	€	€				€
Inventory	-40,000					40,000
Payables	30,000					-30,000
Receivables		-56,000				56,000
	-10,000	-56,000				66,000
	x	x				x
Discount factor	1	0.909				0.621
Present value	-10,000	-50,904				40,986
Net Present Value	**-19,918**					

Table 3.3 Calculation of working capital requirement

Year	**0**	**1**	**2**	**3**	**4**	**5**
Sales		80	100	100	30	0
Total working capital requirement at 10% of sales		8	10	10	3	0
Change in working capital requirement		8	2	0	−7	−3
Figure transferred to project cash flow forecast	**−8**	**−2**	**0**	**+7**	**+3**	**0**

A useful check is to ensure that the sum of the working capital 'cash flows' on your spreadsheet totals zero, as all the working capital will be recovered at the end of the project.

3.3 Taxation

Obviously, our project is likely to be subject to tax, and this needs to be taken into account in the project spreadsheet. As always, the timing of the cash payments needs to be taken into consideration—some countries will levy tax in the year following that in which the profit is made, others might charge an approximate amount during the year the profits are being made (perhaps based on the previous year's result). Remember also that we are looking at the impact of the project on the whole enterprise, so if our project makes a loss for tax purposes in a particular year, there is a good chance that those losses can be offset against the profits of the rest of the business, thus reducing the tax bill of the business as a whole. Whereas tax paid is of course a 'minus' on our spreadsheet, this saved taxation is a 'benefit' of the project and should be regarded as a 'plus' in the spreadsheet—not because the tax authorities pay us cash but because the company pays less tax (hence a 'failure to outflow'). If the whole enterprise, as well as our project, is loss-making in a particular year, in some countries the loss can be carried forward to offset against future years' profits, or even carried back to reduce the tax of previous years, in which case a 'real' cash flow might be received in the form of a refund from the tax authorities.

The next important point relates to the depreciation of fixed (non-current) assets purchased as part of the project. Remember that *depreciation is not a cash flow item.* From a cash flow point of view, we are only interested in how much the asset was purchased for, how much it will be sold for, and when. This will determine what will appear on the cash flow statement. If there was a row for depreciation as well, this would lead to a double counting of the expense—once when it was purchased, and again as it gets depreciated over time. So, we ignore depreciation on the spreadsheet. However, it becomes significant if the tax authorities in the project's country allow depreciation of the particular asset for tax purposes. It is very unlikely they will allow the *whole* cost of the, for example, machinery, against profits in the year in which it is purchased, but they may well allow the cost to be written off via depreciation *over time*. So, the depreciation should not appear as such on the spreadsheet, but it does affect the amount of tax paid each year. We would recommend that, if you are new to this topic, the tax calculation be done separately from the main spreadsheet, so as to avoid confusion as to which rows are to be included in the totals and which not. Remember that if the calculations show that a positive amount of tax is payable, this will be a *negative* cash flow!

As an example, let us return to the Nellam truck project from the previous chapter (Example 2.7). We will assume that (i) the truck can be depreciated over its useful life on the straight-line basis, (ii) the purchase of the truck is made at the start of the first year (not the end of the previous year, which might mean the tax relief is received in year 0), (iii) tax is paid in the year the profits are made, (iv) the tax rate is 20% and (v) the rest of the company makes a profit such that any losses of the project can be offset against the company's total profits (Table 3.4).

Note that, unsurprisingly, the NPV is worse (a higher negative!) than in the previous chapter (which showed about $-3k), as, apart from in year 1, the tax has reduced the net cash flows. Also, as we will see in a later chapter, the presence of tax might well have reduced the discount rate to be used—a complication we have not taken into account here.

In practice, when calculating the tax in the spreadsheet, it is clearly important that the tax regulations of the country where the project is to take place are taken into consideration—and quite possibly the regulations that apply in the country of the holding company will be relevant as well.

Many countries use a system other than the straight-line basis to determine the depreciation that is allowed against tax each year—sometimes giving a more generous allowance in the early years of the life of the asset in order to encourage investment in productive assets. For example, at the time of writing, the United States uses a system called MACRS (Modified Accelerated Cost Recovery System) which, for assets such as computers deemed to have a five-year life (there are different deemed lives for different asset classes), the 'depreciation' rates for tax purposes are as shown in Table 3.5. [Readers for whom the US system is relevant, are advised to check on the latest position.]

Example 3.1 A US company is thinking of buying a computer system, which, if purchased today for $100,000, is anticipated to have a five-year life and save the company $32,000 per year over its lifetime. The saving is assumed to increase profits (rather than decrease losses). The company uses the modified accelerated cost recovery system (MACRS) as shown in Table 3.5.

At a discount rate of 8% and a tax rate of 21%, is the investment worthwhile? The calculations are shown in Table 3.6.

Table 3.4 Tax calculation for Nellam Truck Project ($'000)

MAIN CALCULATION

Year	0	1	2	3	4
Truck cost	-52				
Net cash inflows		12	14	16	18
Tax from below		0.2	-0.2	-0.6	-1.0
Net cash flows	-52	12.2	13.8	15.4	17
Discount factor at 8%	1	.926	.857	.794	.735
Present value	-52	11.3	11.8	12.2	12.5
NPV	*-4.2*				

TAX CALCULATION

Year	0	1	2	3	4
"Profit" from main calculation		12	14	16	18
Depreciation allowance (52/4)		-13	-13	-13	-13
Taxable profit		-1	1	3	5
Tax at 20%		-0.2	0.2	0.6	1.0

Table 3.5 Macrs (Modified Accelerated Cost Recovery System)

Year	% Allowed
1	20
2	32
3	19.2
4	11.52
5	11.52
6	5.76

3.4 Comparing Projects of Unequal Length

What should we do if we are trying to decide which one of two projects of unequal length to go for? Consider the following projects (Project C is the same one that was considered in Example 2.3 in the previous chapter) (Table 3.7).

Table 3.6 Calculation for example 3.1

	Main spreadsheet							
	Year	**0**	**1**	**2**	**3**	**4**	**5**	**6**
1	Initial investment	-100,000						
2	Yearly savings		32,000	32,000	32,000	32,000	32,000	
3	Tax (see below)		-2,520	0	-2,688	-4,301	-4,301	1,210
4	**Net cashflow (1+2+3)**	**-100,000**	**29,480**	**32,000**	**29,312**	**27,699**	**27,699**	**1,210**
5	Discount factor 8%	1.000	0.926	0.857	0.794	0.735	0.681	0.630
6	**Present value (4*5)**	**-100,000**	**27,298**	**27,424**	**23,274**	**20,359**	**18,863**	**762**
7	NPV (sum of line 6)	**17,980**						
	Tax calculation							
	Year	**0**	**1**	**2**	**3**	**4**	**5**	**6**
a	Profit before tax (PBT)		32,000	32,000	32,000	32,000	32,000	
b	*% allowed by Macrs*	100,000	*20.00%*	*32.00%*	*19.20%*	*11.52%*	*11.52%*	*5.76%*
c	Macrs depr'n (b*100k)		20,000	32,000	19,200	11,520	11,520	5,760
d	Taxable profit (a-c)		12,000	0	12,800	20,480	20,480	-5,760
e	Tax (d*tax rate) at 21%		2,520	0	2,688	4,301	4,301	-1,210

Table 3.7 Projects of unequal lengths

	£000		**Project C**		
	Year	**0**	**1**	**2**	**3**
a	Investment outflow	-15.00			
b	Cash receipts		10.00	8.00	6.00
c	**Total cash flow**	**-15.00**	**10.00**	**8.00**	**6.00**
d	Discount factor @ 8% a year	1.000	0.926	0.857	0.794
e	Present value (c*d)	-15.00	9.26	6.86	4.76
	Net Present Value	**5.88**			

	£000			**Project D**			
	Year	**0**	**1**	**2**	**3**	**4**	**5**
a	Investment outflow	-15.00					
b	Cash receipts		9.00	7.00	5.00	4.00	2.00
c	**Total cash flow**	-15.00	9.00	7.00	5.00	4.00	2.00
d	Discount factor @ 8% a year	1.000	0.926	0.857	0.794	0.735	0.681
e	Present value (c*d)	-15.00	8.33	6.00	3.97	2.94	1.36
	Net Present Value	**7.60**					

It's not immediately obvious which one is better. Project D has the larger NPV, but it will take five years to get there! Project C has a smaller NPV but achieves it in just three years.

If the two projects are independent of each other—that is, we could do either, both, or neither of them—it is usually best to rely on the straightforward NPV calculation. But if they are mutually exclusive—that is, if we do one, we can't do the other for whatever reason—then the answer is to calculate the Equivalent

Table 3.8 Projects of unequal lengths (continued)

Project C																
Year	**0**	**1**	**2**	**3**	**4**	**5**	**6**	**7**	**8**	**9**	**10**	**11**	**12**	**13**	**14**	**15**
		10	8	6	10	8	6	10	8	6	10	8	6	10	8	6
	-15			-15			-15			-15			-15			
	-15	10	8	-9	10	8	-9	10	8	-9	10	8	-9	10	8	6
	Net Present Value			**19.53**												
Project D																
Year	**0**	**1**	**2**	**3**	**4**	**5**	**6**	**7**	**8**	**9**	**10**	**11**	**12**	**13**	**14**	**15**
		9	7	5	4	2	9	7	5	4	2	9	7	5	4	2
	-15					-15					-15					
	-15	9	7	5	4	-13	9	7	5	4	-13	9	7	5	4	2
	Net Present Value			**16.30**												

Annual Annuity (EAA) for each project. That is, the *equal* amount received in each of the either three or five years that would generate the actual NPV of each project. In the previous chapter we saw that the NPV of an annuity was derived by multiplying the annual cash flow by the appropriate annuity discount factor. But now we *know* the NPV, but we don't know the annual cash flow. So let that cash flow for Project C be c. The year 3 discount factor for an annuity at 8% is 2.577. So 2.577c = 5.88 (project C's actual NPV), therefore c = 2.28. Let the annual cash flow for Project D be d. The year 5 discount factor for an annuity is 3.993, so 3.993d = 7.60 and d = 1.90.[2] are the equivalent annual annuities for Projects C and D, respectively, and we can see that the EAA of project C is higher. This would normally, therefore, be regarded as the superior project.

This is particularly true if the projects are repeatable. In that case, an alternative method is also available, which is to take the lowest common multiple of the project lives—in our example, 15 years—and run project C five times (which would take 15 years) and Project D three times (also taking 15 years). Thus both projects have been run over the same time period of 15 years in total and should be comparable, see Table 3.8.

Again, Project C has the higher NPV (note, the NPV calculations are not shown). Readers might justifiably feel however that such circumstances are fairly unfeasible in real-life, and prefer to stick to the simple rule of choosing the project with the higher/highest NPV.

[2] Note that in Excel®, you could use the *pmt* function, that is: = pmt(rate,nper,pv), to find the EAA. Inside the brackets of the *pmt* function you need to specify *rate*—the discount rate; *nper*—the number of years and *pv*—the present value, or the total amount that a series of future payments is worth today. For example, for project C: = pmt(8%, 3, −5.88) would yield 2.28. We enter the NPV of the project with a minus sign, so that the resulting EAA would be positive.

3.5 Capital Disinvestment

3.5.1 Why Projects End

Capital disinvestment means disposing of assets a business holds. This may result in receiving sales proceeds for 'second-hand' assets; it may not involve any cash receipts; or it may even require making cash payments to someone for collecting or demolishing the asset or for 'tidying up' after a project has finished (e.g. mining or nuclear energy). At the time of writing, the French energy company EDF has on its Balance Sheet provisions for nuclear plant decommissioning and suchlike totalling €62 billion! Possible limits to a project's life may stem from the following:

1. *Physical exhaustion of equipment. The question may be whether or not to replace the equipment (and if so, when).*
2. *Technical obsolescence of equipment or process. This implies the end of the asset's 'economic' life though not of its physical life.*
3. *Market factors, such as changing consumer tastes. It may not always be possible to extend a product's life cycle by suitable refinements.*
4. *Lapse of time, such as a lease for a finite period or expiry of a patent.*
5. *Political factors, e.g. banning the sale or advertising of a product.*

The nature of a capital project may change over time, especially if its expected life extends for several years. Sometimes a firm may need to abandon a project early, if conditions or estimates have changed—perhaps even before it comes on stream. (For example, a new drug where a competitor has got to market first.)

Technically one can compare the NPV of the ongoing project's remaining life with the NPV of stopping it and selling the assets. One question to analyse may be not whether but when to stop. Another option for self-contained projects might be to sell them as a going concern to another company. A project which no longer seems attractive enough to Company A might still be of interest to Company B. (This is like any voluntary market exchange, where the different subjective valuations of buyer and seller mean that both parties normally expect to benefit.)

It might sometimes seem easier to carry on with a project—effectively throwing good money after bad—than to cut one's losses when something has gone wrong with it. Even though the original decision to go ahead may be a 'sunk cost'—and therefore theoretically irrelevant—in practice, managers can be quite emotional about projects they have championed.

3.5.2 Capital Recovery

Amounts recoverable at the end of a project's life may represent the proceeds of assets: 1. value of land or buildings; 2. scrap or second-hand value of equipment; 3. working capital, such as inventory and receivables. Or the ongoing value of the project itself to another buyer. These amounts will appear as positive cash inflows

Table 3.9 Extending horizon period from 15 to 50 years at 15 per cent a year

years→ rate↓	10	15	20	25	30	35	40	45	50
5%	7.722	10.380	12.462	14.094	15.372	16.374	17.159	17.774	18.256
10%	6.145	7.606	8.514	9.077	9.427	9.644	9.779	9.863	9.915
15%	5.019	5.847	6.259	6.464	6.566	6.617	6.642	6.654	6.661
20%	4.192	75	4.870	4.948	4.979	4.992	4.997	4.999	999

at or beyond the terminal date, together with any tax-related cash flows. Of course, a firm must discount back to present value any amounts (terminal values or residual values) it expects to recover at the end.

The longer the life of the project, the further away in time the terminal date will be, and for any given discount rate, the lower will be the present value. That is why young people are often rather bored by questions about pensions, while those about to retire find the topic strangely fascinating! (It is an intriguing question how, if at all, one's personal real discount rate varies over the course of one's life!)

In appraising long-life projects, it is normal to use an arbitrary horizon period of ten or, perhaps, fifteen years as a rule. Firms do not explicitly consider cash flows beyond the horizon, even if they expect the project to last longer. But of course, including a 'terminal value' at the horizon date in effect does extend the life of the project (though possibly in a different form).

With a fairly high discount rate, this approach seems sensible, since it would make little difference to the amount of the present value. For example, with a 15 per cent a year discount rate, more than trebling a project's horizon period, from 15 to 50 years, would increase the present value of equal annual cash inflows by only 0.814, or 14 per cent. As Table 3.9 shows, the discount factor would increase only from 5.847 to 6.661.

3.6 Inflation

3.6.1 What Inflation Means

So far, we have ignored the effect of inflation on the cash flows of capital projects. But it can be significant. Given that many projects last for more than ten years, a 5 per cent annual rate of inflation means that by year 15 prices may be at least twice as high as at the start.

Inflation is not just a technical detail affecting the numbers: it can have a profound impact on business projects. For example, if one country has faster inflation than others, sooner or later its currency will have to devalue against other currencies. Meanwhile there will be much economic and political uncertainty. A devaluation may have a major effect, for example, on export prices; on the cost of imported materials; and so on. Or high domestic inflation may lead in the future, as it often has in the past, to some form of general price control. This too can devastate business profits since it often amounts to compelling firms to cut their prices in real terms.

3.6.2 Inflation and Capital Projects

In principle there are two different ways to cope with the effect of inflation on capital project appraisal. The key thing is to be consistent: either to discount money cash flows at a money (nominal) discount rate, or to discount 'real' (that is, excluding inflation) cash flows at a real discount rate. (Note that the discount rate derived in Chapter 7 is the *nominal* discount rate.)

Forecasting all cash flows in money terms means allowing for any expected specific money price changes. One then needs to discount the future money cash flows at a money discount rate which includes an inflation premium to allow for general inflation. If the rate of inflation varies from year to year, it may be rather messy using a different money discount rate from year to year over a project's life (for the net present value method). (When using the internal rate of return method, of course, one cannot vary the discount rate either between years, or between items—say of different riskiness—in the same year.)

The alternative is to forecast the cash flows without allowing for inflation, then discount them at the real discount rate. The real discount rate should be lower than the money discount rate by the expected rate of inflation. For example, if the money discount rate is 12 per cent and we expect 3 per cent inflation (which the money discount rate of 12 per cent includes), then the real discount rate would be only 9 per cent. (Strictly speaking it should be $1.12 \div 1.03 = 1.0874$ [i.e. 8.74 per cent], but when inflation rates are fairly low simple subtraction is accurate enough.)

It might seem less trouble merely to forecast cash flows in real terms throughout (in effect in terms of 'Year 0 dollars'), and then just discount by the same real discount rate each year. But such an approach has three snags, as follows:

1. General inflation means an increase in the average level of prices. If 'general' inflation is 5 per cent, some items may go up 8 per cent in price, others 3 per cent, and others may go down by 2 per cent. Selling prices, material costs and wage rates may be critical for a capital project's success or failure. So, one does need to forecast specific price changes. It will nearly always be too simplistic to assume that inflation will affect all items in the same way over a period of years; though forecasting the precise differences may not be easy.
2. For tax purposes, depreciation allowances relate to the original money cost of certain fixed assets, without adjustment for inflation. Hence, in times of inflation, tax depreciation allowances will be falling in real terms. The effect of inflation on tax may not be simple: even if the money amount of sales revenue and cash expenses were to increase exactly in line with general inflation, the

amount of taxable profits (and therefore of tax payable) would increase by somewhat more than that rate.

3. Investment in working capital is also subject to inflation. Inventory levels which stay constant in physical terms will require an increasing level of money investment. Likewise, if receivables days outstanding remain constant, the money investment in receivables will grow as selling prices increase in terms of money. (And payables will tend to grow as suppliers' prices increase.)

3.7 Capital Planning

3.7.1 Capital Spending

In addition to ways of looking at each project's likely profits or future cash flows, companies need a system of capital budgeting. This involves planning aggregate capital spending over the next year or two and splitting it into monthly or quarterly amounts forming part of the cash budget. Among other things, this helps to arrange suitable financing (where necessary) in good time.

Both the amount and the timing of capital projects can change quickly. Business and financial conditions may make it desirable either to speed up or to slow down capital spending. In extreme cases, firms may even have to cancel projects after they have begun, though that can be very expensive.

Capital spending takes time. This, more than limited finance, may account for companies sometimes imposing capital rationing. As discussed in Chapter 2, under conditions of capital rationing, companies may use the profitability index (PI) to rank projects: where not all projects with a positive net present value can go ahead, a company may prefer those with higher PIs (rather than those with higher absolute NPVs).

Many capital projects are risky, so businesses tend to be cautious about capital spending. Once under way, projects may not be reversible. For specialized plant and equipment, there may be almost no second-hand market, and even a potential buyer might only offer a very low price.

That is why companies look carefully before they leap and insist on thorough procedures for capital project proposals. The larger the amount of money involved, or the greater the strategic importance, the higher up in a company projects must go for approval. Such approval may sometimes seem to be merely 'rubber-stamping', but this is probably because extensive informal discussions have already taken place before the formal submission of the project. In most firms, what goes on informally is at least as important as the formal system, even though it is not so visible. The internal politics of capital budgeting can be crucial.

3.7.2 Evaluation Before and After

Table 3.10 compares methods for looking at capital projects in advance and those used for business performance appraisal after the event. Clearly there are several differences.

It has been suggested that using cash flows as the basis for ex-post performance appraisal (rather than accounting profits) could avoid many of the differences. (The asterisks in Table 3.10 show which way cash flow accounting would probably tend.)

Items 1a and 4 would remain difficult items to overcome. After the event it may often be hard to identify incremental amounts resulting from specific projects which the ongoing business has thoroughly absorbed. (This is a major problem in post-project audits: see below.) Nor will it be easy to make useful guesses after the event about the actual level of risk involved. (This is not easy before the event either, but at least ex ante one can hardly be unaware of uncertainty.)

Figure 3.1 illustrates the first point: the contrast between looking at incremental amounts relating to discrete projects over a project's whole life and looking at overall totals relating to the whole business unit for a single accounting period.

3.7.3 Post-Project Audits

Some larger companies arrange post-project audits for some of their capital projects. As soon as a project is on stream, they can check the amount and the timing of the capital spending. But the audit may be more ambitious and try to review operating cash flows too.

Normally such audits take place when a project may still have most of its life to run. It would make little sense to wait until a 10-year project was over before having an audit. Conditions would have changed too much, the people involved

Table 3.10 Ex ante project appraisal versus ex post performance appraisal

In advance	After the event
Main methods: NPV, IRR	Main method: Return On Investment (ROI)
1a. Incremental amounts	*1a. Overall totals
1b. relating to discrete 'projects'	*1b. relating to whole business unit
1c. over all (or most) of project's life	*1c. for a single period (often one year)
*2a. Cash flows	2a. Profits (or losses)
*2b. after tax (but before interest)	2b. often before tax (and before interest)
*2c. ignoring depreciation	2c. after charging depreciation
3a. May be constant purchasing power	*3a. Usually monetary Units
3b. usually discounted	*3b. not discounted
3c. reinvestment assumption (implicit or explicit)	*3c. No reinvestment assumption
4. Uncertainty clearly relevant	4. Uncertainty often ignored

Note *Indicates which way cash-flow accounting would probably tend

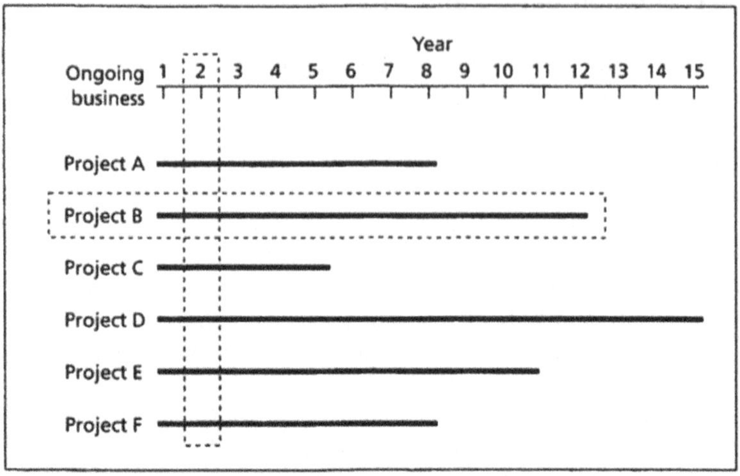

Fig. 3.1 Project lives and accounting periods

might have moved on, and any lessons might be out of date. Thus, an audit may take place after a project has been running, say, about 1 year. It can compare original estimates with actual outcomes for capital spending and perhaps for the first year's operations. But for later years any comparison may simply be with most recent estimates of future results.

A post-project audit need not be entirely backward-looking. It may sometimes be possible to reassess a project's future as a result. Probably only larger projects, or projects with problems, will be subject to audit. It may not be easy to measure a project's impact after the event. That implies a need to specify the purpose of post-project audits. It might be dangerous to allocate blame where things have gone wrong. That might induce a risk-averse attitude in managers. It is probably more useful to try to learn what went right as well as what did not and how to do better in future. Important aspects to review might include: capital spending, assumptions about market size and market share, operating costs, the timing of events, estimates of project life and so on.

3.7.4 International Aspects

Where, for example, a Eurozone company proposes to invest in a capital project outside the zone, it must estimate incremental net-of-local-tax cash flows in the local currency. It probably doesn't matter whether the company assesses projects' net present values in terms of local currency or in Euros. But any extra tax payable in the home country must be allowed for—both the amount and the timing. This might arise, for example, if the local tax rate is less than the home country's tax rate. There is, of course, no need to plan for actual conversion into Euros, though we assume there are no exchange restrictions.

If a company expects more inflation in the local currency (than in Euros), the nominal local discount rate should be higher (than a Euro discount rate) to allow for the extra inflation premium. Translation of local currency cash flows into Euros should use the exchange rate expected at the time when the local cash flows arise. The amounts in Euros should thus reflect any expected decline in the local currency's exchange rate against the Euro. (But in the short run exchange rates may not fluctuate precisely in line with differences in rates of inflation.)

3.8 A Concluding Note

In Chapter 2 we introduced the basics of discounting and how this method can be used to evaluate projects. In this chapter we extended the discussion to consider complications such as taxation, inflation, choosing between projects of unequal length and disposing of assets. We also discussed how to treat working capital in the project evaluation process, as well as other issues relating to capital planning and budgeting more generally.

Don't forget, however, that the essence of project appraisal is to consider future cash flows that arise from the project in order to assist the firm's managers to determine whether the investment is worthwhile. The elephant in the room is, of course, the uncertainty associated with future cash flow. In the next chapter, we turn our attention to this topic.

3.8.1 Problems

Problem 3.1 Stephen Collier Inc is considering an investment project requiring the investment of $50,000 in new fixed assets and $12,000 in additional inventory, the latter of which can be recovered in full at the end of the project. The annual sales revenue for the project is forecast to be $80,000, and the annual running costs $60,000 (including straight-line depreciation of $10,000). The project's life is expected to be five years. Ignoring tax:

a. show the cash flows year by year
b. should the project be accepted if the firm's cut off rate is 20 per cent?
c. what is the internal rate of return on the project?

Problem 3.2 Refer to Problem 3.1 above. Additional information is as follows:

- In order to make room for the new equipment, existing assets which the firm currently use need to be sold and can fetch $2,000, subject to capital gains tax of 30% which is payable upon realization of the capital gains.

- Tax at 30 per cent is assumed payable on *profits* on the last day of the year in which they are earned.
- For tax purposes, straight-line depreciation is used.

a. Show the net cash flows year by year.
b. Should the project be accepted if the firm's after-tax cut off rate is 20 per cent?
c. What is the project's internal rate of return?
d. To what figure could the current £30,000 annual pre-tax operating cash inflows fall, and the project still be acceptable?

Problem 3.3 Colin Park is enthusiastic about a new machine (A), which he thinks would enable Park Products to reduce operating costs by €20,000 a year (before tax of 30 per cent). The machine costs €60,000. For tax purposes, straight-line depreciation over the life of the asset is permitted (Ignore any tax time-lags). At the end of its expected five-year life, the machine could probably be sold for about €5,000 (Ignore any tax consequences of this point). The company normally requires a return of at least 12 per cent a year (after-tax) on this kind of investment.

Should Park Products buy the machine?

Risk and Uncertainty

4

4.1 Introduction

In business, risk is the possibility that future profit will differ from expectations which, in extreme situations, may even result in the firm going bankrupt.

Sometimes a distinction is made between risk and uncertainty. Risk is when we know the chance of each possible outcome occurring (as in roulette or with dice). Uncertainty exists where, as is usual in business, one can only estimate the odds (that is, guess). In practice it is very unlikely that the managers of a business know the possibility of each outcome. In fact, they often rely on past data, experience or gut feelings to attach probabilities to possible future outcomes. It is for this reason that we shall treat risk and uncertainty as identical in this chapter and use the two terms interchangeably.

The causes of business risk are many and varied. They include external factors relating to events outside of the firm such as socio-economic or political changes. For example, an economic crisis may reduce demand for the firm's products. Likewise, technological innovations may render the company's products obsolete. Other risk factors may relate to the industry the company is in. For example, the rise of a competitor, or new industry regulations that make production excessively expensive. On top of these external factors, there are also internal risk factors to which the firm is exposed. Bad management is one such factor, which could have serious implications for the company's profit levels and survival.

A firm can reduce business risk in a number of ways. Table 4.1, which is certainly not comprehensive, lists three kinds of business actions: contractual, flexible and uncertainty-reducing. Some actions may either reduce risk or increase it, such as diversifying into different (less familiar) businesses or building spare capacity.

Sometimes business risk is subdivided into various types. Environmental risk, security risk and country risk are some examples. Another type of business risk is the risk associated with capital budgeting or with specific projects. Risk in capital

R. Manos et al., *Corporate Finance for Business*,
https://doi.org/10.1007/978-3-030-92419-5_4

Table 4.1 Ways of reducing uncertainty

	Contractual	Flexible	Uncertainty-reducing
Sales	Produce goods only against firm orders, not for stock	Avoid over-dependency on a few customers or products	Research market before launching new products
Purchases	Arrange long-term supply contracts	Arrange more than one source of supply	Stockpile raw materials
Assets	Insure as much as possible	Use general-purpose rather than highly specialized equipment	Retain high liquid resources
Employees	Contract work out rather than use full-time employees	Pay partly by bonus or commission rather than flat rate	Promote from within rather than hire from outside

budgeting may include unexpected changes in unit costs or in demand for the product, timing issues or supply chain delays.

Regardless of its type, business risk generally relates to how a business invests its resources. In contrast, financial risk relates to how the business finances its investments. Borrowing to finance assets is risky because the business must legally make regular interest payments and must repay the amount borrowed on the due date. For any change in operating profits (before interest), such financial gearing increases the volatility (= risk or uncertainty) of the profits for equity shareholders. In contrast, equity capital is less risky for the business since it implies no legal commitments in terms of dividends or capital repayments (see Chapter 8).

In this chapter we discuss risk in capital budgeting. We begin in Sect. 4.2 by explaining how to adjust the Net Present Value (NPV) to account for risk. Section 4.3 deals with capital budgeting techniques that are useful in assessing and further understanding the risks and uncertainties inherent in the project being evaluated. From risk assessment we move to Sect. 4.4 and 4.5 where we discuss how to manage risk and real options respectively. After that, in Sect. 4.6 we turn to dealing briefly with foreign exchange risk—that is, the risk associated with cash flows that arise in foreign currencies. Finally, Sect. 4.7 offers a concluding note followed by some practice problems.

4.2 Risk-Adjusted Net Present Value (NPV)

4.2.1 Expected Values

Suppose that, for a new product, a firm reckons that annual sales levels of 400, 250 or 100 units are possible and that the chances of each outcome (in order) are 0.1, 0.6 and 0.3. (Of course, in practice we would not expect such discrete outcomes.) What figure should be discounted in calculating the Net Present Value (NPV)?

Table 4.2 Subjective probabilities and 'expected values'

(1)	(2)	(3)	(4)	(5)
Sales volume	Estimated net cashflow in £'000	Estimated probability	'Expected' volume of sales [(1)*(3)]	'Expected' net cashflow in £'000 [(2)*(3)]
400	130	0.1	40	13
250	40	0.6	150	24
100	-50	0.3	30	-15
		1.0	**220**	**22**

By weighting the possible outcomes by their estimated chances of happening, we can calculate an 'expected value' of sales volume of 220 units (see Table 4.2). We can do the same for the estimated net cash flows (after allowing for costs) at each level of sales, to arrive at an 'expected net cash flow' of £22,000; and in principle we could use the same approach to compute an 'expected Net Present Value' for the whole project and make a decision on that basis.

Attaching subjective probabilities to uncertain future events allows manipulation of the numbers. But that hardly makes the process 'scientific'. What confidence can we have in guesses about the chances of various outcomes? Can we even be sure we have considered every possible event? Experience suggests that events which in advance seemed quite impossible often appear afterwards to have been inevitable. (For example, the collapse of the Berlin Wall or the Great Lockdown following the outbreak of the Coronavirus.)

If we know the true odds, there is no uncertainty, only risk. But we are not safe in extrapolating frequencies for future events from statistics of past occurrences in similar cases. (For example, the millennium bug wasn't much of a problem at the end of the first millennium.) For we are then merely assuming that the past will repeat itself. But trends go on … until they stop! And what about unprecedented events? These are more typical of major business opportunities ('the chance of a lifetime'). What are the odds against the United Kingdom re-joining the European Union in the next fifteen years? Nobody knows.

A further problem is that, when dealing with unique events, we can never know if our estimate of the odds was correct—even after the event. Thus, learning from events is not always easy.

Still, given our estimate of future possible outcomes and their probabilities, we can compute an expected value as we have done in Table 4.2. If we wanted to calculate the NPV of the project, we need to account for the fact that what we are going to discount is not the future net cash flow next year, but rather, the expected net cash flow. We could adjust for the risk in those cash flows by increasing the rate at which we discount future cash flows.

4.2.2 Risk-Adjusted Discount Rate

When computing a project's NPV we have to pre-select a discount rate which normally reflects a company's weighted average cost of capital (WACC): the average of the company's cost of debt and its cost of equity, weighted according to the proportions of each that it has. The costs of debt and equity are the rates of return required by the company's lenders and shareholders respectively. This is discussed in depth in Chapter 7. For our purposes now, though, the important point is that the average cost of financing, the WACC, gives the appropriate discount rate for a project of average risk. Some companies use different discount rates for various kinds of projects, to allow for *differences* in risk. For example, they may regard cost reduction projects as low-risk, and new product projects as high-risk. (Conversely, one large company uses a lower discount rate for certain high-risk technical projects, as a deliberate safeguard against falling behind in the technology race.) How much to adjust the 'average' discount rate (the WACC) to allow for high- or low-risk projects is hard to judge.

The same might be done for different periods or for different kinds of cash flows. For example, it may be that the early years of a project are riskier than the later years. Or the expected cash flow resulting from tax depreciation allowances on capital expenditure may be a good deal less uncertain than cash inflows estimated from future sales revenues. One could allow for this by discounting tax benefits at a lower rate (with a smaller risk premium), and thus, in effect, valuing them more highly. However, as a rule, for projects judged to be of the same risk class as the company's average project, the company's WACC is used as the risk-adjusted discount rate in computing NPVs.

Calculating risk-adjusted NPV using expected cash flows and a risk-adjusted discount rate (the WACC, if the project being evaluated is of the same risk as the average project of the company, or another risk-adjusted discount rate, otherwise) provides an acceptable solution to capital budgeting under conditions of uncertainty. However, management often wishes to further investigate the complexities, risks and uncertainties relating to projects that it is considering. A number of techniques have been developed for this purpose.

4.3 Risk Assessing Techniques in Capital Budgeting

4.3.1 Decision Trees

When facing a complex problem, such as whether to make an investment today when future cash flows are uncertain, it is often helpful to break it down into a number of simpler sub-problems. That is the idea behind decision trees.

A decision tree is a tree-like flow chart of alternative sequential decisions and the various possible outcomes of those decisions. It is common to incorporate subjective estimates of probabilities of outcomes in order to determine 'expected values' for each decision alternative. By 'rolling back' from the ultimate outcomes,

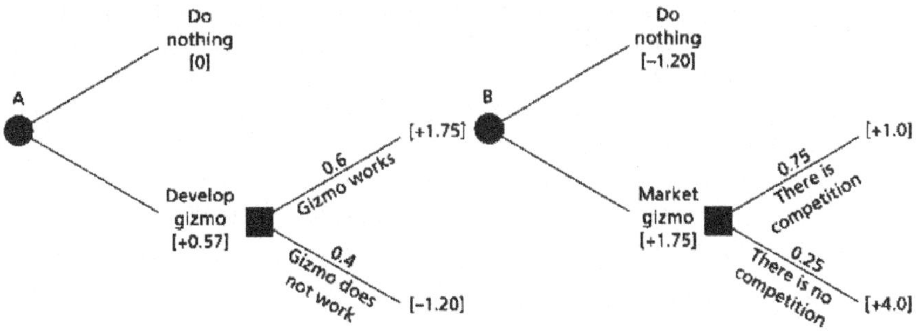

Fig. 4.1 Decision tree for Zing's gizmo

one can (in theory) then simply choose the decision alternative with the highest expected value.

Example 4.1

Zing plc is considering developing and marketing a new gizmo. Development will cost £1.2 million to be paid immediately and will take one year. There is reckoned to be a 60 per cent chance that, at the end of that time, the gizmo will work. If it does, marketing the product will then be an option. It is not clear whether there will be a competing product in the market. If there isn't, the NPV of expected after-tax cash flows is estimated at +£4.0 million. If there *is* competition, the expected NPV is only + £1.0 million. There is thought to be a 75 per cent chance of competition.

Figure 4.1 portrays the decision tree, distinguishing between decisions [•] and events [■]. By rolling back the expected values of the various outcomes and giving effect to the estimated probabilities of each outcome, we can 'value' each decision. Obviously, if we believe all the numbers, we will choose the decision with the highest positive net present value.

Figure 4.1 suggests that the value of developing the gizmo is +£0.57 million, so on the face of it the decision should be to go ahead with development.

Starting from the end and rolling back, the calculations in Fig. 4.1 which yield the NPV of +£0.57 million relating to the decision to develop the gizmo are as follows. At decision point B, if Zing decides to abandon the project and not invest further in marketing, then the firm suffers a loss totalling £1.20 million NPV. But we want to calculate the NPV of the decision to market the gizmo. So, at point B, the expected NPV is:

$$0.75 \times £1m + 0.25 \times £4m = £1.75m$$

Rolling further back to decision point A, if we decide not to invest then the NPV is zero. But we are interested in calculating the NPV of the decision to start the gizmo project. If we go ahead with the project and it fails, the loss is £1.20 million in present value terms (the cost of the investment). If it is successful, the expected NPV is = £1.75*m* as we calculated at decision point B. The problem is that the chances of success or failure are 60 per cent/40 per cent in favour of success. So, the NPV at decision point A is the weighted average of these two scenarios:

$$0.60 \times £1.75m + 0.40 \times (-£1.2m) = £0.57$$

◀

Of course, we can vary some of the estimates and use sensitivity analysis (see below) to test how much difference it makes, for example, if we revise our estimate of the odds (or of anything else). In practice it may be that one of the benefits of decision trees is not so much the numerical 'result', but the pictorial representation of the key decisions and events that affect the decisions.

4.3.2 Sensitivity Analysis

Business managers usually must plan, control and make decisions relating to projects on the basis of uncertain estimates about the future. They may know some figures, such as suppliers' prices for the next few months, but about others they may feel very unsure. Where adverse events could badly impact a big project, this could result in great damage to the business as a whole. It is thus important that managers consider the range and likelihood of possible outcomes. The same is true in respect of favourable outcomes. It would not be very sensible to embark on a project without having any idea that, if everything worked out right, it could be not just modestly successful, but hugely profitable.

Sensitivity analysis is a popular approach to deal with future uncertainties in capital budgeting which amounts to assessing the sensitivity of the proposed project to various inputs and assumptions. It helps to deal with the uncertainty in the project because it points to variables to which the project is particularly vulnerable.

The first step in sensitivity analysis is to make a single 'best estimate' ('best' = most likely, not 'optimal') for each item. One might then also make 'optimistic' and 'pessimistic' estimates for each. The spreads may not be symmetrical. For instance, under the optimistic estimate there may be capacity constraints which would prevent a firm from exceeding budgeted sales volume by much, whereas under the pessimistic estimate—for example, economic recession—there could be a sharp decline.

Instead of making overall optimistic and pessimistic estimates, a sensitivity analysis may involve varying the most likely estimate for each item in turn, to see how much it would affect the result. It is not much use to try changing each item by a fixed percentage (say, 10 per cent); for some items could vary by much more, while others may be unlikely to change by nearly as much. Moreover, some smaller items will not matter much even if they change by a large percentage. So, one needs to identify the critical items, where even a fairly small percentage change could make quite a large difference to the overall result.

Sometimes firms carry out sensitivity analysis by identifying key variables and calculating by how much each in turn (holding the rest constant) can change before the project is rejected. That is, before the NPV of the project is equal to zero. Example 4.2 illustrates the application of sensitivity analysis.

Example 4.2—Sensitivity Analysis

The Hair Factory company is considering the production of a new product with a life expectancy of 4 years. This is a new hair treatment oil which is expected to fetch a price of $12.50 per unit and requires an immediate investment of $2.5 million in equipment. Variable costs include the cost of production—estimated at $3 per unit—and selling costs which are likely to amount to 4 per cent of sales revenue. There are also advertising costs, anticipated at $50,000 in year 1, but reducing by 10 per cent per year throughout the project's life. The company sells mainly to other businesses (hair salons) and expects to sell 120,000 units in the first year (year 1), reducing by 10 per cent in each year of the project's life.[1] Depreciation—an expense allowable for tax—is to be charged on the equipment using the straight-line basis over 4 years, to a salvage value of zero. It is also known that the company's discount rate is 10 per cent per year, while tax on net income is charged at 20 per cent, payable in the year in which it was generated.

a) Calculate the NPV of the proposed project, and comment upon its viability.
b) Conduct a sensitivity analysis to determine by how much each of the following variables would have to change before the company would change its mind about going ahead with the new product:

   1. The percentage reduction in yearly sales volume
   2. Selling price per unit
   3. Advertising costs in the first year
   4. Rate of tax
   5. Discount rate

Table 4.3 displays the cash flow forecast and NPV calculations. The NPV is positive, indicating that the firm should go ahead with the project. But although the discount rate includes consideration for risk, the firm may wish to look more closely at its estimates. For that purpose, Table 4.4 presents the sensitivity analysis for each of five key inputs by presenting the value and percentage by

[1] Note that it is the number of units which are reduced by 10 per cent each year.

which each should change for the NPV to equal zero. Note that the workings are not shown.

As can be seen, the percentage reduction in yearly sales volume can increase by 53 per cent, before the project is no longer viable (from 10 per cent per year to 15.3 per cent). This is quite a large margin. In contrast, the firm has little room for manoeuvre with the pricing of the product. A small drop of 5 per cent in the price per unit, from $12.5 to just under $12, will result in the NPV turning negative. The sensitivities of the project to other key variables, including advertising costs, the tax rate and the discount rate are quite low.◀

Example 4.2 illustrates one of the approaches we discussed to sensitivity analysis—assessing by how much each variable needs to alter for the decision on the project to change. The tax rate must change by quite a bit (double) for the NPV of the project to become zero. Does it mean that the company can ignore the tax rate?

Table 4.3 Cashflow forecast and NPV calculations (in $'000)

		0	1	2	3	4
Equipment		-2500				
Sales			1500	1350	1215	1094
Production Costs			-360	-324	-292	-262
Selling costs			-60	-54	-49	-44
Advertising costs			-50	-45	-41	-37
Tax (see below)			-81	-60	-42	-25
Net cash flow		-2500	949	867	791	726
	10%	1	0.909	0.826	0.751	0.683
PV		-2500	863	716	594	496
NPV		**169**				
Tax Calculation						
Profit before depreciation			1030	927	833	751
Depreciation			-625	-625	-625	-625
Taxable profit			405	302	208	126
Tax		20%	**81**	**60**	**42**	**25**

Table 4.4 Sensitivity analysis

Item	Original value	NPV = 0 value	Change	% Change
Percentage reduction in yearly sales volume	10%	15.3%	5.3%	53%
Selling price per unit	12.5	11.9	−0.6	−5%
Advertising costs in year 1	50.00	127.00	77.00	154%
Tax rate	20%	40%	20%	100%
Discount rate	10%	13%	3%	30%

What if the government indicated it was considering changing the tax regime, so that the tax rate will increase dramatically? In that case, the apparent low sensitivity of the project to the tax rate is irrelevant. This illustrates an important point about sensitivity analysis: it may help to answer the question: 'What if… ?'—but it does not say how likely 'if' is.

It is true that guessing the odds of possible changes in key items is itself not at all easy. For example, it may be difficult to attach a figure to the likelihood of the tax rate exceeding 40 per cent, or to the likelihood of the rate of interest increasing so that the discount rate rises to 13 per cent. However, let's assume we are willing to estimate the odds of bad things happening. Even then, simply combining the pessimistic estimates of the most sensitive items would be far too gloomy and unjustified. For example, assume that the five key variables in Example 4.2 are independent of each other and that the chance of the worst case for each of them is 1 in 10 (0.1). Under these assumptions, there would be only a 1 in 100,000 chance (0.00001) of the worst outcome materializing on all five.

It is, of course, very unlikely that the various items that make up a project *are* completely independent of each other. To illustrate, in Example 4.2, it is fair to assume that the yearly volume of sales, the selling price per unit and advertising costs are all mutually dependent. However, by looking at each item at a time, holding the other items constant, sensitivity analysis does not allow for interdependence. This may be overlooking reality and a good reason to use scenario analysis instead.

4.3.3 Scenario Analysis

Scenario analysis is similar to sensitivity analysis although it is a more sophisticated approach to assessing the risk in proposed projects, as it considers a change in more than one variable at a time. Specifically, scenario analysis involves predicting new estimates for all input items given a particular state of the economy, the industry and the business. For example, the firm may think of a scenario when a recession occurs impacting demand, prices, costs and interest rates. In Chapter 1, Box 1.1, we illustrated the usefulness of scenario analysis with respect to planning for unpredictable changes in market conditions. (The article presents the case of Nando's Chicken's disruptions to supply chains which were triggered by the COVID-19 crisis. Scenario analysis—or scenario planning as it appears there—is suggested as a tool for controlling such disruptions.) In addition, Example 4.3 continues Example 4.2, by describing two possible scenarios and calculating the NPV of the project under each assumption.

Example 4.3—Scenario Analysis

The firm is considering the project described in Example 4.2. The 'best estimate' ('best' = most likely, not 'optimal') for each item is unchanged, so that the expected NPV is as before. However, an election is due next month, the result of which could have a great impact on government attitudes and policies towards the business sector.

The management of the firm draws up two alternative scenarios under each of two possible election outcomes. First, if the existing pro-business government is replaced by one that is more hostile to the business sector, this could result in a hike in the corporate tax rate, reduction in tax allowances on investment spending and overall reduction in demand by businesses. So the firm builds a scenario where depreciation on the type of equipment in which it needs to invest for the project is no longer allowed as a tax-deductible item. Moreover, the corporate tax rate increases to 22 per cent, and demand by the target clientele, which are other businesses, is reduced due to the change in the government's willingness to create a business-friendly environment. Thus, demand in year 1 reduces from 120,000 to 100,000.

Alternatively, if the pro-business government wins the election, it is expected to enhance its support for business by reducing the corporate tax rate to 15 per cent and allowing accelerated depreciation as a tax-deductible item of 50 per cent in each of years 1 and 2 of the project. Under that scenario, demand in the business sector increases, and the firm would enjoy an increase in demand for the project, from 120,000 to 140,000 units in year 1.

Table 4.5 shows the NPV calculations under the first scenario.◀

Taxable profit is computed as sales revenue less the sum of production costs, selling costs and advertising costs. We ignore depreciation as it is no longer an expense allowable for tax. The tax charge is calculated as 22 per cent on taxable profit. The results indicate that a change in the political environment, providing that the estimations under this scenario are accurate, will turn a value-enhancing project into a value-destroying one!

Let's now have a look at the second, more optimistic scenario. Table 4.6

Table 4.5 Scenario Analysis under the assumption that a business-friendly government is replaced by one which toughens up business conditions (in $'000)

		0	**1**	**2**	**3**	**4**
Equipment		-2500				
Sales			1250	1125	1013	911
Production Costs			-300	-270	-243	-219
Selling costs			-50	-45	-41	-36
Advertising costs			-50	-45	-41	-37
Tax (see below)			-187	-168	-151	-136
Net cash flow		-2500	663	597	537	483
	10%	1	0.909	0.826	0.751	0.683
PV		-2500	603	493	403	330
NPV		**-671**				
Tax Calculation						
Profit before depreciation			850	765	688	619
Depreciation			0	0	0	0
Taxable profit			850	765	688	619
Tax		22%	**187**	**168**	**151**	**136**

Table 4.6 Scenario Analysis under the assumption that a business-friendly government is re-elected and makes good on its promises to further support the business sector (in $'000)

		0	1	2	3	4
Equipment		-2500				
Sales			1750	1575	1418	1276
Production Costs			-420	-378	-340	-306
Selling costs			-70	-63	-57	-51
Advertising costs			-50	-45	-41	-37
Tax (see below)			6	24	-147	-132
Net cash flow		-2500	1216	1113	833	750
	10%	1	0.909	0.826	0.751	0.683
PV		-2500	1105	919	626	512
NPV		**662**				
Tax Calculation						
Profit before depreciation			1210	1089	980	882
Depreciation			-1250	-1250	0	0
Taxable profit			-40	-161	980	882
Tax		15%	**-6**	**-24**	**147**	**132**

presents the NPV calculations under the positive scenario where the pro-business government is re-elected and makes good on its promises.

Comparing Table 4.3 with Table 4.6, we see that under the positive scenario where the tax rate is reduced to 15 per cent and accelerated depreciation is allowed for tax purposes, the NPV of the project has increased to $662,000.

Up to this point we looked at how we can measure and assess risk in project appraisal. Before turning to how risk may be managed, we should mention one caveat concerning our calculations in the above examples. Some firms argue that in carrying out scenario analysis (or for that matter, sensitivity analysis), one should discount forecasted cash flows at a risk-free rate and not at the discount rate which encompasses compensation for risk. The reason is that by carrying out scenario or sensitivity analysis, we are directly accounting for risk, hence using a *risk-adjusted* discount rate amounts to double-counting risk. Having mentioned this point, we are now ready to look at how risk could be managed.

4.4 Managing Risk with Derivatives

4.4.1 Forward Contracts and Futures

Suppose a British company exports to Germany and is owed 5 million euros due in three months' time. There is absolutely no need to do anything. The company could simply wait for three months and then receive 5 million euros. But if the company wishes to protect itself against a fall in the euro between now and then it might enter into a three-month forward contract with a bank. The deal would be that the company agrees to pay the bank 5 million euros in three months' time in return for receiving in three months' time a sum in pounds sterling agreed *now*. Thus the company protects itself ('hedges') against an unwelcome fall in the euro.

In a sense, one might argue the company is needlessly speculating on the strength of the euro if it does nothing.

Another example might be a firm which manufactures chocolate bars, for which it needs large quantities of cocoa. It could simply buy the cocoa on the commodities exchange when it needs it for manufacturing purposes. In that case the firm is vulnerable to an increase in the price of cocoa. An alternative would be to buy forward, at a price agreed now. This reduces the risk of suffering from a price increase, though of course it also means the firm will lose out if cocoa prices fall. Such a company might take the view that its core business is making and selling chocolate bars, rather than speculating on the price of cocoa. It may thus choose to eliminate some of the risk of changes in the cocoa price.

In the above two examples the company was using a forward contract to protect (hedge) itself. A forward is a contract between two parties to buy or sell an asset at a specified future date under specified conditions including price, delivery method, quantity of the asset, etc. The terms of the forward contract are normally determined by the two parties involved, allowing them to tailor the deal to their specific needs. This makes forward contracts particularly useful as a hedging instrument. Futures are a standardized version of forward contracts, but unlike forward contracts, they are traded on exchanges and are thus more suitable as speculative tools.

Both forward contracts and futures are derivatives. That is, they are financial instruments whose value is 'derived' from underlying assets and their performance depends on the behaviour of the underlying asset. Derivatives are often more closely associated with speculation than with hedging and are often used to bet on changes in prices (such as share prices, commodity prices or interest rates). Indeed, there have been a number of spectacular losses connected with derivatives. A well-known UK case is Barings Bank's loss of some £900 million on the Japanese Nikkei stock exchange index in 1995 via contracts on the Singapore and Osaka derivative exchanges. That led to the bank's collapse. The problem in Baring's case seemed to be that top management was not aware of what was going on and had inadequate internal control mechanisms.

Many argue that there is nothing necessarily wrong in speculating in business if it is a calculated risk. Indeed, one could argue that most business activity contains an element of speculation. The main reason for the enormous growth of activity in derivatives over recent years, however, is to do with the power of derivatives to *reduce* business risk rather than increase it.

4.4.2 Options

Another type of derivative is options. An option is a contract giving the holder the right (but not the obligation) to buy (a Call option) or sell (a Put option) a financial instrument or other asset at a given ('exercise' or 'strike') price on, or sometimes before, a given date in the future. While the holder of an option has the right to exercise it (to buy in the case of a Call and to sell in the case of a Put), or not, the seller (or *writer*) of the option has the obligation to perform the other side of the transaction if required to do so. Thus, if the holder of the option stands to benefit from exercising its right, the writer of a Call/Put has to sell/buy the underlying asset at the exercise price.

The option contract specification will indicate whether it is an American option or a European option. An American option is one that can be exercised on any trading day up to and including the expiration date. A European option can be exercised only on the expiration date. The option contract will also specify whether the option involves physical delivery or cash settlement.

Many companies use options as part of their risk management strategies. Indeed, a 1998 survey of non-financial American firms found that even back then, 68 per cent of derivatives users were using options (Bodnar et al. 1998). A more recent study, from 2009, which analyzed the North American gold mining industry, found that the choice of hedging instruments is correlated with market conditions (Adam 2009). In particular, under the belief that the gold price is likely to return to its long-term average level, managers prefer to hedge with a Put option rather than to lock in a relatively low price with a forward contract. If the price of gold reverts upwards towards its mean, then the gold will be sold on the market and the Put option not exercised. But if gold prices continue their downward trend, the firm can exercise the Put and sell at the exercise price. Thus, when gold prices decline, using a Put rather than a forward contract allows the firm to hedge the downside risk while still maintaining the upside potential. For this reason, options are normally more expensive than futures.

Private investors may also choose to use options. For example, an investor may decide to speculate with Call options, risking a relatively small amount of money in the hope of a large gain. To illustrate, suppose you thought it likely that convincing scientific evidence would shortly be published showing that smoking cigarettes did not cause lung cancer. One way to 'cash in' on this expectation might be simply to purchase shares in tobacco companies. So, for example, you might invest £120,000 in buying, say, 20,000 shares in British American Tobacco (BAT) at 600p per share. Let us suppose you expect the share price to double from 600p per share to 1,200p per share when the news is announced. In that case, if all goes to plan, your 20,000 shares would become worth £240,000, and you would have made a profit of £120,000 (100 per cent) on your investment.

An alternative would be to buy Call options in BAT. Let us suppose that a 3-month Call option would cost 60p per share, while a 6-month Call option would cost 80p. If you go for the 3-month option, for £120,000 you could purchase options to buy ('Call') 200,000 shares in BAT with an exercise price of 600p each. If the news you expect is duly announced within three months, then you could buy 200,000 BAT shares for 600p, costing a total of £1.2 million. But you would be able to sell those 200,000 shares at once for 1,200p each (assuming you were correct in expecting the share price to double), thus yielding £2.4 million. Your profit would be £1,080,000 (£1.2 million less the £120,000 cost of the options) on your investment of £120,000. That amounts to a profit of no less than 900 per cent!

Of course, if your expectation is wrong—either the news is not announced within the period of the option, or, if it is, but the share price does not increase as much as you expected—then you may not do so well. In particular, if you get the timing wrong and the share price *falls* to, say, 500p, you will let the option lapse (you don't want to pay 600p per share under the contract if you could pay 500p on the normal market!), and you will have lost your entire 'investment' of £120,000 in Call options. If you had instead chosen to buy 20,000 BAT shares outright, at least you would still own the shares. They might not (yet) be worth 1200p per share, but they might still be worth about 600p per share.

What factors determine the value of an option? In general, an option (Call or Put) will increase in value the greater the volatility of the underlying asset and the longer the time period involved. The reason for that is that investors are risk-averse and—unlike linear strategies (e.g. forwards)—holders of options can always choose not to exercise if prices in the market move in their favour.

The higher the exercise price, the greater the value of a Put option, because a Put gives its holder the right to sell the underlying asset at that exercise price. But the value of a Put option will decline with an increase in the market rate of interest because the Put gives its holder the right to sell the underlying asset later, which implies that the money from the sale cannot be invested today at the going rate of interest.

In contrast, the higher the exercise price, the lower the value of a Call option, because a Call gives its holder the right to buy the underlying asset at that exercise price. The value of the Call will increase as the market rate of interest increases because the Call gives its holder the right to buy the underlying asset later, which implies that in the meantime the money can be invested to earn interest. Many companies give their managers and key employees Call-like options. These are termed warrants. Warrants are issued by the company and when the employee exercises their right to buy the company's shares, the proceeds go to the company.

Another option-like instrument is real options. A real option is the choice of action available to managers undertaking a business project which involves investment in a real (rather than financial) asset. While not traded on financial markets like 'ordinary' options (i.e. Calls and Puts), real options can be valuable in capital budgeting, particularly under conditions of high uncertainty. This is the topic of the next sub-section.

4.5 Real Options

In previous chapters we discussed at length the Discounted Cash Flow (DCF) method for valuing projects and determining whether to invest in real assets. One problem with the DCF method is that it ignores managerial flexibility which may be relevant when making capital investment decisions under great uncertainty (i.e. when estimates regarding future cash flows are likely to be inaccurate). In such cases, the firm may have the opportunity to change its course of action as it progresses with the project and more information becomes available.

To illustrate, the firm may be able to invest more in future, or to abandon failing projects, after the outcome of particular events has become less uncertain. For example, companies often choose to invest in new markets, even though the immediate prospects for profit may not be good. They are probably positioning themselves to prosper in the new market many years down the line and are assuming that if they do not start now, they may seriously damage their prospects for the future. If, after some time, their assumptions turn out not to materialise, they will have the opportunity to abandon the project and may still be able to sell the asset they initially acquired.

This type of managerial flexibility is commonly referred to as a 'real option', to reflect the fact that it offers the firm an option which is associated with investment in real (rather than financial) assets. Real options may often be more suited to or at least complement the use of basic DCF techniques. For example, under the DCF method, the higher the uncertainty of future cash flows, the higher is the discount rate to be used. This approach may underestimate the value of the project because while it emphasizes the possibility of actual future cash flows being much lower than expected, it ignores the possibility that they will be much higher than expected. Thus, instead of simply discounting at higher rates to account for risk, managers may try to capture the flexibility embedded in the project. This is the real option approach which aims to avoid underestimating the value of projects, thereby missing out on good investment opportunities.

The flexibility in project analysis can be thought of as providing management the opportunity to buy an option and decide later whether to exercise it. As the project progresses and some uncertainty resolves, the firm will have the right (but not the obligation) to expand the investment (a Call option) or to abandon the project and sell the initial asset (a Put option).

Assessing how firms adjust for risk *in practice* when engaging in capital budgeting is an empirical question. For example, a survey of 146 large UK companies (Ho and Pike 1991) finds that about 40 per cent often or very often used sensitivity analysis, 39 per cent a subjective-intuitive assessment of risk, and 17 per cent probability analysis. Methods of adjusting for risk (of the 133 companies that did so) most frequently included raising the required rate of return (42 per cent), shortening the payback period[2] (34 per cent), and adjusting estimated future cash flows subjectively/intuitively (63 per cent).

A more recent survey of 400 executives in ten countries in Central and Eastern Europe (Andor et al. 2015) reports that 83 per cent (333 firms) performed formal capital budgeting analysis, but of those only 40 per cent used sensitivity analysis and just 17 per cent used real option analysis. The study further shows that large companies were significantly more likely to use sensitivity analysis than small and medium firms (47 per cent versus 22 per cent, respectively). The results of

[2] The payback method is discussed in Chapter 2. As a quick reminder, the payback period is the length of time until the investment recovers the initial cost in terms of accumulated net cash inflows. Some firms determine a length of time by which investments must recover the initial cost, and all investments which are not expected to comply by the rule are rejected.

the survey are consistent with the notion that the use of advanced capital budgeting techniques, including risk assessment and management methods, is positively associated with firm size. This conclusion is consistent with results of prior studies for the United Kingdom, the United States, and Canada.[3]

One risk that companies nowadays need to pay attention to is foreign exchange risk. Indeed, with globalization, increased overseas trade and flexible (or floating) foreign exchange regimes, foreign exchange risk is potentially an important factor in determining the success of projects. The next sub-section provides a quick overview of foreign exchange risk assessment and management.

4.6 Foreign Exchange Risk

Foreign exchange risk is the risk associated with exchange rate fluctuations and their financial impact. Often this risk is classified into three categories: transaction exposure, accounting exposure and economic exposure.

4.6.1 Transaction Exposure

Transaction exposure (or risk) arises when money amounts are receivable or payable in terms of a foreign currency. If the exchange rate changes, so does the equivalent in domestic currency. Suppose a UK company invoices a credit sale abroad in US dollars for \$120,000. If the exchange rate at the date of sale is £1 = \$1.50, the sterling amount due is: \$120,000 ÷ \$1.50 = 80,000. But if the exchange rate at the date of payment is £1 = \$1.60, then the sterling amount is only: \$120,000 ÷ \$1.60 = 75,000. There has been a loss of £5,000.

Whenever a company invoices sales (or is invoiced by suppliers) in a currency other than its own domestic currency, there is uncertainty relating to how much it will actually receive (or pay) in its own currency. Thus, transactions in foreign currencies expose the firm to the risk of loss if exchange rates move in the wrong direction. Of course, the company may also 'gain' when exchange rates move the other way.

It is hard to predict future spot rates (rates for immediate delivery), and thus to decide whether to hedge the transaction exposure (e.g. by entering a forward transaction or purchasing options on foreign currencies). Indeed, in the long run, it may be best simply to convert foreign currencies into the domestic currency when received, without attempting to hedge in order to avoid the transaction risk. The trouble is that in the short run, there may be significant exposure; and risk-averse finance managers might prefer to hedge, even at some cost.

[3] See Pike (1996), Sangster (1993), and Graham and Harvey (2001).

4.6.2 Accounting Exposure

When a group consolidates the accounts of its foreign subsidiaries, there is the question of what exchange rate to use for translation. ('Translate' means 'restate for accounting purposes', whereas 'convert' means 'exchange one currency for another'.) The choice affects the reporting currency amounts in the group accounts.

Should one use the current exchange rate prevailing on the balance sheet date? This would normally be the exchange rate for monetary items such as cash, loans, payables and receivables, while non-monetary assets such as fixed assets would be translated using the historical rate prevailing when the assets were purchased.

Moreover, what about the income statement? Should one translate at the closing rate, an average rate for the period, or the rate prevailing at the time of each transaction? Ideally the last of these, but averages are also sometimes permitted. Similar to the impact of translating items on the balance sheet into the reporting currency, variations in exchange rates are also likely to impact the income and profit reported.

There is reason to think that purely accounting differences, such as would arise from using one method rather than another, have no real effect (for example, on share prices). Hence accounting exposure should not really matter. But many finance managers seem reluctant to accept this conclusion and prefer to hedge away this risk.

4.6.3 Economic Exposure

Economic exposure means that the present value (in terms of domestic currency) of future operating cash flows may vary due to exchange rate changes.

The direct impact works as follows. When the domestic currency strengthens against foreign currencies, and the local firm is an exporter, two scenarios are possible. First, if the exporting firm maintains the local currency equivalent price of its product, then—compared with foreign companies—its prices once converted to the foreign currency would be higher. The firm's competitive position may thus be hurt. Second, if the exporting firm maintains the foreign currency price, then the income from the foreign sales—once converted to the local currency—would be lower. Table 4.7 illustrates this dilemma with a British exporter to the United States which faces a strengthening pound.

Table 4.7 Effect of strong pound on British exporter

Scenario	Strategy	GBP/USD	Amount in GBP	Amount in USD	Conclusions
UK firm exporting to US		1.5	£160,000	$240,000	
GBP appreciates v. USD	Maintain GBP price	1.6	£160,000	$256,000	USD price increases and the firm's competitive position may be hurt.
	Maintain USD price		£150,000	$240,000	GBP price reduces, and the firm's income in local currency terms is hurt.

Table 4.8 Effect of weak pound on British exporter

Scenario	Strategy	GBP/USD	Amount in GBP	Amount in USD	Conclusions
UK firm exporting to US		1.5	£160,000	$240,000	
GBP depreciates v. USD	Reduce USD price	1.4	£160,000	$224,000	GBP income is unchanged, and the firm gains competitive advantage
	Maintain USD price		£171,429	$240,000	GBP price increases, and the firm enjoys higher income in terms of local currency

Continuing with the above example, what will be the situation if the pound weakened against the USD? The British exporter could reduce the USD price of its product, maintaining the same income in GBP, but gaining competitive advantage over its competitors. Alternatively, the British exporter could maintain the USD price of its product, increasing its income in GBP terms. These two scenarios are illustrated in Table 4.8.

In addition, there may be an effect on the sterling cost of imported goods (in the opposite direction). Questions also arise about the price-elasticity of demand and about the permanence of any change in exchange rates. There may also be other less direct effects.

It is obvious that trying to calculate all the likely effects is very complex. One possible way to get some protection might be by means of suitable foreign currency financing. This would aim to roughly match the finance with the foreign currency exposure.

4.7 A Concluding Note

In this chapter we discuss risk and how it is managed. We focussed primarily on business and project risk from the point of view of the firm. However, investors in the company (both equity and bondholders) are also exposed to risk. From the point of view of an investor in the company, risk is defined as the possibility that the return on the investment will differ from the expected return. In general, the higher the risk of the investment, the higher the return (or compensation) investors demand on the project. If a company goes bankrupt and its assets are liquidated, shareholders are last in line to receive any of the proceeds. Lenders to the company are exposed to the risk that the firm will be unable to pay back interest and principal. However, if there are assets left, the company's debtholders will be paid before shareholders. More on that in the next chapters.

4.7.1 Problems

Use the following case to answer problems 1 and 2

Centric Brands Group, an American multiple fashion brands house, is considering a four-year-long lease on a large office complex in the Arts District of Los Angeles. Currently, all brands under the Centric Group have small separate offices around the country. However, under the new proposal, all employees will work from the five-storey complex—each brand having a dedicated space and even its own entrance. This move is expected to save operational time and allow for easier sharing of resources among the brands in the group.

The proposed investment includes an immediate outlay of $2,000,000 (non tax-deductible). In addition, the yearly rent on the new office complex is $1,400,000 in the first year, increasing by 10 per cent each year in years two to four. This is reasonably cheap as rental prices for offices in New York have dropped recently due to the 2020 Covid pandemic and on the background of companies like Airbnb closing headquarters deemed no longer necessary. Indeed, according to Bloomberg, New York office rent prices have fallen 14 per cent since the pandemic began, dwarfing drops in other cities including London, Hong Kong and Singapore.

Cost savings due to the move to the new office complex are expected to amount to $3,000,000 in the first year, reducing by 5 per cent per year over the 4-year duration of the project. Corporate income tax is 30 per cent, payable in the year in which the income was earned, and the company's discount rate is 20 per cent.

Problem 4.1

(a) Calculate the NPV of the proposed project, and comment upon its viability.
(b) Conduct a sensitivity analysis to determine by how much each of the following variables would have to change in order for the company's management to change its mind about going ahead with the project:
1. The initial outlay
2. The rent in the first year
3. The percentage yearly reduction in cost savings
4. Rate of tax
5. Discount rate.

Problem 4.2 While Centric Brands Group is quite optimistic about the project, it decided to consider an alternative scenario where the economy recovers and demand for office space in New York gets back to its pre-COVID era levels and beyond. Specifically, if the economy recovers, the yearly rent in the first year is likely to increase from $1.4m to $1.8m, further increasing by 12 per cent each year. Moreover, the increased economic activity would convince the government to reduce the tax rate from 30 to 25 per cent, while higher public demand for fashion would mean that the yearly cost savings is maintained at $3m per year over the four years of the project.

Calculate the NPV of the proposed project under the alternative scenario and its IRR.

Problem 4.3 Bloomingdale's Inc., an American luxury department store, has just signed a contract to buy €500,000 worth of top brands from Officine Générale, a French fashion house. According to the contract, payment is due in three months' time in euros. The current spot exchange rate is $1.22/€ while a 3-months forward is

$1.21/€. Put and Call options on euro, with an exercise price of $1.22/€ are selling for $0.03/€ and $0.01/€, respectively.

(a) Explain how Bloomingdale's can hedge the foreign exchange risk to which the contract with the French fashion house exposes it. Show the cash flows involved under a forward hedge and under a hedge strategy that involves purchasing options.
(b) Officine Générale is now considering entering the US market by opening an actual store and an office in New York. Why should a European fashion house consider establishing operations in the United States, given the foreign exchange risks to which this activity exposes the firm?

References

Adam, T. (2009). Capital expenditure, financial constraints, and the use of options. *Journal of Financial Economics, 92*, 238–251.

Andor, G., Mohanty, S. K., & Toth, T. (2015). Capital budgeting practices: A survey of Central and Eastern European firms. *Emerging Markets Review, 23*, 148–172.

Bodnar, G. M., Hayt, G. S., Marston, R. C. (1998). 1998 Survey of financial risk management by US nonfinancial firms. *Financial Management, 27*, 70–91.

Graham, J. R., & Harvey, C. R. (2001). The theory and practice of corporate finance: Evidence from the field. *Journal of Financial Economics, 60*(23), 187–243.

Ho, S. S., & Pike, R. H. (1991). Risk analysis in capital budgeting contexts simple or sophisticated? *Accounting and Business Research, 21*(83), 227–238.

Pike, R. (1996). A longitudinal survey on capital budgeting practices. *Journal of business finance & accounting, 23*(1), 79–92.

Sangster, A. (1993). Capital investment appraisal techniques: A survey of current usage. *Journal of Business Finance & Accounting, 20*(3), 307–332.

Part II

An Introduction to the Financing Decision

Up to this point in the book we have dealt mainly with the corporate investment decision. In the previous chapter (Chapter 4) we also looked at risk in corporate investment and how to manage (hedge) it. The second part of the book deals with the question of how to finance corporate investments, that is, the financing decision. The aim now is briefly to introduce this topic.

Before we embark on this introduction, however, it is important to understand that these three key corporate decisions (concerning investments, risk management and financing) are jointly determined. Froot et al. (1993) provide a possible explanation of how.

Their argument starts with a firm that does not manage risk (by hedging). Under this scenario, there will be some variability in the cash flows generated by the firm's current investments. This variability in internal cash flow will lead to either variability in the amount of money raised externally, or in the amount of future investment. Variability in future investment is undesirable because it is likely to reduce the firm's output and profit. Given this, the optimal solution appears to be to leave investment plans unaltered, covering the financing gap that arises due to fluctuations in internal cashflows by raising external funds (equity or debt). Unfortunately, raising external funds is often more costly than using internal funds (see Chapters 7 and 8 and the discussion below). Consequently, a shortfall in internally generated cash may lead the firm to decrease its investments. Fortunately, because risk management (hedging) can reduce this variability in cash flows, hedging can solve the problem of fluctuating cashflows, allowing the firm to undertake good projects and increase its value. Thus, the investment, financing and hedging decisions are intertwined.

Bearing this in mind, we can now introduce the second part of the book, which is concerned with the financing decision. Obviously, the firm can finance its investment plans using internal sources—that is, using retained earnings. Alternatively, it can raise funds externally. If it opts for the latter, then it basically has two choices: raising equity or debt. Equity finance refers to shares (or common stock) that represent proportional ownership of the issuing company. In fact, when the firm uses internal funds (that is, retained earnings), it is using equity financing because retained earnings belong to equity holders (shareholders). Thus, equity funding can be either internal (retained earnings), or external when the firm issues new shares to the public. Debt finance, in contrast, refers to money borrowed from banks or other financial institutions (loans) or to debt securities (bonds). The latter are traded securities that represent a promise of a series of payments (i.e. interest) by the issuing company to the investor holding the security.

The process described above is the financing decision—the process of determining how to finance investment: the choice between external and internal sources, the selection between equity and debt, and in the case of the latter, the decision regarding the type of debt to raise. The aim of the financing decision is to determine the cheapest way to finance the firm's investments.

At first glance this dilemma may appear trivial. After all, raising external equity or debt generally involves commission paid to investment bankers for arranging the issuance, including management and underwriting fees. Registration fees and printing, legal and auditing costs are additional direct costs of raising external finance. There is, however, a more significant cost associated with finance which the firm must bear whether it uses internal or external finance. This cost relates to the fact that providers of funds require a return on their investment. Indeed, they expect to be adequately compensated for the risk they are taking by providing the firm with funds for investment.

The compensation that equity holders receive comes in the form of dividends and share price appreciation while the compensation debt holders receive comes in the form of interest payments and the repayment of the principal. These are the returns that equity and debt holders expect to receive, respectively, for providing the firm with finance for investment. From the firm's perspective, this is the cost of capital which obviously it aims to minimize.

Linking this discussion to our previous chapters (e.g. Chapter 2), the cost of capital is often the discount rate that the firm applies to its projects in calculating their Net Present Value (NPV). Thus, the lower the cost of capital, the more likely it is that a project will have a positive NPV, thereby creating additional value to shareholders. This emphasises the importance of the financing decision.

The second part of the book, then, deals with this financing decision. Chapter 5 is devoted to debt while Chapter 6 discusses equity, so that the reader has a full understanding of the choice of financing methods available. In Chapter 7 we learn how to work out the company's cost of capital and in Chapter 8 we look at how the choice between debt and equity—in particular, the proportions of each (that is, the company's capital structure)—impacts its overall cost of capital. Finally, in Chapter 9, we synthesize what we learnt on project evaluation with our recently acquired knowledge of financing, capital structuring and the cost of capital, to briefly present and discuss company valuation, acquisitions and mergers.

Reference

Froot, K. A., Scharfstein, D. S., & Stein, J. C. (1993). Risk management: Coordinating corporate investment and financing policies. *The Journal of Finance, 48*(5), 1629–1658.

Corporate Borrowing

5

5.1 Introduction

During the summer of 2019 and following a report by the Bank for International Settlements (BIS), publications in the media warned that corporate borrowing—and particularly borrowing by firms with low credit scores—had increased dramatically.[1] Indeed, according to a study by the OECD, non-financial corporations around the world borrowed in 2019 an additional USD 2.1 trillion in the form of corporate bonds (Çelik et al. 2020). This was partly due to a return to more expansionary monetary policies in early 2019, and added to the build up of corporate bond debt since 2008.[2] Thus, by the end of 2019, the global outstanding stock of non-financial corporate bonds reached an all-time high of USD 13.5 trillion.

The BIS report warned that although the increase in corporate debt was mainly due to borrowing by low credit firms in the United States and United Kingdom, it had the potential to destabilize the global financial system leading to a crisis in a manner similar to how the US sub-prime crisis of the early 2000s led to the global financial crisis of 2008. The ink was barely dry on the BIS report, when a global pandemic broke out in early 2020, bringing with it social distancing and collapse in economic activity. The prolonged COVID-19 crisis saw an increase in corporate defaults, putting at risk particularly those firms which utilized the post-2008 low interest rate environment and borrowed heavily.

In this chapter we shall consider corporate borrowing, including types of debt; pricing and valuation of debt; and the risks associated with debt and borrowing.

[1] The BIS Annual Economic Report, June 2019 is available at: https://www.bis.org/publ/arpdf/ar2019e.htm.

[2] Expansionary monetary policy aims to boost economic activity, stimulate aggregate demand and create economic growth by cutting interest rates and/or increasing the money supply.

R. Manos et al., *Corporate Finance for Business*,
https://doi.org/10.1007/978-3-030-92419-5_5

Specifically, in the next Sect. 5.2 we shall help you find your way in the wide-ranging world of corporate debt, by describing common methods by which it is classified. We make the distinction between bank loans and debt securities, the principal of which are corporate bonds. The following two sections focus on corporate bonds. We start by depicting the key features of bonds (Sect. 5.3) and move on to bond valuation (Sect. 5.4). In Sect. 5.5 we discuss further issues relating specifically to corporate bonds, in Sect. 5.6 we look at other types of debt while in Sect. 5.7 we focus on government debt securities and risk-free assets. Section 5.8 concludes the chapter, followed by problems for readers to work through.

5.2 Classification of Corporate Borrowing

Companies borrow money to finance business activities such as the purchase of land, equipment or other businesses. The amount of money borrowed is called **debt** and the act of borrowing is often referred to as raising debt. The debt agreement (contract) specifies the future date or dates when the borrowed sum (the principal) is to be repaid, and the amount and timing of interest that is charged. Thus, the borrowing company must repay amounts borrowed as they become due and pay the regular agreed amount of interest on the debt outstanding. Failure to do so entitles the lender to take legal action at once to recover the principal and any unpaid interest. When the borrower is a company, the debt is referred to as corporate debt. However, debt is also raised by other entities such as international organizations, governments, municipals, financial institutions and individuals. Our focus here is on corporate debt.

Corporations can raise debt of various forms, and the choice a company makes depends on several factors including the purpose for which the funds are needed (e.g. amount needed, what is to be financed or the length of time); the characteristics of the borrower (e.g. creditworthiness, size, collateral that can be offered, etc.) and market conditions (e.g. expectations regarding future interest rates, inflation and business activity). To find your way in the universe of corporate debt it is helpful to refer to various classifications. For example, debt is often classified as either a loan or a debt security. Alternatively, corporate debt is also classified based on its length of life/maturity, its quality or the creditworthiness of the borrower. In what follows we explain some of the most common classifications of corporate debt.

5.2.1 Classification Based on Loans Versus Debt Securities

A loan is an amount of money borrowed from another entity, usually a financial institution such as a bank. The main characteristic of a loan is that the terms of the contract are determined privately between the two parties and are tailored to the needs of the borrower. For example, the terms may specify that the loan is repayable on demand (an overdraft) or at the end of a term (a term loan).

Sometimes, when the amount borrowed is very large, the lending entity may be a syndicate of banks.

A debt security is a loan raised from investors in financial markets. This means that, unlike bank loans, a debt security is a tradeable financial asset that can be traded between investors (on exchanges or over the counter). The borrowing company which raised the debt securities is also referred to as the issuing company. It will normally pay interest to the investors holding the debt securities as well as repaying them the amount borrowed on (or by) the date when the debt security matures. There are various types of debt securities which differ from each other mainly in terms of their time to maturity. For example, bonds, which are the best-known debt securities, usually have maturity of more than one year, while commercial paper has maturity of less than one year.

5.2.2 Classification by Maturity: Short-, Medium- and Long-Term Borrowing

The Maturity of a debt security is the date when the principal amount borrowed becomes due and may vary from overnight to infinity. Unfortunately, opinions differ as to what precisely is classified as short, medium or long-term debt except that any debt that is due for repayment within a year is referred to as short-term while anything beyond 10 years is referred to as long-term debt. Anything between 1 and 10 years might be referred to as short, medium, or long, according to context!

Short-term debt, if it is defined as debt that is due within twelve months, will be listed in the company's balance sheet under current liabilities (creditors due within one year). This is amounts due arising from the firm's normal business activity or it may be that part of longer term debt that has become due for repayment in the coming year. For example, a bank overdraft is a popular form of short-term borrowing that is convenient and flexible for borrowers. It is not fully accurate to describe an overdraft as short-term because it may continue beyond one year. However, because it is legally repayable 'on demand', balance sheets show overdrafts as current liabilities (creditors due within one year). Only the amount actually overdrawn bears interest, though there may be a small 'commitment fee' on the agreed maximum limit. Interest accrues from day to day, at a rate that varies with market conditions. It is often expressed as 'x per cent over base rate'. Note that debt that is due in 1–5 years is sometimes still described as short-term, but this will appear on the Balance Sheet as a non-current liability.

Medium-term debt is normally defined as debt that is due for repayment within five to ten years. Because the risk associated with medium-term debt is higher than that on similar short-term debt, the interest rate charged on medium-term debt is normally also higher than that on short-term debt. The best-known medium-term debt is term loans which may provide for borrowing in tranches, and for repayment by instalments (rather than a single 'bullet' repayment on maturity). In project finance the timing of repayment may depend on how well a project performs. Term loans are usually more expensive than overdrafts, often with a penalty on early repayment. Interest rates on term loans often vary during their 'lives' because volatile rates of inflation can make fixed rate loans risky both for lenders and for borrowers.

Long-term debt (often called debentures, from the Latin 'they are owed') is principally a financing tool to enable the firm to grow and expand. It is listed in the company's Balance Sheet under non-current liabilities. Sometimes, when medium-term debt is defined as debt repayable between one year to five/ten years ahead, then long-term debt would be defined as any debt with maturity longer than that. Although long-term debt may be perpetual (irredeemable), most long-term debt must be repaid one day. This means that what starts as long-term debt ends up eventually as short-term.

Due to its longer maturity, long-term debt is considered riskier than similar medium- or short-term debt. The borrowing firm must typically repay the whole amount on the due redemption date. If its financial position has worsened, the firm may find it hard to repay the amount due or to arrange new borrowing (refinance). Inability to repay debt is one of the main causes of corporate failure. For this reason, the interest on long-term debt is usually higher than that on shorter-term debt. This is also the reason why long-term debt may require security. Moreover, in order to reduce the risk to the lender, long-term debt is sometimes arranged with partial repayment at regular intervals. Likewise, although subsidiaries of a large group often plan investment in fixed assets themselves, borrowing is usually arranged centrally by the whole group. This is partly to reduce the lender's risk (and therefore the interest rate), since the whole group's assets, not just a single subsidiary's, will then be available as security.

Long-term debt of large companies is normally listed on stock exchanges just like government borrowings. The original lender can then recover the investment, not by the corporate borrower repaying, but by selling the debt security to another investor. At the maturity date, the borrowing company will repay the principal amount to the current holders of the debt security. (Some companies start to buy in their own debt securities towards the redemption date to reduce the total amount of cash needed on final maturity.)

Instead of raising debt from investors on the market, smaller firms may arrange loans from banks, insurance companies, pension funds or private investors. With only a single lender, it may be possible to renegotiate certain loan conditions if circumstances change. That is not feasible with listed debt where the lenders might be widely dispersed members of the public.

5.2.3 Risk, Classification Based on Creditworthiness, and the Role of Credit Rating Agencies

We shall begin this section by looking at factors that affect the riskiness of all forms of debt, whether bank loans taken out by small companies or very substantial bond issues by multinational corporations, and the methods that can be used to mitigate the risk. We then go on to look at the role of the credit rating agencies in assessing the risk of major debt instruments.

5.2.3.1 Reducing the Lender's Risk

General Considerations

In general the return to lenders is fairly low (unlike possible gains on equity investments); so most lenders only want to take small risks. Hence they will be concerned with the margin of safety on business lending. For example:

- How far might the borrower's profits and cash inflows fall in a downturn?
- To what extent could the company reduce planned spending at lower levels of output?
- How quickly could the borrower liquidate current assets if need be, to pay loan interest or to repay principal?
- In a crisis, how quickly could the borrower sell-off fixed assets? How low, at worst, could their second-hand value be, if the whole industry is in a downturn?
- Is the borrower both honest and competent? What is their track record? What about their character: would a possible default really concern them? If their financial position were to get much worse, would they continue to provide regular accurate up-to-date reports?
- What sort of business is it? Profitable? Risky? Stable? How good is the management, especially financial management and management control? Is there adequate *depth* of management?

Personal Guarantees

In a limited company the liability of the shareholders is limited (hence the name) to the nominal amount of the issued ordinary share capital. So when the shares are 'fully-paid-up', shareholders have no further potential liability to the company. In contrast, the creditors of partnerships or sole traders ('unincorporated' businesses) can, if need be, look for repayment to the private assets of the individual proprietors (owners), in addition to any assets of the firm itself. Thus the potential liability of sole owners or partners in a firm is normally unlimited.

A small business is likely to be risky, especially if it is new. So anyone lending money to a small limited company may want to get a personal guarantee of repayment from the main shareholder(s). This will put the lender in the same position as if they were lending to a sole trader or partnership.

The reverse side of this coin is that giving a personal guarantee is a major step. At the time, it may seem almost like a 'free' way of improving a small company's credit rating. But giving a personal guarantee fundamentally changes the legal position of whoever gives it (whether the controlling owner, a director or a friend or relative). If things go wrong, the consequences may be extremely serious. In acknowledgement of this, in 2020, during the early stages of the Covid pandemic, the UK Government banned lenders from requiring personal guarantees for loans under £250,000.

Security

Another way for a lender to reduce their risk of loss is to arrange for certain assets to serve as formal collateral for the loan. This is dealt with in Sect. 5.3 under the subheading 'Collateral'.

Covenants

Corporate lenders usually insist on certain conditions (covenants). The conditions included in the covenant may be negative, prohibiting the borrowing company from taking certain actions, or they may be affirmative, requiring the borrowing company to undertake certain actions. Negative covenants may include restrictions on the amount of directors' salaries; limitations on dividend payments; prohibiting the sale of substantial parts of the business; or barring the granting of prior claims on assets to other subsequent lenders. Affirmative covenants may include the requirement to undertake maintenance of certain financial ratios at stated levels, or the maintenance of physical assets in good condition. They may also require the borrowing company to provide regular up-to-date financial information to lenders/bondholders.

Breaches of the covenant (like failure to pay interest when due) can entitle the lender to require immediate repayment of the loan or to charge a penalty on the violation. But a breach may simply act as a 'trigger': it alerts the lender to an unexpected event and suggests a need to discuss the current state of the business with the borrower. In that sense, the covenant is an important risk management tool for lenders.

5.2.3.2 Credit Rating Agencies

Publicly traded debt, such as corporate or municipal bonds, are often classified on the basis of their creditworthiness. That is, by assessing the risk that the borrower would fail on their promise to make payments (of interest and principal) as they become due. Credit rating agencies are financial-services companies that provide opinions about the credit risk of various entities, and on the credit quality of individual debt issues. These opinions are expressed in terms of credit ratings that reflect the risk of default. For example, the rating of a corporation is based on an analysis of its current and prospective financial strength and operating performance, while the rating of a particular debt issue is based on its seniority and guarantees.

To illustrate, the risk quality of an issue assessed by S&P Global Ratings[3] is expressed by a letter code that ranges from AAA to D. A high rating score, in the range between AAA to BBB is considered investment grade, and anything from BB to D is considered non-investment (sub-investment/speculative/junk) grade. Investment grade bonds are issued by well-established companies, such as Microsoft, that carry low probability of defaulting on their debt. For instance, a rating of AAA by S&P Global Ratings indicates that the bonds are very safe.

[3] https://www.spglobal.com/ratings/en/.

In contrast, junk bonds are bonds issued by companies with credit rating below investment grade. A junk bond has a greater price volatility and higher likelihood of default. These bonds pay a higher yield than investment grade bonds to compensate for their higher credit risk.

Credit rating firms belong to a highly concentrated industry. The three leading rating agencies are Moody's, S&P Global Ratings and Fitch (*the Big Three*) which together control 95 per cent of the ratings business.[4] In recent years, driven by lessons learned from the global financial crisis of 2008 and new regulations that were subsequently enacted, *the Big Three* have introduced changes to improve the quality, transparency, and integrity of their ratings. This followed a damning report by the Financial Crisis Inquiry Commission (FCIC),[5] which concluded that '*the failures of credit rating agencies were essential cogs in the wheel of financial destruction*' (see Box 5.1).

Box 5.1: Moody's: "Given a Blank Check", A Case Study in: FCIC Final Report, The Mortgage Machine, Chapter 7, pp. 118–122[6]

In its final report, the FCIC points—among other players—to the *Big Three* credit rating agencies as responsible for the financial meltdown of 2007–2008.

The report concludes that the mortgage-related securities at the heart of the crisis could not have been marketed and sold without the approval of the rating agencies. This is because investors relied on those ratings or were obligated to use them, while regulatory standards were often based upon them. Furthermore, the *Big Three* also awarded high ranking to insolvent financial institutions such as Lehman Brothers which subsequently failed.

The FCIC report examines Moody's as a case study. It notes that in the period 2000–2007, Moody's rated nearly 45,000 mortgage-related securities as triple-A. In particular, in 2006 it gave a triple-A rating to 30 mortgage-related securities *every working day*! This is in stark contrast with the post crisis era of early 2010, when only 6 private-sector US companies were awarded this high rating. The results of this inflation in ratings were disastrous according to the FCIC report. For instance, 83 per cent of the mortgage securities rated triple-A in 2006 were subsequently downgraded.

The FCIC report analyses the causes of the problems at Moody's, pointing to flawed computer models; conflicts of interest arising from the company's business model; the insistence on relentlessly increasing the firm's market share; lack of resources; and the absence of adequate regulatory supervision.

[4] Moody's and S&P Global Ratings controlling 40 per cent of the global market each while Fitch controls the reminder 15 per cent. Source: The UK Government, Actuary's Department, Monthly Bulletin, June 2018. Available at: https://assets.publishing.service.gov.uk/government/uploads/system/uploads/attachment_data/file/718731/May_2018_update.pdf.

[5] The FCIC was appointed by the US Congress to investigate the causes of the 2008 global financial crisis. The commission's report is available from http://fcic.law.stanford.edu/.

[6] The Financial Crisis Inquiry Report: Final Report of the National Commission on the Causes of the Financial and Economic Crisis in the US, Submitted by The Financial Crisis, Inquiry Commission, January 2011.

Criticism over the failures of the rating agencies during the financial crisis of 2008 often focusses on their issuer-pays business model under which issuers of securities pay the rating agencies for providing a rating. This gives rise to conflicts of interest because the rating agencies may be reluctant to give low ratings to securities issued by the entity which pays them. From the point of view of the rating agencies, there are at least two good reasons for the issuer-pays model. First, it promotes transparency by allowing ratings to be free to all users, and hence constantly analysed and examined by players in the market including the media and academia. Second, the issuer-pays model facilitates access to high-quality information that might not otherwise be available. Arguably, this enhances the quality of the rating agencies' analysis.[7]

Nonetheless, following widespread criticism over the issuer-pays business model, S&P Global Ratings, and others, have implemented safeguards to manage potential conflicts of interest. These safeguards include, for example, the separation of the commercial and analytical functions or imposing restrictions on communications between sales personnel and ratings analysts.[8] However, notwithstanding these efforts, and regardless of the damning US FCIC report, little competition has developed in the aftermath of the 2008 global financial market crash within the credit ratings industry. Indeed, global investors still rely mainly on the *Big Three* for ratings and informed analysis of the risk associated with debt securities.

Investors in bonds carefully study the credit ratings of issuers, and select bonds based on their own risk-return preferences. Highly risk-averse investors are likely to prefer investment grade bonds, while those who are willing to take more risk—in return for higher expected return—are likely to prefer bonds below investment grade.

We could go on to categorize debt based on other features. For example, debt can be classified according to how interest is received. Thus, there are interest-bearing debt securities which pay interest at regular intervals, the rate on which can be fixed, floating (by reference to some other rate) or variable (e.g. fixed for a period of time followed by floating). In contrast there are zero-coupon debt securities that bear no interest but instead are issued at a discount to the redemption value that the borrower receives when the debt matures. Some of these securities will be discussed in the next sections, but we leave interested readers to delve more deeply into these issues, while we move on to focus on the most common debt securities, namely bonds, and describe their key features.

---

[7] See S&P Global Ratings website where the business model is explained and rationalized: https://www.spglobal.com/ratings/en/about/understanding-credit-ratings.

[8] See S&P Global Ratings website for detailed explanation, at: https://www.spglobal.com/ratings/en/index.

5.3 Key Features of Bonds

As discussed above, the most common debt security is the bond, a loan raised from investors in financial markets. Possibly the most important feature of a bond is its contract—generally referred to as the bond indenture. The bond indenture specifies the terms, conditions and characteristics of the bond. These include such elements as the term to maturity; collateral; par value; coupon (interest) rate; the frequency of payments as well as the currency in which the bond is denominated. Starting with the bond indenture, we discuss these features in this section.

5.3.1 The Bond Indenture

A bond indenture is the contract between the issuer of the bond and the investors that hold it. It specifies the terms and conditions of the bond, including maturity date, the rate of interest—or how it is calculated, frequency of interest payments, and other details. The most important section of the indenture contract is the section of the covenant. Basically, this is a set of conditions that the issuing/borrowing company must fulfil.

The covenant is designed to reduce possible conflicts between bondholders and other stakeholders in the firm (e.g. managers or equity holders). Typical conditions included in the covenant are set out in the previous section.

5.3.2 Term to Maturity

As discussed in Sect. 5.2, debt—including bonds—is often classified based on the length of time during which the holder expects to receive periodic interest payments, ending when the principal is repaid. In general, short-term bonds mature within five years, medium-term bonds have maturity of between five to ten years and long-term bonds have maturity of ten years or more. Long-term debt may even be perpetual—also referred to as irredeemable bonds. For example, Britain first issued consolidated bonds—better known as consols—in 1752 and used them to finance various wars including the Napoleonic Wars and World War I. Originally carrying an interest rate of 3 per cent (later reduced), the British consols were known as perpetuals because they had no redemption date. They were, however, *callable* (redeemable) at the option of the government, which—starting around 2014—exercised this option as a strategy to remove its perpetual obligation.

Thus, long-term bonds are often callable which means that the issuer can redeem the bond before the maturity date (see Box 5.2 further below, for an example of callable bonds). Because the decision to redeem early lies with the issuer (borrower), the investor is compensated with a higher rate of interest. Obviously, issuers will decide to call the bonds early when market conditions are in their favour. For example, when the rate of interest in the market is low relative to the rate of interest stated on the callable bond, the option to call allows the lender to refinance at a lower rate. Likewise, convertible bonds which can be converted into shares of the issuing firm, as well as bonds with put option which allow their holders to sell them back to the issuing company, also imply that these bonds may never reach their maturity date.

5.3.3 Collateral

We saw in the previous sub-section that including a callable option in the bond's indenture allows issuers (the borrowing company) to reduce their risk by redeeming the bond before its maturity. Alternatively, issuers may attempt to reduce the risk borne by lenders—and thus to reduce the compensation the lenders require—by naming certain assets as formal collateral for the loan. On liquidation of the business—that is, if the company is wound up and its assets sold—the collateral gives the lender security in the shape of priority claim on the proceeds from selling the assets that serve as collateral. In other words, the proceeds from selling those assets will go first to repay any secured loans. Anything left over will go into the company's general pool of funds to pay other, unsecured, creditors. What if the proceeds from selling assets serving as collateral do not cover the full amount of a 'secured' loan? To the extent of any shortfall, the creditor will be classed as unsecured.

Debtors (also known as receivables), some kinds of inventory, and general equipment can serve as collateral for loans, as well as land, buildings and marketable investments. For highly specialized assets there may be no resale market and thus such assets do not serve as good collateral. Assets that represent good collateral include those with easily transferable legal title and fairly stable and easy-to-determine value. Furthermore, to serve as good collateral, the value of the asset should cover the amount of the loan it backs, by a considerable margin.

Instead of securing a loan on specific assets, a lender may obtain a floating charge on all a borrower's assets. This comes into effect ('crystallizes') only if a company goes into liquidation. In other words, a floating charge permits the sale of assets in the normal course of business, until the point when it crystallizes, when the floating charge becomes fixed. This differs from securing a loan against a specific asset, in which case that asset can only be sold in the normal course of business if the lender agrees. On a winding-up, certain debts (for example, certain wages and taxes) come before the claims of unsecured creditors. They also have priority over any floating charges—though not over a fixed charge on a specific asset.

Thus, secured bonds are backed by collateral which can be a specific asset or a floating charge. Moreover, secured bonds are often further ranked in order of seniority for repayment in the case of the company's defaulting. Specifically, senior secured bonds provide their holders priority in repayment over other secured bondholders. In contrast, an unsecured bond has no collateral backing it, and in the case of default by the company, its holders rank last in the line of debt holders for repayment.

5.3.4 Par Value

Par value—also referred to as nominal value, principal value, face value or redemption value—is the stated value of the bond. It is the amount that the bond issuer promises to pay to the holder of the bond (i.e. the lender) on maturity. For example, a bond with a $1,000 par value will pay the investor holding it $1,000 on the date it matures. Moreover, the par value also determines the amount paid on the bond as interest—the bond indenture specifies the interest payments on the bond as a percentage of its par value. This is the coupon rate, which is discussed in the next sub-section.

However, although the par value is the amount paid by the issuing company upon redemption of the bond, it is not necessarily the price that the investor will pay to purchase the bond when it is first issued. Nor is it the price at which the bond will change hands between investors in the secondary market during its life. For example, a bond with face value of $1000, due for redemption in 4 years, may be currently trading in the secondary market at $1100, i.e. at a $100 premium to par. The price at which the bond changes hands in the market is its market value, determined by demand and supply. Demand and supply for the bond, in turn, are driven by the prevailing market conditions such as the rate of interest and the issuing company's perceived risk of arrears or default (more on this in Sect. 5.4).

Thus, the price of the bond in the market may be below, above or equal to the bond's par value. Accordingly, the bond is said to be trading at a discount to par, at a premium to par or at par respectively. As the bond approaches maturity, its value approaches the amount that the holder of the bond will receive on maturity, i.e. par value. The simplest example is a zero-coupon bond, which makes no interest payments. The bond is issued at a discount to par and holders receive par value upon redemption. During its life, the market price of the zero-coupon bond increases towards the par value that will be received upon redemption (although the price will fluctuate with market conditions).

Notwithstanding the discussion above, sometimes the issuer may redeem the bonds at a price different to the bond's par value. A good example is in the case of callable bonds discussed above, which allow the issuer to redeem the bonds before the stated maturity (see Box 5.2).

Box 5.2: Example of a Callable Bond Redeemed at a Premium to Par, Where the Redemption Is Financed by Secured Callable Floating Rate Bonds[9]

Gamigo AG gives notice of conditional early redemption of its EUR 50 million bond maturing in 2022

Gamigo AG is a leading publisher of free-to-play online and mobile games, headquartered in Hamburg, Germany. On 13 November 2020, it announced that it was going to exercise its right to make an early redemption in full of its EUR 50 million bond maturing in 2022. This was in accordance with the terms and conditions specified in the bond's indenture. The Bonds were to be redeemed on 10 December 2020 at a price of 103.875 per cent of par—i.e. at a premium to par—plus accrued but unpaid interest. This was to be paid to each person registered as owner of the bonds in the debt register as of the end of business day on 3 December 2020 (the record date).

It was also announced that the early redemption in full was conditional upon the success of a bond issue by Media and Games Invest Plc (MGI), the parent company of Gamigo AG. The planned bond issue by MGI was for EUR 80 million senior secured callable floating rate bonds with maturity date of December 2024. In particular, MGI intended to use part of the net proceeds from the new bond issue to redeem Gamigo's bond. Following the redemption, the Gamigo's bonds would be delisted from Nasdaq Stockholm and Frankfurt Stock Exchange Open Market.

5.3.5 Coupon Rate and the Frequency of Payments

Closely related to the concept of par value is the coupon rate. In the case of bonds, the coupon rate is specified in the bond indenture. In the case of other types of debt, e.g. bank overdrafts, it is referred to as the stated rate of interest and specified as part of the debt contract or terms. The coupon rate is the rate of interest that is applied to the par value, to give the periodic interest payment by borrowers to lenders. The terms of the bond or debt will also specify the frequency of interest payments. This may be annual, semi-annual, quarterly, monthly or any other frequency. For example, a holder of a 10-year, £100 par value bond with a coupon rate of 10 per cent, paid on an annual basis, will receive £10 every year for 10 years, until the bond matures and the principal (par value) of £100 is redeemed.

The coupon rate/stated interest rate should not be confused with the rate of interest prevailing in the market (the market rate of interest). In particular, the coupon rate is specified in the terms of the bond and is fixed throughout the life of the bond—or at least the formula that determines it is fixed. The market rate of interest, in contrast, is likely to change during the life of the bond and such changes will impact the market price of the bond. However, regardless of how far the bond market price is from its par value, the interest payments are unaffected.

[9] Source: Extracted on 19.11.20 from Yahoo Finance at: https://uk.finance.yahoo.com/news/gamigo-ag-gives-notice-conditional.

The reason is that the periodic interest payments are determined by applying the coupon rate to the par value and not to the market price of the bond.

In terms of its meaning, the coupon rate reflects the compensation lenders seek for advancing the loan. In other words, it reflects the riskiness of the borrowing firm and of the type of investment for which the money is intended. It is thus normally the case that coupon rates on long-term borrowings are higher than coupon rates on short-term debt of the same company, to account for the extra risk that lenders bear when they invest in long-term debt.

Furthermore, the coupon rate/stated rate of interest may be fixed or floating (floating means that the *formula* for determining the rate is fixed but the rate itself varies). Fixed interest rates do not change during the life of the debt. In contrast, floating rates, which apply for example to most bank loans, may change since they are linked to a benchmark rate. Thus, a debt instrument might define the interest rate as '1 per cent over base rate'. Then when the base rate changes, the interest rate on that debt will change too. Fixed rate debt became unpopular in the 1970s, when in many countries inflation rates were high and volatile. Often neither borrower nor lender was keen to speculate on future changes in the rate of inflation. Allowing the rate to float meant that changes in inflation rates would penalize neither party. However, this unpopularity faded as inflation came under greater control.

Box 5.3 provides a real-life example of green bonds which aim to raise money to be invested in environmental projects. The green bond described in Box 5.3 has a fixed interest rate that is paid on a semi-annual basis.

Box 5.3: Example of a Green Bond with 10-Year Maturity, and Semi-Annual Interest Payments[10]

J-Power sets terms for JPY-20bn green bond issue

Japan's Electric Power Development Co. Ltd., known as J-Power, today unveiled the terms and conditions to issue JPY 20 billion worth of green bonds in its first offering of such securities in the domestic market.

Funds from the placement will enable J-Power to support the development, construction, operation and improvement of its clean energy projects and assets, the company previously said.

The offering and subscription started on January 15 with closure set for January 21, 2021. As part of the proposed transaction, J-Power will issue green bonds with a 10-year maturity, scheduled for January 20, 2031.

[10] Published by Renewables Now, January 15, 2021. Author: Lucas Morais: https://renewablesnow.com/news/j-power-sets-terms-for-jpy-20bn-green-bond-issue-728018/.

The securities have an interest payment date set for January 20 and July 20 of each year at an annual coupon rate of 0.350 per cent.

Mizuho Bank Ltd., was appointed as trustee, while SMBC Nikko Securities Co. Ltd., Mizuho Securities Co. Ltd., and Daiwa Securities Co. Ltd., will act as lead managers.

J-Power is active in the Japanese and overseas renewables industry with wind, solar, biomass and hydropower plants.

5.3.6 Currency

The currency in which the bond is denominated is also a feature specified in the bond indenture. Companies with overseas assets may choose to borrow in foreign currencies rather than in the home currency, as protection against exchange rate risk (i.e. the risk arising from fluctuations in the company's local currency against foreign currencies in which it has assets or liabilities), also known as currency risk. In particular, if the company has income in a foreign currency, it can use that income to service its interest payments that are denominated in the same foreign currency thereby hedging itself from fluctuations in the exchange rate.

Bonds that are denominated in foreign currency come in many forms. First, foreign bonds are bonds that are issued by a foreign entity in the domestic market and denominated in the domestic currency. These bonds have nicknames to indicate the currency and market in which they are trading. For example, a bulldog bond is a bond issued in London by a non-British company and denominated in pounds sterling. Similarly, a samurai bond is denominated in yen and issued in the Japanese market by a non-Japanese company. For example, in the summer of 2020, Indonesia raised 100 billion yen by issuing samurai bonds in the Japanese market to help the government finance its response to the Covid pandemic.[11] Around the same time Hungary issued the equivalent of €500 million of samurai bonds (by definition denominated in Japanese yen and on the Japanese market). Green bonds accounted for one-third of Hungary's samurai bonds issue, making it the first foreign sovereign issuer to enter the yen-denominated green bond market.[12]

Alternatively, a company may issue Eurobonds, which are bonds issued outside of the country where the currency in which the bond is denominated is the legal tender. For example, Eurodollar bonds are bonds that are issued outside of the United States and denominated in US dollars. To illustrate, in October 2020,

[11] Indonesia raises $930m in samurai bonds to fund pandemic response, by Adrian Wail Akhlas in *The Jakarta Post* (3, July 2020) obtained from: https://www.thejakartapost.com/news/2020/07/03/indonesia-raises-930m-in-samurai-bonds-to-fund-pandemic-response.html.

[12] Hungary issues samurai bonds. *Budapest Business Journal*, 11.9.20: https://bbj.hu/economy/finance/debt/hungary-issues-samurai-bonds.

Gazprom, Russia's natural gas giant, issued its first corporate perpetual subordinated Eurobonds in dollars on the Irish Stock Exchange. The issue was undertaken as part of the company's strategy to improve its financial stability and deal with challenging trends in energy markets.[13] Being subordinated meant that Gazprom's Eurodollar bonds were unsecured and ranked below more senior debt for repayment. Furthermore, the coupon rate on these bonds was set at 4.6 per cent, paid on a semi-annual basis. As illustrated in Box 5.4, Gazprom's Eurobond debut issue in October 2020 was followed by a series of further issues aimed at raising $7 billion on the backdrop of political tensions and US sanctions.

Box 5.4: The Eurobond Market[14]

MOSCOW, February 10 (Reuters)—Gazprom returned to the bond market on Wednesday with a new 1 billion euro ($1.21 billion) Eurobond issue, Gazprombank said, in a sign of investor confidence in the state-controlled Russian gas producer despite tensions with the West. The new bond deal comes just three weeks after Gazprom raised $2 billion also via a Eurobond issue.

Russia's relations with the West have deteriorated over the past few weeks after the imprisonment of the Kremlin critic Alexei Navalny, which has led to tit-for-tat expulsions of diplomats.

Gazprombank and J.P. Morgan are joint global coordinators and bookrunners of the issue. Denis Shulakov, Gazprombank's first vice president, said the order book for the issue has generated more than 2.45 billion euros. He added that 210 investors from Germany, Switzerland, France, Great Britain and other European countries, as well as from Russia, Asia and the Middle East have taken part in the issue.

Gazprom is leading the $11 billion Nord Stream 2 gas pipeline project from Russia to Germany, which Washington opposes. The project is under US sanctions which have delayed its construction. Despite the tensions, Gazprom placed an 8-year Eurobond worth $2 billion last month which attracted strong demand and investors have come back for more, shrugging off the political issues surrounding Russian borrowers.

Gazprom has set the final yield for the new issue at 1.5–1.55 per cent, down from the initial guidance of 1.75–1.875 per cent, as demand exceeded 2 billion euros for the 6-year deal, Interfax news agency said. Fitch Ratings, which had assigned the proposed Eurobond a rating of 'BBB', said Gazprom is expected to use the proceeds for general corporate purposes. 'Gazprom's strong competitive position in Europe is supported by low production cost, enormous gas reserves, and long-term contracts with take-or-pay provisions, which are, however, likely to become less prominent as legacy contracts expire'.

Before its recent issues, Gazprom had last tapped the market in October, raising $1.4 billion in perpetual bonds at a yield of 4.6 per cent and another 1 billion euros at 3.9 per cent. It plans to raise a total of 512 billion roubles ($7 billion) both in Russia and abroad this year.

[13] Debut issue of Gazprom perpetual Eurobonds closed. *Financial Times*, 27.10.20: https://markets.ft.com/data/announce/detail?dockey=1323-14733966-15P2D7ILO3GI3VIR1KVQSGIOJU.

[14] Update1—Gazprom taps Eurobond market again with 1 billion euro deal, by Vladimir Soldatkin, 10.2.21, Reuters: https://www.reuters.com/article/gazprom-eurobond-idUSL1N2KG25F.

However, notwithstanding the hedging advantage offered by foreign currency bonds, the issuing company needs to consider a number of risk factors. First, the interest rate on foreign bonds may differ from that on bonds in the home currency, depending mainly on the expected relative rates of inflation. Second, different term structure of interest rates in the home and foreign market (i.e. the different relationship between interest rates and length of maturities) may also be relevant. For example, around mid-August of 2019, the US government bond market had experienced an inversion of the yield curve, as the rate on two-year bonds was slightly higher than on ten-year bonds. (You may remember that normally the longer the maturity, the *higher* the interest rate.) At around 1.6 per cent, dollar rates were nonetheless much higher than sterling rates which were at less than 0.5 per cent at around the same time. Third, if the exchange rate changes during the term of the loan, then the true cost of borrowing comprises the interest payable plus or minus any gain or loss on exchange. Consider samurai bonds issued by an American company. The size of the interest payments in dollar terms depends on the exchange rate between yen and dollar. Specifically, if the yen weakens against the dollar, then yen interest payments are cheaper in dollar terms, while if the yen strengthens, then they are more expensive. Fourth and last, borrowing in foreign currencies can be risky if overseas earnings/assets do not fully cover the interest and principal.

The currency in which the bond is denominated, as well as the par value, the collateral and the other key features included in the bond indenture, are part of the terms of the bond and do not change over its life. In contrast, the bond market price as well as its yield to maturity constantly change in response to market conditions. We now turn to discuss how the value of a bond is determined in the market and how this relates to the yield to maturity.

5.4 Valuing Bonds

You may remember that in Chapter 2 we looked at valuing annuities, and mentioned that although there might not be many instances in capital projects where the same amount of cash flows in or out each year, there are other examples of where that is indeed the case, and a bond is one of them. If I buy a €100 face value 5-year bond with a coupon rate of 6 per cent, my cash flows will be.

Year	0	1	2	3	4	5
	−100	6	6	6	6	106

[Note that year 5 consists of 6 in interest and the redemption value of 100.]
Or, to show them as an annuity,

Year	0	1–5	5
	−100	6	100

If I discount these cash flows at 6 per cent,

Year	0	1-5	5
	-100	6	100
6%	1	4.212	0.747
	-100	25.3	74.7
NPV	**0**		

The NPV is zero—in other words, I get no more and no less than the 6 per cent that was my required return when I bought the bond. But remember two important points—the bond is tradeable during its lifetime, and its coupon (=interest) rate (and, normally, frequency of coupon payments and redemption value) is fixed. However, the going rate of interest in the market for bonds of similar risk is likely to change during the bond's life. If, instead of having bought the bond at the time it was issued, I bought it at the very start of its third year of life, and at that time the going rate of interest was no longer 6 per cent but 8 per cent, I'm not going to be satisfied with paying €100, receiving coupon payments of €6 per year, then getting €100 back at the end. We know from the logic above that this would represent a 6 per cent return, when I need 8 per cent (and could get this easily enough by investing, for example, in a different, *new* bond). So, how do I get the required 8 per cent? The only way is by paying less than the face value, so that I make, in effect, a capital gain on the bond when it matures. The coupon payments plus the capital gain should give me an 8 per cent return. So how do I calculate how much I should pay now? Simply by solving the following:-

Example 5.1—Finding the Bond Value

Year	0	1-3	3
	X	6	100
8%	1	2.577	0.794
	X	15.5	79.4

That is, X = −94.9 to make the NPV equal to zero.◀

If I pay €94.9 for the bond, I get my required 8 per cent return. We have valued our bond part-way through its 'life'! Naturally I can't expect to pay any less than €94.9, because if I did, my positive NPV on the deal would mean a negative NPV for the bond's seller.

A bond trading at less than its face value is said to be trading at a discount. Obviously, if in our example the going rate of interest had not increased, but *reduced* to, say, 4 per cent, I would have to pay *more* than its face value (the 6 per cent coupon is offset by a capital loss to give 4 per cent), and it is said to be trading at a premium. Note the very important point regarding capital markets that as the going rate of interest increases, the value of bonds reduces, and vice versa.

5.4.1 Yield to Maturity (YTM)

The previous section enabled us to calculate the intrinsic value of a bond—that is, its true worth irrespective of its current market price (although these should be the same). If, however, we *know* the current market price, we can work out the bond's yield to maturity (YTM). The YTM is the rate at which future payments promised on the bond are discounted to arrive at its market price. In other words, it is the average annual return expected on the bond if the bond is bought at today's market price, held until maturity, and makes all payments (interest and principal) as scheduled. It is that discount rate which equates the present value of all future payments expected on the bond to its current market price—thus, the internal rate of return (IRR) of the bond. Sometimes the YTM is referred to as the redemption yield to indicate that it is the annual rate of return on the bond if held until redemption.

The YTM differs from the current yield which is the ratio of the periodic interest payment to the current market price of the bond. The main difference between the current yield and the YTM is that the latter considers all future payments (i.e. including the redemption value) and also takes into account the time value of money.

Example 5.2—Finding the YTM

A bond with 5 years remaining, and with a coupon rate of 5 per cent paid annually, and par value of £100, is trading for £104.45. The next coupon payment is due next year. What is the YTM and the current yield on the bond?

The cash flows for a buyer of the bond are:-

Year	0	1	2	3	4	5
	−104.45	5	5	5	5	105

Using the Excel® formula (=IRR) or trial and error, this gives an IRR of 4 per cent. This is the yield to maturity—the effective rate of return you will get if you buy a bond with these cash flows. This is an example of where interest rates on similar-risk investments have gone *down* since the bond was issued.

Like the YTM, the current yield has also gone down, but not all the way to 4 per cent (because the current yield ignores the redemption value): $\frac{100*5\%}{104.45} = 4.79\%$. The current yield moves in the same direction as the YTM, only it does so less aggressively.◀

5.5 Further Consideration of Corporate Bonds

Companies (even large ones) are normally riskier to lend to than governments, which have control of the printing presses (see Sect. 5.7). Hence the required rate of interest will include a risk premium, though it may be fairly small as indicated in Box 5.5.

Box 5.5: Apple Sells $14B of Bonds[15]

At the start of February 2021, Apple Inc. sold $14 billion of bonds with maturities ranging from 5 to 40 years. For example, the 5-year bonds were sold with a coupon of 0.7 per cent, about 0.1 per cent higher than 5-year US Treasury notes which at the time were selling with yields of just 0.6 per cent. Apple were apparently seizing the opportunity of historically low borrowing rates to secure cheap long-term financing as the market was expecting Treasury yields to rise and influence the rates at which Apple and other companies would be able to borrow.

In its prospectus, Apple indicated that the proceeds from the issue would be used to repurchase shares, pay dividends, repay existing debt and for other corporate uses. However, the yield on the five-year bonds at 0.7 per cent, exceeded the dividend yield of 0.6 per cent on Apple's shares. Thus, using the bond issue proceeds to repurchase stock, at first glance, seemed unreasonable. In particular, why would Apple use the costlier bonds to repurchase shares, when it could use cash reserves which it had plenty of at that time? The reason is that interest expenses are tax-deductible, so that the after-tax cost of debt was actually less than the dividend yield, since dividend payments are not tax-deductible.

The risk premium on Apple 5-year bonds over the risk-free rate (US Treasury notes) stood at 0.1 per cent. If the riskiness of Apple were to increase, then so would the required risk premium. This would increase the required rate of return of Apple's investors and reduce the market value of its bonds. It should be obvious that the market price of Apple's long-term bonds will be more sensitive to a change in interest rates than will the market price of the 5-year bonds.

[15] By Mark Kolakowski on February 3, 2021 at: https://www.investopedia.com/apple-aapl-sells-usd14b-of-bonds-5101660.

As we saw in Example 5.2, there is an inverse relationship between the market rate of interest and bond prices. When interest rates in the market rise, bond prices generally fall. This is called interest rate risk and is the reason why bonds with longer maturity have higher coupon rates than short-term debt. For example, while the 5-year bonds issued by Apple in February 2021 (Box 5.5) carried a coupon rate of 0.7 per cent, its 40-year bonds were issued with a coupon of 2.8 per cent. Bonds with longer maturities expose investors to more interest rate risk—the risk that a bond's price will fall if interest rates rise.

To give another example, the low interest rate environment which followed the 2008 global financial crisis encouraged companies, including those with lower credit ratings, to increase their leverage ratios. To illustrate, over the three years 2016–2019, the lowest investment grade (BBB) bonds had grown to account for over 50 per cent of all new investment grade bond issues, exposing those firms to the risk of a rise in interest rates on new debt. Indeed, if interest rates in the market were to rise, bond prices would fall, sending yields up and increasing borrowing costs. Likewise, in case of a downturn—a situation which materialized in 2020 with the COVID pandemic—the credit ratings of those highly levered firms would be downgraded, sending their bond prices down and borrowing costs up (see Box 5.6). Moreover, downgrading BBB-rated corporations implies reclassifying their bonds as non-investment grade (junk bonds), thereby limiting their ability to raise funds for investments or refinancing and possibly triggering a rise in default rates.

Box 5.6: Bond Insights: 2020 Mid-Year Outlook on Corporate Bonds by Collin Martin[16]

Corporate bond prices began to tumble early in 2020 due to concerns about the economic impact of COVID-19. As the economy ground to a halt, and cash flows were plunging, it became increasingly more difficult for companies to make timely interest or principal payments. The increased risk to corporate revenues and profits, as well as the possible defaults or arrears in paying interest, resulted in corporate bond prices dropping during February and March.

A turnaround came on March 23rd, when the Federal Reserve (Fed) announced unprecedented action to increase liquidity in the corporate bond market in response to the woes brought on by the COVID-19 pandemic. Specifically, two corporate bond-buying facilities were announced, allowing the Fed to purchase bonds in the primary market, where the bonds are initially issued (PMCCF) and in the secondary market where bonds are traded following initial issuance (SMCCF).[17] The SMCCF allowed the Fed to buy up to $750 billion of corporate bonds which it began to do on June 16th. Some restrictions were imposed on what bonds were eligible for purchasing. For example, only bonds that on or after March

---

[16] Charles Schwab, June 23, 2020, at: https://www.schwab.com/resource-center/insights/content/2020-mid-year-outlook-corporate-bonds.

[17] PMCCF stands for *Primary Market Corporate Credit Facility*, while SMCCF stands for *Secondary Market Corporate Credit Facility*. Note that in practice, as the Fed could not directly buy

22nd were rated investment grade (BBB or above) could be purchased, including those that have subsequently been downgraded to non-investment grade. Indeed, the Fed purchased bonds issued by companies from a range of industries (e.g. tobacco, video games and energy), including companies that were downgraded from investment grade to junk bonds (termed *fallen angels*) such as Ford.

Knowing that the Fed was going to purchase corporate bonds helped alleviate the concerns about companies failing to repay or refinance their debts. Subsequently, bond prices rose, and yields dropped. However, while the Fed's support allowed corporations to issue more bonds, it also raised their risk over the long run.

5.6 Other Types of Debt

5.6.1 Leases

Leases allow a user (the lessee) the use of an asset (e.g. property, equipment) in return for regular payments of lease rentals to the lessor, who remains the legal owner. Unless the lease is for a very short period (less than 12 months) or for very small amounts (in which cases the lease payments may, at the company's option, simply be charged to the Income Statement) they are regarded as, in effect, putting the lessee in almost the same position as if they had borrowed the money and purchased the asset outright. So, the lessee's balance sheet capitalizes finance leases and shows fixed assets at 'equivalent cost' matched by long-term 'liabilities'. The annual accounts treat part of each year's lease rental as interest expense and part as repayment. (In addition, depreciation is charged on the fixed asset.) A similar approach applies to hire-purchase deals where, for example, following a 20 per cent down payment, firms acquire assets by instalments over up to five years.

In capital project appraisals, one may discount future finance lease payments ('deferred investments') at a very low discount rate (suitable for debt), or else replace them with a 'payment' at the start of the project equivalent to the capital cost of the asset. In either case, tax treatment of the lease payments needs to be taken into account.

5.6.2 Preference Share Capital

Preference shares are essentially shares with a (usually) fixed dividend rate based on their par value, where the dividends must be paid by the company before any dividends are paid to the ordinary shareholders, and which rank above ordinary

corporate bonds, it lent money to special purpose vehicles (SPVs) that were established to do the purchasing. For more information see: https://www.schwab.com/resource-center/insights/content/feds-corporate-bond-buying-programs-faqs.

shares in the event of the winding up of the company. As a form of corporate finance, preference share capital lies in between long-term borrowing (debt) and ordinary share capital (equity). From a financial point of view many of its features are similar to debt, but legally it forms part of shareholders' funds. (These are now split between 'equity'—normally ordinary share capital—and 'non-equity'—which would certainly include preference share capital.)

Debt interest must be paid before there can be any question of declaring preference dividends; and until a company has repaid lenders in full on winding-up, the preference shareholders will get nothing back at all. But, as stated above, preference capital has priority over ordinary capital, both with respect to dividends and with respect to ultimate capital repayment. Both the amount of any preference dividend and the amount of preference capital repayable on redemption (when the preference shares are paid back by the company) are normally fixed money amounts.

Mainly because they are not deductible for tax purposes, preference dividends are usually more expensive for a company to pay than debt interest. Where preference shares exist, failure to pay preference dividends will prevent payment of any ordinary dividends. No company contemplates that except in dire crisis, so in practice preference dividends may seem nearly as much a commitment as debt interest. Yet if the worst comes to the worst, there is a big difference between a company being highly embarrassed if it has to omit preference dividends for a period or two, and being liquidated if it fails to pay interest due on its debt.

It may be better to view preference share capital as an alternative to ordinary share capital, not to borrowing, and as a useful way to increase what is, in effect, financial gearing without too much risk. Indeed, preference shares will be much cheaper than ordinary shares (being so much less risky to the holders), yet (from the company's viewpoint) much less risky than debt.

5.6.3 Convertible Loans

Some long-term loans may be convertible into ordinary shares at the holder's option on pre-arranged terms. As long as a loan is not converted, it counts as debt on the balance sheet. It continues to incur regular interest payments and ranks as a creditor in the event of winding up. But upon conversion it ceases to bear interest and becomes ordinary share capital ranking for dividends. The value of the option to take up equity if the company prospers will reduce the nominal interest rate payable on convertible loan stocks. Where it makes much difference, earnings per share and book amount of equity per share may be computed both as they are now and as they would be on a fully diluted basis (that is, after taking account of the new shares that would be issued on conversion of the loan).

5.6.4 Income Bonds

Income bonds are debt instruments which promise to pay back the principal, but on which interest is payable only if sufficient profits are earned in a period (although borrowers have to accumulate any missed interest payments and make them up later). The terms of the bond specify when the borrower is deemed to have earned income out of which interest is to be paid to the lender. Some people argue that income bonds offer all the advantages of preference share capital (see Sect. 5.6.2), together with the tax advantages of debt. Unlike preference shares, the issuer must redeem income bonds at a fixed amount on a specific date.

5.6.5 Asset-Backed Securities

Asset-backed securities (ABS) are created by pooling non-tradable, often illiquid assets into a single security which is then sold to investors. The underlying assets can be mortgage loans, student loans, credit card debt, automobile loans or similar income-generating assets. The issued ABS are, by definition, backed by the underlying assets so that income earned on the assets is used to make interest and principal payments on the ABS. This pooling process is called securitization and is normally managed by a special purpose vehicle created in order to allow the institutions that originally held the underlying assets to remove them from their books. The pooling of many risky assets also facilitates diversification, thereby reducing the risk of the individual assets. Typically, the newly created asset is divided into tranches with different levels of risk and returns. For example, holders of lower risk-return tranches receive payments before holders of higher risk-return tranches. ABS are considered one of the main drivers leading to the 2008 financial crisis, and subsequently ABS holders suffered significant losses during that period. The crisis revealed that many ABS holders did not appreciate the risk involved in the securitization process.

5.6.6 Catastrophe Bonds

Catastrophe (CAT) bonds are bonds that are issued primarily by insurance companies to transfer insurance risks to market participants (mainly institutional investors). These bonds were first issued in 1997 in the wake of large-scale failure of insurance companies following natural disasters such as the 1992 Hurricane Andrew in Florida (Polacek 2018). In essence, CAT bonds promise to pay interest and principal as long as a predefined natural disaster, such as a hurricane or an earthquake, does not occur. If, however, the catastrophe event occurs, payments would cease, so that the insurance company could use the funds to pay policyholders. For institutional investors, such as pension funds, CAT bonds are attractive because they characteristically promise high coupon, while allowing the investors to diversify their portfolio risk by investing in an asset which is typically uncorrelated with market returns.

Box 5.7 provides an example of a specific type of CAT bond, namely pandemic bonds, which were issued by the International Bank for Reconstruction and Development (IBRD), part of the World Bank. It highlights the typically high coupon which CAT bonds offer and their popularity with institutional investors and also the fact that CAT bonds can represent a portfolio diversification instrument.

Box 5.7: Coronavirus to Trigger Pandemic Catastrophe Bonds by James Fernyhough, from the Australian Financial Review.[18]

Coronavirus is set to test the nascent pandemic bond market, as the virus triggers the insurance mechanism resulting in investors losing their principal investments, says international ratings agency DBRS Morningstar. Marcos Alvarez, a UK-based analyst with DBRS Morningstar, said $US320 million ($484 million) was tied up in pandemic bonds globally and it was likely that much of this would be lost as the disease spreads.

Pandemic bonds are a type of catastrophe bond, or insurance linked security—an investment vehicle issued by insurance companies, financial institutions, and governments—to protect against the costs of a sudden pandemic outbreak. Investors receive a higher-than-average coupon in compensation for the risk that they will lose some or all of their principal in the case of a pandemic. While most catastrophe bonds cover natural disasters such as hurricanes, cyclones, and earthquakes, and are issued by insurers and reinsurers, the only issuer of pandemic catastrophe bonds is the International Bank for Reconstruction and Development, part of the World Bank.

The market was launched in 2017 following the Ebola outbreak in West Africa in 2014, as a way of transferring some of the cost of international aid from the coffers of the World Bank on to capital markets. The high-coupon securities immediately proved popular with investors, and the $370 million issuance in 2017 was 200 per cent oversubscribed.

Mr. Alvarez said it was now highly likely that the catastrophe bonds would be triggered for the first time. "It is still to be seen if investors will remain attracted to pandemic bonds after payouts are activated, but past experience with catastrophe bonds illustrates that interest remains even after large natural catastrophes affect this asset class".

Fermat Capital Management managing director, John Seo, said they are a way of diversifying credit risk. Traditional natural disaster catastrophe bonds are both entirely uncorrelated to traditional financial risks such as interest rates and global financial shocks, and are also geographically specific, meaning an investor can spread the risk by purchasing bonds that cover a range of different regions.

The IBRD issued two types of pandemic bond in 2017; one in which 17 per cent of the principal is lost when triggered, and one in which the entire principal is lost. Dedicated catastrophe bond investors in Europe and the United States are by far the biggest holders of pandemic catastrophe bonds, followed by pension funds and non-specialised asset managers.

[18] *The Australian Financial Review*, March 9, 2020, at: https://www.afr.com/companies/financial-services/coronavirus-to-trigger-pandemic-catastrophe-bonds-20200309-p5483y.

5.6.7 Peer to Peer Lending

Peer to peer lending (also known as P2P lending or crowdlending) is an online platform that allows individuals and businesses to borrow and lend funds directly to each other. By cutting out the financial intermediary, P2P lending reduces overhead costs and allows borrowers to enjoy cheap rates while lenders benefit from previously inaccessible investment opportunities. The P2P platform provider takes a fee for its services which may include credit screening of potential borrowers, calculating risk-compatible interest rates, proposing borrowers to lenders and vice versa and maintaining the platform so that it can handle all transactions. Notwithstanding these services, compared with traditional banks the fees charged by the platform provider are typically low. Moreover, P2P lending provides access to credit to individuals and small businesses that find it difficult to access traditional credit. The first P2P lending platform was Zopa, a UK platform that was founded in 2005. Another well-known UK P2P lending platform is Funding Circle, which focusses on lending to small businesses worldwide, pooling lenders that include individuals as well as local and national governments and financial institutions. P2P lending platforms that operate from the United States include Lending Club and Prosper Marketplace.

5.7 Government Debt Securities and the Risk-Free Asset

Readers with an interest in risk-free securities, and in particular, government bonds, might wish to read this section. If not, please jump directly to the conclusion, Sect. 5.8.

A risk-free security is one that offers future cash inflows which are certain. There is no possibility of a default by the issuer, and the price at which the security could be sold at any time is known.

The closest thing to a risk-free security is short-term government debt obligations. The reason is that governments are the least likely to default on their obligations (although this sometimes happens, see Box 5.8). Moreover, by shortening the maturity of the obligation, the issuer reduces the risk that the market price would change during the security's life. For example, US treasury bills (T-Bills) are considered risk-free because they are redeemed within one year and are issued by the US treasury department which means that they are backed by the US government. T-Bills often have a face value of $1000, and instead of making coupon payments, they are issued at a discount to par value. It is for this reason that T-Bills are also known as Treasury zeros. For example, a 3-month US T-Bill may be selling for $985, to be redeemed at par. In fact, because the price is traditionally quoted as a percentage of par, our T-bill would be quoted at 98.5 (i.e. 98.5 per cent of 1000 = 985).

Box 5.8: Lebanon to Default on Debt Payments for First Time as Crisis Deepens[19]

Lebanon is to default on a foreign debt payment for the first time in its history as the country struggles with a major financial crisis.

Prime Minister Hassan Diab said Lebanon would not be making a bond payment of $1.2bn (£900m) due on Monday. 'The debt has become bigger than Lebanon can bear, and bigger than the ability of the Lebanese to meet interest payments', Mr. Diab said.

Lebanon has been struggling since the value of its currency plummeted. The Lebanese pound has been losing value against the dollar for months, in part because the country's banks have been reluctant to convert local pounds to dollars—leading to an increase in demand for the latter. This issue with foreign exchange has led to importers having difficulty accessing goods, which have become more expensive. Those with savings have also been affected by the drop in value of the local currency.

In a live televised address on Saturday, Mr. Diab said that negotiations to restructure the country's debt, which stands at more than $30bn, would continue 'with all creditors ... in a manner consistent with the national interest'. Mr. Diab added that more than 40 per cent of the population could soon be in poverty as Lebanon tackles its worst economic crisis in decades.

The 61-year-old became prime minister in January as part of a new government that formed after protests over the failure of leaders to deal with the economic crisis turned violent.

In October, anti-government protesters took to the streets in response to rising prices, high youth unemployment, poor public services and corruption. The crisis has severely hit public services, with electricity and water supplies frequently disrupted and rubbish left to pile up on the streets. With Lebanon remaining heavily in debt, economists suggest that a rescue deal with the International Monetary Fund (IMF) is the only way forward—and real reforms would be needed for that to happen.

T-Bills can be considered risk-free, provided that the holder does not need to exchange the dollar payments into another currency. Furthermore, the US treasury department also issues Inflation Protected Securities (TIPS). These are treasury bonds that are indexed to an inflation measure in order to protect future payments from a decline in purchasing power. The periodic coupon payments as well as the redemption value on inflation-index bonds are adjusted in line with movements in the price level to eliminate inflation risk.[20]

T-Bills satisfy the demand for risk-free assets but only for investors interested in short-term securities, because they typically have maturities of one year or less. Alternative risk-free assets with longer maturities are STRIPS. These are zero-coupon securities that are created from issued Treasury bonds under a programme called the Separate Trading of Registered Interest and Principal Securities. Although created from Treasury bonds, STRIPS are not issued by the Treasury, but by dealers in US Treasury bonds who transform Treasury-backed, long-term,

[19] BBC, 7 March 2020: https://www.bbc.com/news/world-middle-east-51785690.

[20] More precisely, the coupon rate on TIPS is fixed, while the principal is adjusted for inflation. Interest payments are also inflation adjusted because for calculating the periodic payment, the fixed coupon rate is applied to the inflation-adjusted principal.

coupon-bearing bonds into a set of zero-coupon bonds. This process is called stripping. Stripping involves selling each individual coupon and the par value separately as zero-coupon bonds. Just like other zero-coupon Treasury securities (e.g. T-Bills), STRIPS are sold at a discount, so that the implied interest is the difference between the face value of the coupon or principal and the discounted price.

Example 5.3—Zero-Coupon Bonds

A 10-year Treasury bond with face value of $1000 and coupon rate of 4 per cent paid on a semi-annual basis, was stripped into 20 coupon STRIPS and one principal STRIP. If the current interest rate is 3 per cent a year, how much will the principal STRIP cost today?

$$\$1000 = PV \times \left(1 + \frac{0.03}{2}\right)^{10\times 2}$$

where PV is the present value of the principal STRIP today. Note that the periodic (semi-annual) interest rate is $\frac{3\%}{2} = 1.5\%$, and the number of compounding periods remaining on the principal STRIP is $2 \times 10 = 20$. Thus, the present value is:

$$PV = \frac{\$1000}{(1.015)^{20}} = \$742.47$$

◀

STRIPS and other zero-coupon securities make no payments before maturity and therefore do not bear the risk associated with reinvesting intervening cash flows (reinvestment risk). Their market price reflects the present value of the lump sum paid upon maturity, hence, the further away the zero-coupon security is from maturity, the lower is its price. Likewise, the higher the market rate of interest (the discount rate), the lower is the price of the zero-coupon bond. The latter is true, of course, for all bonds and other financial and non-financial assets. However, zero-coupon securities are particularly sensitive to the rate of interest since there are no intervening interest payments.

Zero-coupon treasury bills are also issued by the UK government. These are zero-coupon sterling-denominated instruments of up to 12 months maturity when first issued. Like the US T-Bills, they are issued at a discount and redeemed at par. In addition, the UK government also issues conventional gilts. These instruments, which are listed on the London Stock Exchange, are also considered risk-free as they enjoy similar high issuer's reputation to the US government's securities. More precisely, UK conventional gilts are issued by the Debt Management Office (DMO) on behalf of Her Majesty's Treasury, and it is this primary characteristic that won them the name gilts or gilt-edged securities. They are the simplest form of sterling-denominated bonds, which pay a fixed coupon every six months until the bond matures, and its holder receives the final coupon payment plus £100 par value.

Gilts are issued for periods varying from three months to more than twenty-five years, and in the past some of them were even undated. These undated gilts were referred to as consols and promised to pay a stated coupon rate each year for ever. The consols were callable which meant that the option to redeem them rested exclusively with the government. Indeed, although some of these perpetuities had been in issue for more than one hundred years, all of them were fully redeemed by 2015, following a decision by the Chancellor of the Exchequer. However, following the COVID-19 crisis, there were renewed calls for issuing perpetual bonds, see Box 5.9.

Box 5.9: Let's Finance Britain's Budget Deficit by Issuing Perpetual Bonds, Taking Advantage of the Fact Global Interest Rates Cannot Fall Any Lower, by George Soros, the Chair of Soros Fund Management and the Open Society Foundation[21]

A more contagious variant of Covid-19 has created a new emergency, so all the countries that can ought to issue perpetual bonds to pay for the cost of fighting the virus. The prime candidates for this are the United Kingdom and the so-called Frugal Five: Austria, Denmark, Finland, the Netherlands and Sweden.

These are not normal times. The pandemic has created an emergency situation … with an economic impact worse than the 2008 financial crisis. That requires a bold economic response …I have long championed perpetual bonds. These are bonds that never have to be repaid; only the annual interest needs to be paid. To some, this may sound like a radical idea, yet perpetual bonds have been used for centuries. Britain issued perpetual bonds, called 'Consols' in 1752 and later used 'war bonds', which were also perpetual, to finance the Napoleonic wars. The United States issued Consols in the 1870s.

Perpetual bonds ought to be introduced now, when global interest rates cannot fall any lower. They would lock in that advantage forever. They could be introduced gradually to allow financial markets to familiarise themselves with a new instrument. This presents no problem because an undated bond can be easily sold in tranches.

But countries in Europe have no experience in using this instrument. Britain could render them a great service in this regard by issuing perpetual bonds. It would set a precedent that could be relied on by other European governments. This would help to build trust and cooperation between the UK and the EU. Above all, it would be the right way to finance Britain's budget deficit.

For example, imagine the UK government has issued a risk-free perpetual bond, paying interest of £0.8 per £100 nominal of stock, once a year for ever (a perpetuity). Ignoring tax, what would we expect its market price to be? We know the amount and the timing of all future cash receipts. The only other thing we need to find out is the YTM, i.e. the interest rate at which these cash flows are to be

[21] *The Independent*, 18.1.21, at: https://www.independent.co.uk/voices/perpetual-bonds-coronavirus-response-interest-rates-b1787183.html.

discounted in order to find the bond's present value. The YTM reflects the opportunity cost—the rate of return which could be earned on similar-risk (in this case, risk-free) investments.

Example 5.4—Undated Bonds

A risk-free government gilt pays interest of £0.8 per £100 nominal of stock, once a year forever. If the current rate of interest on perpetual risk-free securities is 1 per cent a year, then the present value of this perpetuity is:

$$PV = \frac{Coupon \quad Payment}{r} = \frac{£0.8}{0.01} = £80$$

If the interest rate were now to rise to 2 per cent a year, investors would sell the £0.8-a-year perpetuity until its market price reached £40 (= £0.8/0.02). In other words, investors would sell the bond until its price reached the point at which it offered the going market rate, i.e. 2 per cent (=£0.8/£40).

Following the change in the rate of interest from 1 per cent to 2 per cent, why would people sell the £0.8-a-year perpetuity if its market price were above £40? Because they would then be able to acquire—risk-free—a larger annual income forever. Suppose the market price remained at £80. By selling the perpetuity and reinvesting the £80 proceeds in a risk-free security yielding the 'going' rate of interest of 2 per cent a year, someone could achieve an income twice that offered on the perpetuity. Specifically, they would earn £1.60 a year for ever (= 2 per cent × £80).

Note that because they have no redemption value, the price of an undated bond is the ratio of the periodic interest payment to the YTM. (In Example 5.4 we have: $PV = \frac{£0.8}{0.01} = £80$.) Likewise, the YTM is equal to the **current yield** of the bond ($YTM = \frac{£0.8}{£40} = 2\%$). The calculations, however, are somewhat more complex where there is a redemption date some years in the future. For example, as we saw in Example 5.1, if the bond has both interest payments and redemption value, then to find its present value, we have to calculate the present value of an annuity, together with the present value of a lump sum to be received in the future. Similarly, as we saw in Example 5.2, if the bond has both interest payments and redemption value, then to find its YTM, we need to use the = irr function in Excel® or by trial and error.

To conclude our discussion on risk-free assets, we saw in this sub-section that US backed debt obligations (e.g. bonds, bills, and notes) as well as debt obligations issued by other governments, such as the United Kingdom, are considered the closest thing to risk-free assets. This is why the YTM on these government securities is used as a benchmark against which to measure other assets. Specifically, the return expected on a risky asset, such as on a corporate bond, is made up of the risk-free return plus risk premium.◄

5.8 A Concluding Note

A firm will finance its activities from internal or external resources. External resources can come in the form of new equity finance or in the form of debt. In this chapter we have looked at corporate debt.

Understanding debt finance is important because of its centrality for corporations. For example, the results of the CFO Signals™ survey of Q2 2021 found that debt attractiveness remained high among CFOs during the COVID-19 pandemic, at 92 per cent. It is thus not surprising that the levels of debt owed by the US and UK companies had risen during the COVID-19 pandemic. For example, while between 2010 and 2019, debt of US non-financial companies grew at an average annual rate of 5.5 per cent, in 2020, growth jumped to 9.1 per cent. The Deloitte's CFO Insights report of August 2021 offers a number of explanations for this trend. First, low interest rates could have driven firms to borrow more. Second, companies may have been forced to borrow to keep operations running during shutdowns. Third, some companies may have increased their borrowing in order to fund investment in technology to support remote work. Fourth, the pandemic increased demand in some sectors such as information technology, health care, consumer products and communication services. Consequently, firms in these sectors borrowed more to finance this growth opportunity.

The CFO Signals™ survey of Q2 2021 also looked at equity financing. It found that CFOs' views on equity attractiveness moved up slightly, from 55 per cent in Q1 2021 to 56 per cent in Q2. Our next chapter deals with this alternative source of financing.

5.8.1 Problems

Problem 5.1

(a) What is the value of a perpetuity of 600p (£6) a year if the interest rate is 12 per cent and the first payment is due in one year's time?
(b) What happens to the value if the interest rate falls to 10 per cent a year?
(c) What happens if the interest rate rises to 15 per cent?

Problem 5.2 The Arcadian government's irredeemable bond is considered risk-free. It pays an annual coupon of 4 per cent on 100 par value, and the next interest payment is due in one year's time.

(a) What is the risk-free rate of interest if the bond is currently trading at 60 Arcadian dollars?
(b) What will the price of the bond be if the interest rate is:
    (i) 5 per cent
    (ii) 3 per cent?

Problem 5.3 You bought a 10-year zero-coupon bond with a face value of $1000, for $853.

(a) What is the yield to maturity on the bond?
(b) What would be the price of the bond after 5 years, if the yield to maturity at that time stood at 1.5 per cent?

Problem 5.4 Some years ago, a company issued a 20-year bond with face value of £100 and coupon rate of 5 per cent, paid annually.

(a) The bond now has 3 years to maturity, the next interest payment is due in one year, and its current market price is £105. What is the yield to maturity on the bond?
(b) The bond now has 2 years to maturity, the next interest payment is due in one year, and the yield to maturity stands at 3 per cent.
   (i) What is the current market price of the bond?
   (ii) What is the current yield on the bond?

References

Çelik, S., Demirtaş, G., & Isaksson, M. (2020), Corporate bond market trends, emerging risks and monetary policy. *OECD Capital Market Series*. Paris. Available at: www.oecd.org/corporate/Corporate-Bond-Market-Trends-Emerging-Risks-and-Monetary-Policy.htm

Polacek, A. (2018). *Catastrophe bonds: A primer and retrospective* (Chicago Fed Letter, No. 405). https://www.chicagofed.org/publications/chicago-fed-letter/2018/405

Ordinary Share Capital

6

6.1 Introduction

A company's market capitalization is the total market value of all its outstanding shares. That is, its share price in the market, multiplied by the number of shares outstanding. At the end of 2020, the global market capitalization (of all companies listed on stock exchanges around the world), stood at USD 109.21 trillion, according to the World Federation of Exchanges.[1] But the year 2020 also saw market volatility levels comparable only to those of the great financial crisis of 2008. These unpredictable and sharp price movements were brought about by increased tension between the United States and China, Brexit negotiations, the US presidential election and ultimately, by the COVID-19 pandemic. However, despite great uncertainties and volatility, the year 2020 also witnessed an increase of over 25 per cent (relative to 2019) in new listings through Initial Public Offerings (IPOs). This increase in the number of private corporations going public by listing their shares on stock exchanges highlights the important role that exchanges play in funding the real economy, particularly during challenging times.

In this chapter we shall explain and discuss terms such as market capitalization and IPOs. The chapter is structured as follows. Section 6.2 reviews the nature of shares, followed by Sect. 6.3 where trading in shares on stock exchanges is discussed. The meaning of IPOs will be made clear in Sect. 6.4 where we outline the methods by which companies go public and raise equity financing. We end the chapter with some concluding notes (Sect. 6.5) followed by practice problems.

[1] See Full Year 2020 Market Highlights published by the WFE Statistics Team on 19.2.21 (https://www.world-exchanges.org/news/articles/full-year-2020-market-highlights).

R. Manos et al., *Corporate Finance for Business*,
https://doi.org/10.1007/978-3-030-92419-5_6

6.2 The Nature of Ordinary Shares

A share is a security issued by a company to investors and is also referred to as common stock, an equity share or an ordinary share. It represents proportional ownership of the issuing company, where this proportion is determined by the total number of shares issued. As the owner of a proportion of the company, the shareholder (stockholder) is entitled to a share of its profits and dividends and to vote on the company's affairs. Thus, in the company's Annual General Meeting (AGM) shareholders hear about the company's plans and performance and can vote on matters including dividend payments, executive pay, the appointment of auditors and election of members to the Board of Directors (BoD).

Box 6.1 illustrates how shareholders in Apple Corporation exercise their voting right during the company's AGM, to determine dividend payments, the election of members to the BoD and executive compensation.

Box 6.1: Apple's 2021 shareholders meeting[2]

Apple Inc. (Nasdaq: AAPL) shareholders have voted to re-elect the company's entire board of directors and also approved the 2020 executive compensation program, CNBC reported Tuesday. The company also plans to increase the dividend.

Apple CEO Tim Cook's 2021 compensation will include a long-term equity award, the first since he was promoted to the top role in 2011, as per CNBC. The equity package was announced in September 2020.

In a proxy filing, Apple's board noted that since Cook's promotion to the role of CEO in August 2011 through September 2020, the company's market capitalization increased by more than $1.5 trillion and total shareholder return, including dividends, was 867%.

Apple shareholders reportedly voted down a proposal that would require the company to reduce executive pay compared with median employee salary across the company.

Cook said that Apple planned to raise its dividend, according to the CNBC report. The iPhone maker had declared a dividend of 20.5 cents per share in the holiday quarter.

The CEO also reportedly noted that Apple employees have been working from home since March and have adapted well to remote work.

Regarding Apple's acquisition strategy, Cook said Apple acquires a company every month or so and has acquired about 100 companies over the last six years.

Why It Matters: Apple has thrived despite the pandemic and reported revenues of $111.4 billion in the recent first quarter, up 21% year-over-year. The tech giant is the biggest listed public company in the United States with a market capitalization of $2.1 trillion.

Price Movement: Apple shares closed 0.1 percent lower at $125.86 on Tuesday.

In the meeting, Apple's management presented information regarding the company's acquisition strategy and reported on its performance, including how it managed its workforce during the COVID-19 pandemic and lockdowns. Apple's

[2] Apple To Hike Dividends, Tim Cook Says by Madhukumar Warrier, Feb 24, 2021, Benzinga, Yahoo Finance (https://finance.yahoo.com/news/apple-hike-dividends-tim-cook-055457834.html).

directors also provided information about the company's performance, including the increase in its market capitalization, a measure of how the company is valued by the stock market and a popular proxy for its size. In Apple's case, with a market price of $125.86 per share and 16.79 billion shares outstanding, its market capitalization is:

$$Market\ Capitalization\ for\ Apple = \$125.86 \times 16.79\text{billion}$$
$$\cong \$2.1\text{trillion}$$

6.2.1 The Return on Shares

As indicated in Box 6.1, Apple's shareholders enjoyed the increase in the company's market capitalization, because the appreciation in the market price of the shares they hold is a capital gain which they can crystallize by selling their shares at a price higher than the price at which they bought them. This capital gain is only part of the return a shareholder receives. The other component is the dividend payment. Thus, the formula for calculating the annual return on a stock/share is the sum of the appreciation in the price (capital gain) over the year plus any dividends paid, divided by the price of the stock at the start of the year for which the return is calculated:

$$Return\ on\ Share = R_{Share} = \frac{Capital\ Gains + Dividend\ Payment}{Price\ at\ start\ of\ year}$$
$$= \frac{(Price\ at\ end\ of\ year - Price\ at\ start\ of\ year) + Dividend\ Payment}{Price\ at\ start\ of\ year}$$

Example 6.1 illustrates how to calculate the return on a stock.

Example 6.1: Calculating the return on a share

In March 2020, the share of Apple was trading at $62. A year later, the share was trading at $120. If Apple paid its shareholders a dividend of $0.8 during the year, what was the total annual return on the stock?

$$R_{Apple} = \frac{(\$120 - \$62) + \$0.8}{\$62} = 94.8\%$$

Note that the total return is made up of two components: capital gain yield and dividend yield. The capital gain yield is the price appreciation divided by the price of the share at the beginning of the period:

$$R_{capital\ gain\ on\ Apple} = \frac{(\$120 - \$62)}{\$62} = 93.5\%$$

The dividend yield is the dividend paid divided by the price of the share at the beginning of the period:

$$R_{dividend\ yield\ on\ Apple} = \frac{\$0.8}{\$62} = 1.3\%$$

◄

6.2.2 The Risk of Shares

Similar to bonds, shares of publicly traded companies can be bought and sold in financial markets. For example, Apple's shares are traded on the NASDAQ stock exchange under the symbol AAPL. In terms of risk, however, shares and bonds are very different.

In particular, as an owner of a proportion of the issuing company (rather than a bond holder who is basically a lender), the shareholder takes on the risk associated with the company. There are in fact two associated risks. First, unlike bondholders to whom the firm is obliged under the bond contract to pay interest and return the principal on due dates, the return to shareholders is highly uncertain. As illustrated in Example 6.1 the return to shareholders comprises both dividends and capital gain (i.e. share price appreciation). The former is at the discretion of the *directors*, and the latter is highly unpredictable. Second, owning equity shares is riskier than lending the company money because on a winding-up, only after the company has repaid all other suppliers of finance in full will ordinary shareholders then get anything that remains. This implies that in a successful company the potential reward for shareholders is limitless, but if the company is unable to pay all its creditors in full, the ordinary shareholders get nothing at all.

Shareholders, however, are protected in a way because in a limited company they cannot be called upon to subscribe any more money. Once the shares are fully paid up, the most that shareholders can lose is what they have already invested. Historically this limitation proved vital in encouraging rich investors to finance companies, knowing that, in a diversified portfolio, only a small part of their wealth was at risk.

Notwithstanding the above, from the *investor's* viewpoint the risk borne by shareholders is greater than that borne by lenders. From the *company's* viewpoint, however, it is the other way round: ordinary share capital (equity) is less risky than borrowing (debt) as a source of funds, for three main reasons:

1. There is no legal commitment to pay any dividend (unlike interest on debt).
2. As long as the company exists it need never repay equity capital to shareholders, whereas it must legally repay debt on the due maturity date.
3. Equity capital is free from the restrictions which lenders often attach to debt by way of covenants.

The difference between equity and debt in terms of the risk borne by both parties—the firm and investors—is reflected in the difference in the returns expected by investors on each of those securities. Shareholders, who bear more risk, expect to receive higher returns (which, you will remember, they receive in the form of dividend and price appreciation) compared with debtholders who receive periodic interest plus return of the principal on maturity. Thus, from the company's viewpoint, the cost of equity (the return expected by equity holders) is higher than the cost of debt (the return expected by debt holders).

6.2.3 Shareholders' Action

As presented in Box 6.1, shareholders in Apple also voted to re-elect the company's board of directors. In theory, dissatisfied shareholders may vote to replace a company's directors at the AGM. But in practice, they will usually simply sell their shares. The trouble is that by then the market price of the shares may have fallen, to reflect past performance and poor future prospects. Large shareholders, in contrast, may prefer to remain as investors and try to find ways to get the managers to improve the company's performance (or to replace the chief executive). In Apple about 60 per cent of shares were held in 2021 by institutions.[3] But Apple is a publicly listed company. In unlisted companies, it may be very difficult to influence a company's policy since the directors are often also major shareholders (with their families). It may also be difficult for an 'outside' shareholder to sell their shares, at least not at anything like the expected price. It is for this reason, and for other reasons too, that companies decide to go public and list on the stock exchange, thereby facilitating public trading in their shares.

6.3 Trading in Shares

6.3.1 The Stock Exchange

The stock exchange is a regulated market on which shares in local and international companies are listed and traded. The stock exchange is actually made up of two markets: the primary market and the secondary market. The primary market is where companies raise capital by way of issuing new shares to the public. Once shares are listed, they are bought and sold in the secondary market by investors who in effect exchange shares amongst themselves.

A company first lists (or floats) its shares in the primary market through a process called an Initial Public Offering (IPO). If it needs more funds, it can later issue more shares through a process called a seasoned equity offering (SEO). In either case, issuing shares in the primary market raises new capital for the company

[3] https://finance.yahoo.com/quote/AAPL/holders?p=AAPL.

by making a portion of its shares (ownership stake) available to the public. Listing shares requires the company to meet the stock exchange's listing rules, which vary from one stock exchange to another. For example, the stock exchange may stipulate the minimum size of the issue, or demand that a prespecified portion/number of the company's shares be in the hands of public investors (i.e. require a minimum public/free float).

The primary market has a crucial role in the economy. It facilitates the mobilization of finance by bringing together companies that need capital to grow with investors who have resources on which they seek to earn returns. Indeed, according to the World Federation of Exchanges, the number of countries with a stock exchange has grown from just over 50 in 1975 to over 160 in 2015, and in December 2020 there were 47,919 listed companies worldwide with total market capitalization of over USD 100 trillion.[4]

Note, however, that it is only in the primary market that listing results in a flow of funds from investors to the firm. In the secondary market trading takes place between investors, detached from the company. Nonetheless, the secondary market concentrates much more activity than the primary market, as most stock exchange transactions involve the exchange of existing securities between investors. Only a small proportion of transactions comprises new issues. But, if the secondary market is not responsible for the funnelling of capital to companies for productive uses, why do stock exchanges develop, supervise and manage the secondary market?

The answer is that the secondary market is important since investors value liquidity. Put differently, investors value the ability to sell quickly at close to current prices if they need the money and the secondary market makes this possible. Thus, the existence of the secondary market makes it possible for companies to raise money on the primary market, because, if investors were denied the facility to sell their shares quickly and easily in the secondary market at close to current prices, they would be unlikely to participate and buy shares in the primary market. It is for this reason that stock exchanges devote much thought and resources to developing trading systems that are attractive to investors. Such trading systems need to facilitate fair and transparent trading to ensure that information is equally available to all, and that access to the trading platform is equitable and not biased against, say, small investors or companies. Figure 6.1 illustrates the flow of cash and shares in the primary and secondary markets.

In panel (a) of Fig. 6.1, the company is issuing new shares to A, B, C and D and receives the cash. In panel (b) the company is not directly involved in the transactions and does not receive any cash. Shareholder A is not dealing; B is selling shares to D; and C is selling shares to E, at the market price at the time of each deal.

Regulated stock exchanges offer companies and investors a secure environment with rules and regulations that aim to ensure a well-functioning market where investors' rights are protected, listing and trading rules are imposed, and good

[4] https://www.world-exchanges.org/.

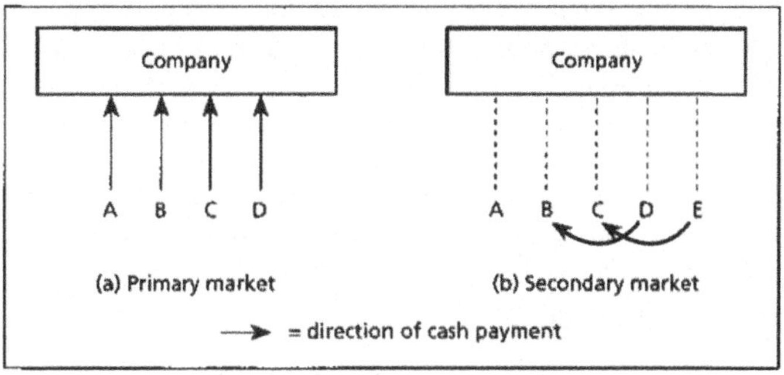

Fig. 6.1 The stock exchange: primary and secondary markets

corporate governance is encouraged. As of 2021, the biggest stock exchanges are the New York Stock Exchange (NYSE) and the NASDAQ stock exchange, both in the United States.

Investors that participate in the activity of the stock exchange include big institutional investors such as banks, insurance companies, pension and hedge funds as well as small private investors. There are some investors that invest for the long term while others engage in short term speculations by dynamically buying and selling shares in the hope of profiting from short term price changes. In particular, bulls buy shares expecting them to rise (probably in the fairly short term), while bears look for prices to fall. The latter either sell shares they do not even own (selling short), hoping to buy them back later at lower prices; or at least refrain from buying yet, planning to do so more cheaply later. If on balance speculators make profits, that implies that their views are somehow 'more correct' than other people's. Their actions drive market prices sooner to levels they would otherwise take longer to reach. In this way—and without intending it—they help improve the trustworthiness of market prices as signals to investors and others. Some people, however, sometimes accuse speculators, and particularly short sellers, of creating market volatility.

6.3.2 Short Selling

Short selling involves borrowing shares that the investor does not own but expects will decline in price. The idea is to buy low and sell high, but in reverse order. Thus, the short seller borrows the shares from a stockbroker (a professional in the business of buying and selling shares on behalf of clients) with whom they have opened a margin account, and sells them on the market. The margin account is a form of collateral and the short seller is required to deposit a minimum amount in that account, determined by the bodies regulating the broker (although the broker may require a higher amount). The short seller will also need to pay interest on the borrowed shares. In addition, the short seller will later need to buy-to-cover—that is, return the number of shares they previously borrowed to the stockbroker who will pass them back to their lawful owners. Closing the short selling position is done by purchasing that number of shares, hopefully at a price lower than that at which the borrowed shares were previously sold, thereby making a profit.

Holding a short position is riskier than holding a long position (i.e., buy and then sell). When one is long on shares, the maximum loss is the price originally paid for the share in the case that the share price drops to zero. With short selling, in contrast, the short seller loses when the price of the share increases, which in theory is limitless. Example 6.2 illustrates a short selling transaction.

Example 6.2: Short selling

An investor with \$10,000 to invest believes that the share price of company S, which is currently trading at \$100 per share, will decline by 10 per cent to \$90 when its competitor, company L, announces a breakthrough in research and development next week. The investor also thinks that the share price of company L, currently trading at \$200 per share, will increase by 10 per cent to \$220 on the news.

The investor decides to borrow 200 shares of company S from a broker and short sell those shares on the market, and invests the proceeds together with their own capital in the shares of company L:

- Proceeds from short selling 200 borrowed shares of company S, currently trading at \$100 per share: $200 \times \$100 = \$20{,}000$
- Investment of own capital plus proceeds from short selling, in the shares of company L: $\$10{,}000 + \$20{,}000 = \$30{,}000$.

  In fact, the investor has invested 300 per cent of their wealth in company L, by short selling the shares of company S to the tune of 200 per cent of their wealth. They now hold $\frac{\$30{,}000}{\$200} = 150$ shares in company L.

  At the end of the week, the shares of company S drop as expected to \$90 per share and the price of the shares of company L increases as anticipated to \$220 per share. The investor decides to close the short position and to sell their holdings in company L.

  Ignoring commissions and interest, their position is as follows:
- Payment made on the buy-to-cover action of 200 shares of company S which they buy from the open market at a price of \$90 per share (to return those shares to the broker): $200 \times -\$90 = -\$18{,}000$
- Proceeds from selling 150 shares of company L, now trading at \$220 per share: $150 \times \$220 = \$33{,}000$
- Overall, they now have: $\$33{,}000 - \$18{,}000 = \$15{,}000$.
- The total return on the investor's initial capital of \$10,000 is: $\frac{\$15{,}000-\$10{,}000}{\$10{,}000} = 50\%$.

We can show that the rate of return they earned on their portfolio of the two companies' shares is the weighted average of the return earned on their holding in each company, where the weights equal the percentage invested in each: $-200\% \times (-10\%) + 300\% \times (10\%) = 50\%$.◀

Because short sellers profit in falling markets, it is sometimes argued that short selling activity escalates downward price trends, leading to crises, and should therefore be banned. Indeed, bans on short selling were imposed by regulators during the global financial crisis of 2008 as well as during the COVID-19 outbreak in 2020. These bans were imposed regardless of research showing that short sellers often establish positions that are *contrary* to prevailing market sentiments. Box 6.2 illustrates the debate.

Box 6.2: Short Selling Ban following the Coronavirus Outbreak in 2020[5]
South Korea is considering an extension of its ban on short selling even as a buying frenzy by retail investors raises fears of a bubble in parts of the stock market.

Regulators in mid-March suspended short selling for six months after the coronavirus outbreak prompted record foreign investment outflows from the export-driven economy. South Korea is one of three countries in the world that maintains such a ban along with Malaysia and Indonesia. Short sellers seek to profit by selling borrowed stock on the expectation its price will fall.

The country's Kospi index has soared more than 50 per cent following the ban, which is intended to curb speculative trading. Retail investors bought a net Won33tn ($25bn) shares in the first half with many betting on an economic recovery after South Korea brought its Covid-19 outbreak under control.

The government plans to hold two public hearings in August where it will hear views from investors and experts ahead of making a decision on whether to extend the ban. It is currently due to expire on September 15.

"It is hard to gauge the impact that the short-selling ban has had on the local stock market, but the measure has certainly helped boost sentiment. We can extend it," said a senior official at South Korea's financial regulator.

"It is a divisive issue. Many experts say the ban should not be extended, given some side effects, but there is strong resistance against lifting the ban among retail investors," the official added.

Analysts say the suspension has contributed to a dizzying surge in healthcare stocks, raising concerns of a bubble. The MSCI Korea Health Care Index jumped nearly 60 per cent in the first half, compared with a 5 per cent fall in the Kospi.

"It is hard to say if there is a bubble in the sector's valuations but their stock prices would not have risen this much if short selling had been allowed," said the regulatory official.

South Korean officials previously said they wanted to divert abundant liquidity away from the property market and into shares. Surging home prices in the greater Seoul area as a result of record-low interest rates have contributed to growing public discontent.

But throwing up obstacles to short sellers could hurt the development of the country's financial markets, as the ban may decrease South Korea's chances of being included in globally important share indices.

[5] Extracts from: South Korea considers extending short-selling ban as market booms, by Song Jung-a, The Financial Times, JULY 23 2020 (https://www.ft.com/content/fd9c321f-a3b6-4aff-b43d-d1a1a3f5600f).

Note in Box 6.2 that the impact of the ban on short selling is assessed with reference to share indices such as the Kospi Index and the MSCI Korea Health Care Index. This is not surprising as stock indices are typically used to gauge market performance and to help investors assess market trends. The Kospi Index, for instance, is the Korea Composite Stock Price Index of all shares that are traded on the stock exchange of South Korea. It is the major stock market index of South Korea and plays a similar role to the Standard & Poor's 500-share index (S&P500) in the United States, or the FTSE100 in the United Kingdom.

6.3.3 Stock Market Indices

A stock market index measures the change in the share prices of a basket of different companies, so that movements in the prices of the underlying shares in the index impact its performance. Stock indices are widely used by investors and financial institutions to analyse the market, to manage investments, and as benchmarks against which to measure portfolio performance. Popular stock indices in the United States include the S&P500 and the Dow Jones Industrial Average (DJIA).

The decision on which companies to include in the index depends on what the index is meant to represent. For example, the MSCI World index is a broad global stock index that captures the performance of large companies across twenty-three developed markets countries. In contrast, a national index represents the performance of the stock market of a single country and is used to measure investors' opinions regarding the state of the local economy. Thus, the Tel Aviv 35 Index (TA-35) is the flagship index of the Tel Aviv Stock Exchange (TASE) in Israel. It tracks the share prices of the 35 most highly valued companies listed on the TASE. Likewise, the DAX is a stock market index consisting of Germany's thirty largest companies that are traded on the Frankfurt Stock Exchange. Other stock indices attempt to track the performance of specific sectors. For example, the MSCI World Health Care Index aims to represent the health care sector by tracking the share prices of large companies in the health care sector across twenty-three developed markets.

Once a decision has been taken regarding the nature and number of companies to include in the index, the constructor of the index needs to decide on the index-weighting scheme. The market capitalization method is the most popular weighting scheme. Under this method, the weight of each share in the index is based on the company's market capitalization, so that companies with the highest market capitalization have the heaviest weight and the largest impact on the value of the index.

In contrast, in a price-weighted index, the weight attached to each share is based on its price relative to the sum of the prices of all shares in the index. It is therefore clear that in a price-weighted index, companies with the highest share price have the heaviest weight and the largest impact on the value of the index. Popular examples of price-weighted indices include the US Dow Jones Industrial Average (DJIA) and the Japanese Nikkei 225.

Finally, a stock index worth mentioning is the Renaissance IPO Index. This stock market index is based upon a portfolio of newly listed US companies, ahead of their inclusion in core equity indices. The index represents the largest 80 per cent of US IPOs, which remain on the index for two years, after which they are removed. The weighting methodology used in constructing the Renaissance IPO Index is based on market capitalization with a 10 per cent cap imposed on the weight of large constituents. Table 6.1 presents the performance of the Renaissance IPO Index in comparison to the performance of the S&P500 index. It is clear that the Renaissance IPO Index offered higher returns compared with the S&P index.

Table 6.1 Performance history of the Renaissance IPO Index[6]

As of Dec 31, 2020	3M	YTD	1 Year	3 Year[a]	5 Year[a]	10 Year[a]
Renaissance IPO Index	24.35%	109.82%	109.82%	32.93%	26.33%	17.49%
S&P 500 Index	12.15%	18.40%	18.40%	14.18%	15.22%	13.88%

[a]Average annual return. Inception date: June 19, 2009

A dedicated Exchange Traded Fund (ETF)[7] that tracks the Renaissance IPO Index provides investors the opportunity to access the US IPO market without having to buy the shares of newly listed US companies individually.

6.4 Issuing Shares

6.4.1 Going Public via an Initial Public Offering (IPO)

As previously noted, an IPO is a method for *going public*. That is, for a company to raise capital by listing its shares on a stock exchange. The process is long and costly, but by the end of it, the company obtains a unique *ticker* symbol meaning that investors can buy and sell the shares on the particular stock exchange which issued the symbol.

In general, a company may wish to list its ordinary shares on the stock exchange for two main reasons: to raise more share capital from the public, or to enable existing shareholders to sell some of their shares. When a company goes public it must issue a prospectus naming the directors and giving the company's history, its recent financial results, and certain other details.

[6] Renaissance Capital, Renaissance IPO Index factsheet (www.renaissancecapital.com).

[7] An ETF (Exchange Traded Fund) is a financial instrument that tracks an index and is traded on an exchange, just like a share. ETFs provide investors a way to buy and sell a basket of shares (or other assets) without having to buy each share individually, thus facilitating a cheap and easy means to diversify.

Normally a company must offer a minimum amount of its ordinary shares to the public, in order to ensure a reasonably liquid market in the shares (i.e. minimum public/free-float requirements). For smaller enterprises, dedicated exchanges are often attractive as they normally have less stringent requirements. For example, while on the London Stock Exchange (LSE) public float requirements specify that at least 25 per cent of the listed securities must be held in public hands, there are no such requirements for companies listed on AIM, a sub-market of the LSE, dedicated to smaller companies.

The costs of issuing shares to the public can be high, ranging between $10 million to $13 million, according to PwC.[8] In a typical IPO, the largest portion of the costs (between 4 and 7 per cent of the money raised) is the underwriting and related fees (e.g. the fees charged by investment banks for taking the company public and raising funds on its behalf from investors). In addition, there are administration costs incurred for preparing the filing documentation; filing costs for registration with the regulatory bodies and marketing costs associated with advertising and promoting the shares to be floated. Furthermore, going public may also involve indirect costs such as having to adhere to a lockup period which prevents employees and early investors from selling their shares during a prespecified period. Another indirect cost relates to underpricing (or mispricing). This relates to when the underwriters offer a price discount to attract buyers, leading to a hike in the share price on the first day of trading and to money being left on the table (i.e. less money is raised for the company than could have otherwise been raised).

Despite the high costs associated with IPOs, most big companies on the main stock exchanges (such as the NYSE or the LSE) got there by going through an IPO. The process involves a roadshow to present the investment opportunity to potential investors, and investment bankers acting as underwriters and helping to determine the issue price for the shares. Box 6.3 illustrates the case of a planned IPO which went wrong.

Box 6.3: WeWork's Failed IPO

WeWork is an office-leasing company founded in 2010. It invests in real estate and provides small office space and supporting services to startups and other entrepreneurs, thereby facilitating access to the benefits of an office at low cost.

In 2019 the company filed for an IPO, hoping to raise over $3 billion. However, information over heavy losses was revealed in its filed IPO documents. Analysts doubted WeWork's ability to become profitable and at the same time criticism was mounting over the company's corporate governance practices, business model and excessive valuation.

[8] Considering an IPO? First, understand the costs: PwC (www.pwc.com/us/en/services/deals/library/cost-of-an-ipo.html#content-free-1-28b3).

Consequently, the value of the company dropped from $47 billion to around $10 billion and the decision was taken to postpone the IPO. An article in Forbes describes the lessons to be learnt from the WeWork IPO withdrawal story[9]:

".....WeWork's withdrawn IPO has been in the news for all the wrong reasons: weak governance, idiosyncratic management, and astronomical valuation. A valuation loss of $40 billion in a matter of months, especially the sufferings of rank and file employees in the process, is not a cause for celebration. But there is a silver lining in this spectacular collapse. WeWork's failure shows that loss-making companies cannot raise billions of dollars of capital in the public equity market without caring about their outside shareholders. Markets spoke.

Well-functioning capital markets must have the ability to separate firms that are worthy of raising capital from those that are not. WeWork's failure bolsters investors' confidence in the markets' ability to do so. The eventual withdrawal of the IPO sends a clear message to entrepreneurs and underwriters that they can no longer ignore shareholders' rights if they want shareholders' money. This bodes well for the long-run efficiency of the IPO market. But beyond that, there is a lesson for seasoned firms' CFOs as well: strengthen your governance structure before you plan to raise money in the Seasoned Equity Offerings (SEOs)...."

Two years after the failed IPO, WeWork decided to try a different route to becoming a public company. In 2021 reports in the media confirmed that the company was planning to merge with a Special Purpose Acquisition Company (SPAC) thereby gaining a listing on the US NASDAQ stock market.

6.4.2 Going Public via SPAC Merger

A SPAC merger is designed to skip the IPO process and take a private company public at lower cost and higher speed compared with the classic IPO. The procedure includes two steps. In the first stage, a Special Purpose Acquisition Company (referred to as a SPAC and also as a blank cheque company) is set up. The SPAC is a company without any activity, and it is established as a publicly traded company by an IPO. Notably, the IPO process for a company without activity or history is cheap and simple compared to the case of an averagely active private firm.

Once the IPO is completed, the capital raised is placed into an interest-bearing account. In the second stage, the SPAC identifies the private company it wishes to acquire. Typically, the SPAC has two years after it has raised financing through an IPO to acquire the private company it wishes to merge into its publicly trading structure.

If the SPAC is unable to make a deal within two years, it has to return the money to its investors. However, providing it does make a deal, the method by which it acquires the privately held company is usually through a reverse merger.

[9] Why We Should Celebrate WeWork's Failed IPO, by Amiyatosh Purnanandam, Forbes, Nov 11, 2019 (https://www.forbes.com/sites/amiyatoshpurnanandam/2019/11/11/why-should-we-celebrate-weworks-failed-ipo/?sh=71fdc96710ea).

The owners of the private company acquire all the shares from the shareholders of the SPAC. The existing shareholders of the private company become the owners of the SPAC, merging it with the active private company thereby transferring it into a publicly traded company (a process sometimes referred to as a De-SPAC transaction).

SPAC mergers have become very popular since 2019, partly because they offer a cheap and speedy route to go public. They are also said to offer more certainty and thus are particularly appropriate during periods of market instability. Moreover, SPAC mergers provide access to the stock exchange to companies that are likely to fail the traditional IPO due to complicated business, troublesome history, or sustained losses. Box 6.4 continues the WeWork story of failed IPO (Box 6.3) to show what the company decided to do once it became clear that it would not be able to resume and complete its planned 2019 IPO.

Box 6.4: WeWork to merge with a SPAC two years after aborted IPO[10]

Troubled shared-office provider WeWork is set to merge with a special-purpose acquisition company two years after its plans to go public ended in spectacular disarray. The planned merger with BowX Acquisition, a publicly listed investment vehicle, values WeWork at $9bn including debt, a far cry from the $47bn WeWork was valued at in a private round of financing from SoftBank Group in 2019.

The company shook up the office rentals market, styling them for a new generation of businesses by adding communal areas with beer taps and foosball tables. It continues to describe itself in tech, rather than property, terms, recently telling investors it is an "asset-light platform for managing and orchestrating flexible space".

In its heyday WeWork's growth was exponential and the company expanded into other areas including private rentals and education. But its losses were also massive—$2.9bn in the three years before its aborted initial public offering. And the erratic behaviour of its founder and former chief executive, Adam Neumann, also put off investors.

The new deal would allow WeWork to raise $1.3bn in new money and comes at a time when some are expecting a return to office life as increasing vaccinations against coronavirus begin to control the COVID-19 pandemic......

Sandeep Mathrani, chief executive of WeWork, said: "WeWork has spent the past year transforming the business and refocusing its core, while simultaneously managing and innovating through a historic downturn. As a result, WeWork has emerged as the global leader in flexible space with a value proposition that is stronger than ever."

Bow Capital Management, sponsor of the special purpose acquisition company (Spac), is run by Tibco Software's Vivek Ranadivé, owner of the National Basketball Association's Sacramento Kings...

Spacs are "blank-cheque" companies that have become an increasingly popular way for companies to go public and offer a cheaper, quicker way for a private company to join the stock markets.

[10] WeWork to merge with investment company two years after aborted IPO, by Dominic Rushe, The Guardian, Fri 26 Mar 2021 (https://www.theguardian.com/business/2021/mar/26/wework-merger-property-company-bowx-acquisition-spac).

6.4.3 Going Public via Direct Listing

A SPAC merger is one way of avoiding the long and bureaucratic process of going public via an IPO. Another alternative is direct listing, also known as direct placement. However, unlike IPOs and SPAC mergers, direct listing does not involve raising new capital or issuing new shares. Instead, the company sells a small number of existing shares direct to the public without the help of underwriters, thereby becoming publicly traded.

The main advantage of direct listing is that underwriters are not required, thereby avoiding the largest chunk of the cost of a traditional IPO (see the discussion above). Likewise, there is normally no lockup period during which employees and other existing shareholders cannot sell their shares. Moreover, because direct listing does not include the sale of new shares, the problem of share dilution does not arise (share dilution occurs when the company issues new shares, thereby reducing the ownership proportion of existing shareholders). Finally, unlike an IPO, the share price is not set in advance. Box 6.5 illustrates the growing popularity of direct listing.

Box 6.5: Companies opt for direct listing in snub to IPOs[11]

"U.S. grocery delivery app Instacart is considering going public through a *direct listing*, concerned that it could leave money on the table through a traditional initial public offering (IPO), according to people familiar with the matter. The move would make Instacart the latest company to snub an IPO, for decades the primary path to a stock market debut, because it risks pricing its offering too low compared to where its shares end up trading. In a *direct listing*, companies go public without raising money through a stock sale.

Shares of newly listed US companies that went public through an IPO ended trading up 36.2% on average on their first day last year, compared to 17.2% in 2019, according to data firm Dealogic.

IPOs have been on a tear since last summer as markets rallied following the Federal Reserve's moves to support the US economy during the COVID-19 pandemic. Yet their popularity has been eroding as more companies choose to go public through mergers with special purpose acquisition companies (SPACs) or direct listings. There were 208 IPOs excluding SPACs last year, the most since 2015, according to Dealogic. By comparison, 249 SPACs went public through IPOs. Two prominent direct listings last year were those of technology firms Palantir Technologies Inc and Asana Inc.

Only a handful of companies have gone public through a direct listing since it was pioneered in 2018 by music streaming platform Spotify Technology SA. US gaming platform Roblox Corp abandoned plans for an IPO earlier this year because it did not want to leave money on the table. It is slated to debut on the New York Stock Exchange (NYSE) next week through a direct listing. US cryptocurrency exchange Coinbase Global Inc has said it is looking to go public through a direct listing. Online broker Robinhood and robotic software startup UiPath Inc are also considering choosing a direct listing over an IPO, according to people familiar with the matter…

[11] Extracts from: Exclusive. Instacart mulls direct listing in snub to IPOs, By Joshua Franklin, Anirban Sen, Krystal Hu. Reuters, March 5, 2021 (https://www.reuters.com/article/us-instacart-directlisting-exclusive-idUSKBN2AX13F).

Once a company goes public through a direct listing, insiders can typically sell their shares immediately rather than be restricted for months, as is the case with IPOs. A company can also sell its shares in the open market to raise capital following a direct listing without restrictions, typically after it has reported quarterly earnings. Some companies opting for direct listings also choose to raise money before they go public through private fundraising rounds. …"

6.4.4 Seasoned Equity Offerings

A Seasoned Equity Offering (SEO) is the issue of shares by a publicly listed company (i.e. post-IPO) in order to raise more equity capital. Unless existing shareholders participate in the SEO by buying the new shares in proportion to their current holding, their ownership will be diluted. Example 6.3 illustrates this point.

Example 6.3: Dilution of ownership

Following its IPO, a company has 100,000 shares held by 100 shareholders. Mr Smith holds 5,000 shares and thus he owns: $\frac{5,000}{100,000} = 5\%$ of the company.

To raise more capital, the company decided to issue 100,000 new shares via a SEO. 100 new shareholders bought the new issue. Mr. Smith still holds 5,000 shares, but his ownership stake has been diluted and he now owns: $\frac{5,000}{200,000} =$ 2.5% of the company. As a result, Mr. Smith also has less voting power.

Although Mr. Smith suffered a dilution in his ownership stake and voting power, providing the new shares were issued at the current market price, Mr. Smith's wealth has not changed. However, if the new issue is at a lower price, then Mr. Smith will also experience a reduction in the value of his investment in the company.

For example, assume the current market price per share is \$10, so that Mr. Smith's investment in the company is worth: $5,000 \times \$10 = \$50,000$.

The new shares are issued at \$9 per share, so after the issue the company's market capitalization is: $(100,000 \times \$10) + (100,000 \times \$9) = \$1,900,000$. The diluted price after the SEO is: $\frac{\$1,900,000}{200,000} = \$9.50$. So, Mr. Smith's investment in the company is now worth: $5,000 \times \$9.50 = \$47,500$, a reduction of $\$50,000 - \$47,500 = \$2,500$◀

6.4.5 Rights Issues

Companies whose shares are already listed often use a rights issue to raise more equity money. This is because the stock exchange regards rights issues as normally being fairest to existing shareholders.

A rights issue offers extra shares to existing shareholders, in proportion to their current holdings, priced at some discount to the current market price per share. (Of course, the offer price of a rights issue must be below the current market price, otherwise anyone who wants to buy more shares would simply do so in the market, not by way of the rights!)

In theory, the price of a rights issue does not matter! An existing shareholder who is unwilling to take up the new shares will be able to sell their rights in the market and thus avoid any loss from dilution (the bigger the rights issue discount from the current market price, the more the rights will be worth). Indeed, in some cases, the company itself will automatically sell the rights on behalf of shareholders who do not take up their rights. Example 6.4 illustrates the workings of a rights issue and shows that existing shareholders stand to neither gain nor lose by either subscribing to the issue or selling their rights (except that if they sell their rights, the proportion of the company that they own will be reduced).

Example 6.4: Rights issue

Thomas Lodge plc has 50 million ordinary shares already in issue, with a current market price of 150p each. The company plans to raise an extra £20 million of equity capital by means of a rights issue. Table 6.2 shows two different ways of achieving this (ignoring transaction costs): either issuing 1 for 1 @ 40p, or else issuing 2 for 5 @ 100p.

Alan Yarrow (AY) owns 1000 shares and decides to take up his rights in full; while Norman Oliver (NO), who also owns 1000 shares, decides to sell all his rights. Table 6.3 shows that in each case the market value of AY's holding goes up to reflect the amount of extra cash (£400) he has invested; and the market value of NO's holding goes down by exactly the amount of cash he receives in each case for selling his rights.◄

Table 6.2 Rights issue: alternative issue prices

	1 for 1 @ 40p	2 for 5 @ 100p
Number of new shares to be issued (50m*new/old)	50 million	20 million
New total number of shares *(# = new + old)*	100 million	70 million
New share price [(50m*£1.5 + £20m) /#) = £95m/#]	95p	135.71p
Value of the rights per share (new share price—issue price)	55p	35.71p

Table 6.3 Taking up or selling rights

	1 for 1 @ 40p		2 for 5 @ 100p	
	AY	NO	AY	NO
Opening holding @ 150p: 1,000 shares	£1,500	£1,500	£1,500	£1,500
Buy 1,000 shares @ 40p	£400			
Buy 400 shares @ 100p			£400	
Sell 1,000 rights @ 55p		(£550)		
Sell 400 rights @ 35.71 p				(£143)
Closing holding @ 95p [135.71 p]				
AY: 2,000 [1,400] shares	£1,900		£1,900	
NO: 1,000 [1,000] shares		£950		£1,357

6.4.6 Bonus Issues and Share Splits

So far, we have been discussing two kinds of share issues on the stock exchange: new listings, which may raise new money for a company, but often the main purpose of which is to go public; and seasoned equity offerings, by which listed companies raise new capital, but which may result in share dilution.

Two kinds of share issues raise no new money for companies but can affect certain stock exchange ratios. They are respectively bonus issues and share splits.

1. Bonus issues (scrip issues) capitalize some of a company's reserves, by transferring them within the balance sheet to called-up share capital. This is purely a book-keeping entry. The total amount of shareholders' funds remains the same as before since the company has raised no new money: it has merely turned some of its retained profits or other reserves into called-up ordinary share capital (so they are no longer available to pay out as dividends).
2. Share splits simply split shares into smaller units without even affecting balance sheet amounts.

Example 6.5 illustrates a share split.

Example 6.5

Giant plc has 600,000 ordinary £1 shares in issue, with a market price of £12 each (1200p). After the company makes a '4 for 1' share split, it will have 2.4 million ordinary shares of 25p each in issue, each with a market price of 300p. Notice that a '4 for 1' share split means 4 new shares instead of each existing share in issue; whereas a '4 for 1' bonus issue means 4 new shares in addition to each existing share held, making 5 in all.◄

In comparing earnings per share (or other 'per share' amounts) over time, one will need to adjust earlier years' figures to allow for subsequent share splits or bonus issues.

What is the purpose of making bonus issues or splitting shares? They 'give' shareholders nothing they did not already own as they do not increase the total market value of the equity capital. One obvious effect is to reduce the per share market price on the stock exchange; but there is no reason—either in theory or in practice—to think this matters.

6.5 A Concluding Note

In this chapter we looked at how equity shares are issued and traded. We also reviewed the risk and return to be expected on equity shares and highlighted how different they are from debt securities in terms of the risk borne by the holder. Together, equity shares and debt securities (e.g. bonds, discussed in the previous chapter) provide the main sources of capital to fulfil the company's long-term investment needs. It is thus the case that the return investors expect to receive on these securities make up the cost of capital to the firm—the topic of the next chapter.

6.5.1 Problems

Problem 6.1

a. Identify three components of the Dow Jones Industrial Average (DJIA) and find the market capitalization of each.

b. Explain the importance of market capitalization and the difference between market capitalization and free-float market capitalization.

Problem 6.2 An investor buys 100 shares of company X at $20 per share. The company pays a dividend of $2 per share. By the end of the year, the shares of company X are trading at $25 per share.

a. Calculate the dividend yield.
b. Calculate the capital gain yield.
c. Calculate the total return to the investor.

Problem 6.3 An investor believes that the share price of company Y is overvalued at $300 and is going to drop in price. As she does not hold the stock, the investor decided to short sell 20 shares of the company.

a. Show the investor's profit/loss on the deal if the shares end up at $250 per share.
b. Show the investor's profit/loss on the deal if the shares end up at $330 per share.

Problem 6.4 Nancy King plc has 240 million ordinary shares already in issue, with a current market price of 330p per share. The company plans to raise an extra £180 million of equity capital by means of a rights issue. Two possible ways of achieving this (ignoring transaction costs) are being considered: either (a) issuing 3 for 2 @ 50p or else (b) issuing 1 for 4 @ 300p.

a. For each alternative, calculate:
   i. what the new total number of shares would be
   ii. what you would expect the new market price per share to be
   iii. the estimated value of the rights.
b. Also calculate the position of two holders of 2000 ordinary shares. The first, Olivia Knox, plans to take up the rights to which she is entitled; while the second, Colin Berry, proposes to sell his rights for cash. Show in each case, and for each of the alternative methods of making the rights issue: how much cash will be paid (by OK) or received (by CB), and how many shares each will own after the rights issue, and what those shares will be worth.

Cost of Capital

7

7.1 Introduction

The purpose of this chapter is to help us work out a company's Weighted Average Cost of Capital (the WACC), which is the appropriate discount rate to use when deciding whether or not to go ahead with an average-risk project using the NPV technique. It is in essence the average of the cost of debt and the cost of equity to the company—but not the simple average derived from just adding them and dividing by 2, but the *weighted* average, where the weighting is the respective proportions of equity and debt. Let's start with an example.

Example 7.1

A company has equity capital with a market value of £120 million and debt capital with a market value of £40 million. So equity has a 'weight' of 75 per cent and debt of 25 per cent. Using, as an example, costs of 13 per cent for equity and 5 per cent for debt, the result is an overall weighted average cost of capital of 11.0 per cent [$(0.75 \times 13) + (0.25 \times 5)$].◄

Notice that the WACC is therefore the proportion of equity multiplied by its cost, plus the proportion of debt multiplied by *its* cost. So there are three main areas to tackle—first, how do we determine the proportions of equity and debt (Sect. 7.2); second, what is the cost of debt (Sect. 7.3); and thirdly, we then tackle the very tricky topic of the (opportunity) cost of equity capital. We look at two methods of approaching the latter: first, in Sect. 7.4 we introduce the Capital Asset Pricing Model (CAPM) and, second, in Sect. 7.5 we consider the Dividend Growth Model (DGM). Then we return to how to combine the cost of debt and the cost of equity to estimate the Weighted Average Cost of Capital (Sect. 7.6). We conclude the chapter in Sect. 7.7, followed by some practice problems.

R. Manos et al., *Corporate Finance for Business*,
https://doi.org/10.1007/978-3-030-92419-5_7

7.2 The Proportions of Equity and Debt

The proportions of equity and debt can be obtained from the company's gearing ratio using Eq. 7.1:-

$$value\,of\,debt \div (value\,of\,debt + value\,of\,equity) \tag{7.1}$$

The result will give you the proportion of debt (say, 35 per cent), and the balance to 100 per cent (here, 65 per cent) will give you the proportion of equity.[1] The challenge is to determine the values of equity and debt. There are three common approaches: using market values; using book values; and using target values.

7.2.1 Market Values

Generally, using *market* values for both debt and equity is the right thing to do, if they are available, because market values reflect current prices and expectations. So for a quoted company, the market value of *equity* is the market capitalization of its shares—that is, the number of shares multiplied by the market price per share. Obviously, if there are different classes of traded shares, the market capitalization of each class should be summed together. The market value of *debt* is often the same as appears on its Balance Sheet, especially if it has been obtained from a bank, but we saw in Chapter 5 that *traded* debt will have a different market value to its issue price if interest rates have changed since it was issued. This market value is the one we should use.

7.2.2 Book Values

With unquoted companies, it is fairly unlikely they will have quoted debt, so the book (i.e. Balance Sheet/Statement of Financial Position) value will be accurate, or accurate enough. As regards equity, however, often there is no obvious market price for the shares as they are not traded on a regular basis. Consequently, we have no choice but to use the book value of equity as a proxy for market value. This can be problematic given the uncertainty around some Balance Sheet values, and the fact that many companies have an actual value of equity well in excess of book value. Even so, using book values as the basis for weighting may not make much difference to the WACC estimate, unless the market value of equity is *very* different from its book value. (We could in principle use the DCF valuation

[1] Aswath Damodaran of Stern School of Business at New York University, collects and calculates debt to capital and debt to equity ratios for US corporations. Access to the data page is via the following link: http://www.stern.nyu.edu/~adamodar/New_Home_Page/data.html.

technique discussed in Chapter 2 to calculate a notional equity valuation of a private company, but whether in practice the management of such a company would wish to do this complex exercise on a regular basis solely for this purpose is doubtful.)

7.2.3 Target Values

Some companies say they have a *target* gearing ratio, and it might be sensible to use this. A French company familiar to the authors had a gearing ratio of around 50 per cent for many years. They then made an acquisition which they financed by an increase in debt and a relatively small increase in equity, leaving them with a gearing ratio of 60 per cent. The Chairman announced at the time that the company intended to reduce that ratio back to 50 per cent within 3 years. Given that they would be using their WACC to perform DCF calculations on projects of well in excess of 3 years' duration, using 50 per cent debt and 50 per cent equity proportions to calculate the WACC might make more sense than the 60/40 that applied immediately after the acquisition.

Finally, it is worth noting that although the use of market values for calculating the proportions of equity and debt is generally recommended, different companies use different methods. Furthermore, sometimes companies combine methods such as using the book value of debt alongside the market value of equity.[2]

7.3 Cost of Debt

7.3.1 Direct Cost

The direct cost of debt is the payment of interest to the lender. It should be noted from the outset that the 'correct' cost of debt (and, for that matter, cost of equity which we examine later) in arriving at the WACC is the *marginal* cost—that is, with debt, the rate of interest we would have to pay if we took out new debt today on top of whatever debt we already had. In practical terms, this is often the same as we are already paying on our existing debt, if the rate is variable and any new debt would not substantially increase the risk to the lender. But what if, for example, some time ago we had been smart, or lucky, enough to take out *fixed* rate debt at a rate lower than would apply to similar-risk debt right now? And what if, in addition, that fixed rate was going to apply several years into the future? Surely that fixed interest rate represents our cost of debt, not the rate we would have to pay if we took out the loan today? The reason this is *not* the case is because if we are going to make a correct decision on whether or not to go ahead with a project today, we need the project to be exceeding the weighted average cost of

[2] See for example, Jacob and Shivdasani (2012).

debt and equity *right now*, because this represents current market conditions. If you're not happy with that, think of it this way: imagine we took out a long-term loan at 5 per cent several years ago that extends several years into the future as well. The *current* rate of interest for a similar-risk loan, were we to take one out, is 8 per cent. Presumably we could, if we so wished, loan out the money we have borrowed to another company—at 8 per cent! Consequently, the debt cost element of our target to beat with our potential project is 8 per cent, otherwise lending the money out would be economically preferable. Our *opportunity cost* of debt is 8 per cent, not 5 per cent.

Readers should note that corporate bonds, as described in chapter 5, fall into precisely this position: they are at a fixed rate of interest throughout, irrespective of any changes in the 'going' rate during their 'lifetime'. Consequently, it is a bond's yield to maturity (see Sect. 5.4.1) that we need to take as the pre-tax cost of debt in the WACC calculation, not the coupon rate.

Debt interest is normally a business expense for tax purposes, but when we create our project spreadsheets, there should not be a row for financing costs, because these are dealt with by discounting the cash flows—so, if there was a row for interest, for example, it (the interest) would in effect be counted twice—once in the interest row and again in applying the discount rate. But if there should not be a row for interest, how do we allow for the tax-deductibility of the interest? The answer is to reduce the cost of debt by the tax relief, meaning that the after-tax cost of debt is usually less than the nominal (coupon) rate of interest.

Example 7.2

Suppose a company pays loan interest of 8.0 per cent a year and tax on profits is 30 per cent. Then the after-tax cost of debt interest is 5.6 per cent a year:

8% x (100% - 30%) = 8% x 70% = 5.6%. The figure of 5.6% is the figure we will use as the cost of debt in the WACC equation.

The after-tax cost of debt (k_{dat}) is given in Eq. 7.2:

$$k_{dat} = k_d \,\text{x}\, (100\% - Tc) \tag{7.2}$$

where k_d is the before-tax cost of debt, and T_C is the corporation tax rate.

Of course, if a company is paying no tax on profits, either because it is making losses or because of high tax allowances against profit, then there will be no reduction due to tax in the direct cost of borrowing.◄

7.3.2 Indirect Costs

The direct cost of debt is the interest payments, taking into account both tax and inflation. But there may also be an indirect cost to a company as the level of gearing rises, in that then the riskiness (volatility) of the returns to equity increases too. So the cost of equity may rise as a result. This is discussed further in Chapter 8.

Whatever the financial cost of debt and equity to the company, as the level of debt rises it is likely to restrict managers' freedom of action. External lenders will tend to demand more stringent covenants. And managers themselves prefer not to borrow too close to the perceived limit in order to maintain some spare borrowing capacity in case of urgent need. (Companies in serious trouble may have to borrow as much as they can get their hands on; but it is internal, not external, decision-makers who normally choose how much companies borrow.)

7.4 Cost of Equity (CAPM)

7.4.1 Modern Portfolio Theory and CAPM

The cost of equity capital is the return required by equity holders (dividends and capital gains), which reflects what they expect to receive in the market on similar-risk securities (also known as the minimum required rate of return on equity). It is normally higher than the cost of debt, because from the point of view of investors, holding the firm's shares is riskier than holding its bonds. The most popular method to estimate the cost of equity is the Capital Asset Pricing Model (CAPM), which is derived from Modern Portfolio Theory (MPT). The CAPM is specified in Eq. 7.3:

$$k_e = r_f + \beta(r_m - r_f) \tag{7.3}$$

where k_e is the cost of equity; r_f is the risk-free rate of return, β is the beta coefficient; r_m is the required return on the market portfolio and $(r_m— r_f)$ is the market risk premium—all of which terms we are now going to explain. Deriving the CAPM can be done by some complex maths which need not concern us here, but the fundamental logic is fairly straightforward. In effect, we are going to build up what the cost of equity must be from first principles.

7.4.1.1 The Risk-Free Rate (r_f)

To start with, clearly shareholders are going to require a return in excess of the return they are likely to receive on a risk-free investment, because the higher the risk, the higher the required return, and an investment in a share or shares is certainly not risk-free. A risk-free investment might be short-term Government Bills, or perhaps long-term Government Bonds (the pros and cons of this choice, and indeed the many other problems with the theory, will be considered later in the chapter). Of course, such investments, especially the longer term ones, are not *entirely* risk-free as one cannot be sure at the outset by how much inflation will have diminished the purchasing power of the principal when it is returned at the end (readers might care to consider here whether they can think of *any* investment that is entirely risk-free!). The return on our as-close-as-possible to risk-free investment is normally shortened to, somewhat confusingly perhaps, r_f. At the time of writing, the risk-free rate of return using US Treasury Bills was about 2.5%, but obviously this number varies both by country and over time. Readers are advised to investigate at the time of calculating the WACC what the risk-free rate is in the relevant country.

7.4.1.2 The Market Risk Premium (r_m—r_f)

So, we know the required return on equity must be higher than r_f. The next item we are going to add on is an *additional* return to compensate the investor for the fact that they are investing in a risky stock market. This is called the Market Risk Premium (or the Equity Risk Premium), a forward looking figure that reflects expectations regarding the extra return equity will yield over the risk-free rate. Hammond and Leibowitz (2015) provide a set of estimates of the equity risk premium which range from zero to 7 per cent! But the truth of the matter is that we don't know exactly what it is. What we *do* know, however, is the average historical difference between the annual return on the stock market and the return on risk-free Government Bonds or Bills. This varies somewhat from stock market to stock market, and according to exactly how it is calculated, but a rough rule of thumb is about 6 per cent.[3] So, *on average*—an average that conceals a very wide range of actual outcomes—an investment in the stock market has generated a return 6 percentage points per year higher than a risk-free investment. The best we can do is assume that this *historical* average actual, realized, premium at least approximately reflects the required *future* premium, which is what we are looking for. This Market Risk Premium is shortened to (r_m—r_f), where r_m is the return on the market as a whole. Remember—it is the *premium* we are looking at: how much *greater* the market return is (or is required to be) than the risk-free rate.

Now, one would think that on top of the risk-free rate plus the market risk premium, we would also want a return to compensate us for the specific risk of the particular share we are considering. After all, some companies clearly operate in much riskier business areas than others, some operate in riskier ways (for example, by structuring themselves with very high fixed costs), and so on. Surely we must require an extra return to allow for this?

[3] See Damodaran On-line at http://www.damodaran.com for historical equity risk premiums or Dimson et al. (2015).

In fact, we *cannot* expect to receive a higher return to allow for this specific risk. This is where Modern Portfolio Theory comes in. According to this, risk can be split into two types of risk: specific risk (also referred to as unique or diversifiable risk) and market risk (also known as systematic, unavoidable or non-diversifiable risk). While equity investors cannot avoid *market* risk, which stems from the uncertainties of the whole economy, in contrast, *specific* risk can, in effect, be diversified away by investing in several different shares (or projects).

An investor who splits their equity roughly equally (in value terms) between 10 to 20 different shares (of companies in different industries) can diversify away a large part of the total risk they would bear if they had invested everything in shares of a single company or just a few companies. In effect, the 10–20 share portfolio averages out the specific risks of the different shares.[4] But regardless of how many different shares they hold, investors cannot diversify away the risk to which all shares are subject—the *market* risk. As Fig. 7.1 shows, increasing the number of holdings beyond about a dozen equity investments makes little further difference in reducing *specific* risk, provided those investments are well spread around the market. The important point is that, as an investor, nobody can force you to diversify your portfolio, but if, to use an extreme case, you choose to invest in only one share, you cannot expect a return to compensate you for the *specific* risk of that company, because most other investors will have a diversified portfolio and therefore will not be bearing that risk to anything like the same extent and therefore will not require an extra return to compensate for it; but there is a *residual* risk inherent in the whole market that cannot be diversified away.

Before moving on, Table 7.1 summarizes the names that the reader might encounter for the two types of risk we have been talking about:

[4] For example, in their 2012 study, Desmoulins-Lebeault and Kharoubi-Rakotomalala investigate the relationship between the number of shares held and the investor's ability to diversify risk away. They find that the consensus opinion is that holding between 10–20 shares fully eliminates the specific risk of the individual shares, although some studies argue that the number is actually between 30–40. In reality, however, it is noted that the number of shares held by household investors is actually much smaller, ranging between 1–5 shares, whereas more sophisticated investors tend to increase the number of shares they hold. Desmoulins-Lebeault and Kharoubi-Rakotomalala explain this anomaly by their findings that during crises or in strong falling markets, most shares in the market will yield negative returns thus limiting the possible benefits of diversification. Therefore, they suggest that investors that expect strong falling markets should limit the number of shares they hold (see Desmoulins-Lebeault and Kharoubi-Rakotomalala 2012).

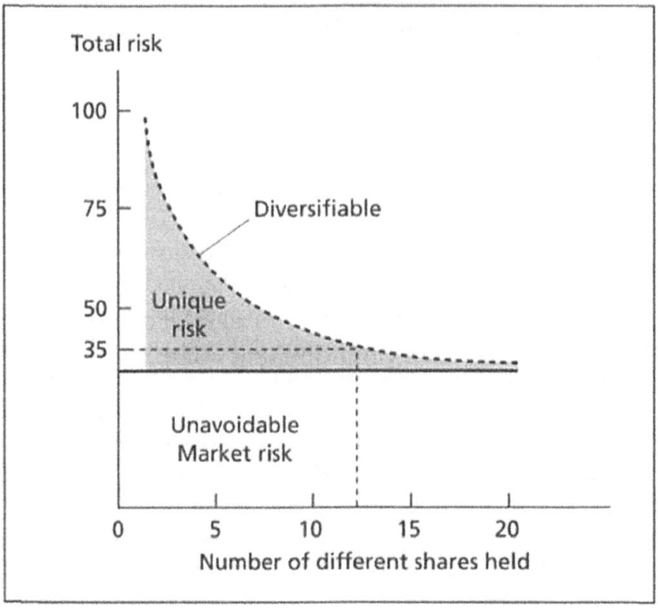

Fig. 7.1 Diversifiable risk and unavoidable risk

Table 7.1 Synonyms for two different kinds of risk

Specific Risk	Market Risk
Unsystematic risk	Systematic risk
Diversifiable risk	Non-diversifiable risk
Unique risk	Unavoidable risk

7.4.1.3 The Beta (β)

So now we have a problem. If investors cannot expect to be compensated for the specific risk of a share, we are back to a required return on equity of the risk-free rate plus the market risk premium. But if that were the whole story, then the required return on all shares would be exactly the same, because neither r_f nor $(r_m—r_f)$ in Eq. 7.3, are company-specific. That cannot be correct because not all shares are equally sensitive to market-wide events. For example, all companies are influenced by oil prices, but airlines are particularly so, hence their share prices are likely to react more aggressively to movements in the price of oil, compared to the share prices of 'average' companies. This is where the final part of the CAPM comes in. The return (dividend plus capital gain) on some shares is more

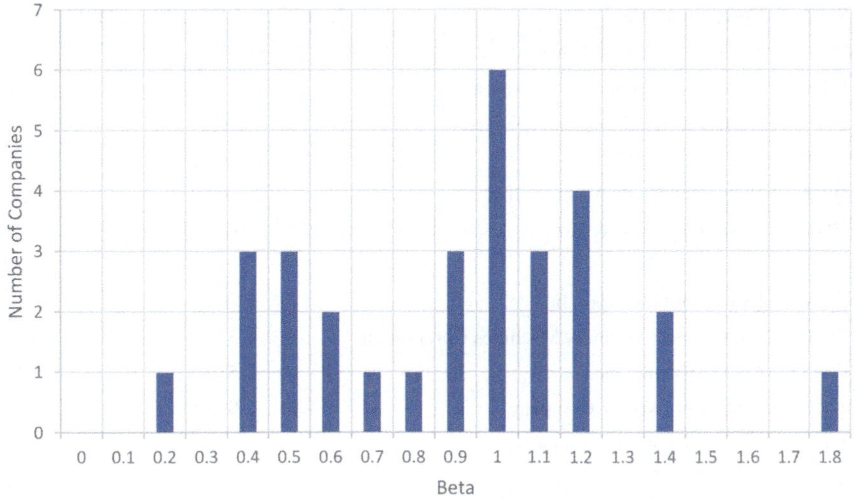

Fig. 7.2 Dow Jones Industrial Average Components: beta estimates from Yahoo Finance as of 11.3.19 (monthly betas over 3 years)

volatile than that on other shares because of their sensitivity to market-related factors. As this volatility cannot be diversified away it needs compensating for. The method used for measuring this volatility is called the beta (β) of the share, and essentially it is a measurement of the extent to which the share price of the specific share varies with the movement of the market as a whole. Thus if, on average, our share increases in price by 1 per cent when the market goes up by 1 per cent, and down by 1 per cent when the market goes down by 1 per cent, it has a beta of 1. But if our share goes up or down by 2 per cent as the market goes up or down by 1 per cent, it has a beta of 2, and so on. An investment with a beta of less than 1.0 is less risky than the whole market; with a beta of more than 1.0, riskier. Figure 7.2 and the table below that accompanies it show the spread of betas for companies in the Dow Jones Industrial Average on 11 March 2019, according to Yahoo Finance.

Symbol	Company name	Last Price (USD)	Beta (3Y Monthly)
HD	The Home Depot, Inc.	181.91	1.22
WMT	Walmart Inc.	98.06	0.64
JNJ	Johnson & Johnson	138.8	0.66
MCD	McDonald's Corporation	180.67	0.39
TRV	The Travelers Companies, Inc.	131.91	1.01
PFE	Pfizer Inc.	41.17	0.51
NKE	NIKE, Inc.	85.39	0.85
PG	The Procter & Gamble Company	99.11	0.22
DIS	The Walt Disney Company	114.9	0.51

Symbol	Company name	Last Price (USD)	Beta (3Y Monthly)
GS	The Goldman Sachs Group, Inc.	197.12	1.16
UTX	United Technologies Corporation	125.27	1.24
UNH	UnitedHealth Group Incorporated	240.07	0.99
MRK	Merck & Co., Inc.	80.75	0.41
WBA	Walgreens Boots Alliance, Inc.	60.63	0.82
JPM	JPMorgan Chase & Co.	104.27	1.04
CAT	Caterpillar Inc.	132.98	1.4
XOM	Exxon Mobil Corporation	80.15	1.04
IBM	International Business Machines Corporation	137.12	1.76
CSCO	Cisco Systems, Inc.	51.84	1.07
AXP	American Express Company	109.61	1.1
VZ	Verizon Communications Inc.	57.41	0.51
V	Visa Inc.	149.92	0.85
CVX	Chevron Corporation	123.88	0.91
MSFT	Microsoft Corporation	112.6	1.02
DWDP	DowDuPont Inc.	55.75	1.1
INTC	Intel Corporation	53.53	0.56
KO	The Coca-Cola Company	45.86	0.37
MMM	3M Company	205.79	1.18
AAPL	Apple Inc.	178.71	0.99
BA	The Boeing Company	389.34	1.36

What the Capital Asset Pricing Model (CAPM) does is to multiply the market risk premium by the beta of the individual share, such that less volatile shares require a lower return on equity than more volatile shares, as we would expect because volatility is quite a good measure of risk. This leaves us with the formula for the cost of equity (abbreviated to k_e) as shown in Eq. 7.3 and repeated here:

$$k_e = r_f + \beta(r_m - r_f)$$

This is the CAPM formula, which we have gradually built up over the last few sections. So how does it work, and is it useful? We'll start with examples from the US stock market, using betas from Fig. 7.2.

Example 7.3

Let's assume that we want to estimate the cost of equity capital for The Home Depot, Inc. Say the risk-free rate is 2.5 per cent, the market risk premium is 6 per cent and the beta of a Home Depot share is given as 1.22. Using the CAPM the estimated cost of equity for The Home Depot is: 2.5% + (1.22 × 6%) = 9.82%. As another example, Walmart's cost of equity is: 2.5% + (0.64 × 6%) = 6.34%.◄

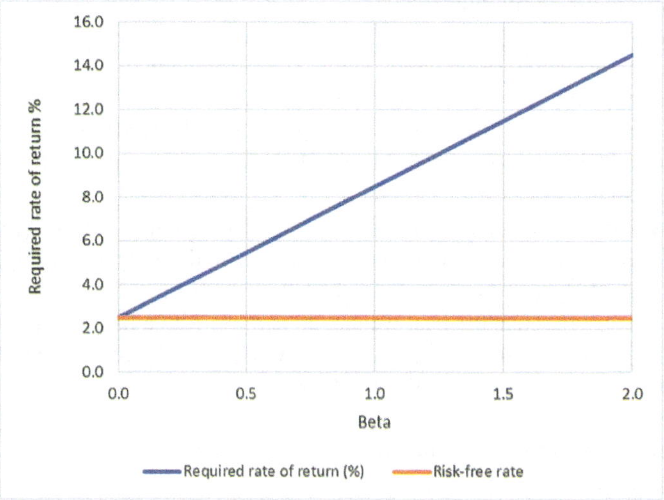

Fig. 7.3 The capital market line

Figure 7.3 shows what is called the 'capital market line' for the US stock market, derived from our formula (Eq. 7.3), with a straight-line relationship between market risk (beta, β) and the required rate of return (k_e). It starts from the risk-free rate of return (assumed to be 2.5 per cent) and adds a risk premium—the market risk premium of 6 per cent multiplied by the company's own beta (both these numbers are only estimates, don't forget). The beta applies *only* to market risk. A company's specific risk is ignored on the grounds that any investor, as discussed above, can choose to avoid that risk by holding a diversified portfolio. It can be seen that a company with a beta of 1 has an equity cost of 8.5 per cent, and a company with a beta of 1.5 has an equity cost of 11.5 per cent, etc.

Unfortunately, though, there are numerous problems with the CAPM, which we now turn to.

7.4.1.4 Problems with CAPM

The CAPM formula for the cost of equity capital is as shown in Eq. 7.3: $r_f + \beta(r_m—r_f)$. We can take each of the three main components in order, to see what problems each gives rise to:-

r_f, the risk-free rate of return

1. What time period should we use? Is it very short-term government securities, such as 90-day Treasury Bills? Or should we be matching the term with the 'typical' life of a project, say ten to fifteen years? (The answer needs to be consistent with the way we define 'r_f' in the expression $[r_m—r_f]$.)
2. What about tax? Should we assume the typical equity investor is a financial institution? Or a personal taxpayer? Their tax positions are likely to be different.

β, the relationship to market risk

3. Is it true (as some researchers claim) that company betas vary 'considerably' depending on which version of the stock market you use? And how unstable are company betas over time? Why is a thirty-six-month past period right to calculate a company's beta, rather than six months or fifty years (= 600 months)?
4. How can we modify the estimated beta of a listed company into a suitable beta for unlisted companies? If a private company actually *had* a regularly calculated share price, its beta is likely to be greater than that of listed companies, but *how much* greater? Perhaps the best we can do is try to find a listed company similar in nature to the unlisted company (quite a challenge in itself), and add, as an extremely rough example, 0.5 to the beta.

(r_m—r_f), the market risk premium

5. There is a great deal of controversy as to the appropriate figure to take for the market risk premium. As previously mentioned, the authors have seen suggested figures varying from 0 per cent to as high as 9 per cent. For example, as of 2018, KPMG estimates a market risk premium of 5.5 per cent. In contrast, Credit Suisse in their Global Investment Returns Yearbook 2018, estimate future equity premium at 3.5 per cent.[5] In the 2022 edition of the Yearbook, the authors (Dimson, Marsh, and Staunton) look at US data from 1914 to 2021 and make the distinction between periods that follow interest rate falls (easing cycles), and periods following interest rate increases (hiking cycles). During hiking cycles, equities gave an annualized real return of 3%, compared with 0.3% on US bills, thus providing an annualized MRP of 2.7%. In contrast, during easing cycles, the annualized real return on equities was 9.7%, less 0.4% on US bills, yielding an annualized MRP of 9.3%. Issues that can lead to the different suggestions include: (i) is it correct to use simply the domestic stock market in order to calculate the required market risk premium? Or should we aim to cover global markets or use a much wider set of assets than just listed securities? Or do we not worry too much about that, because although investors tend to invest in their own markets, in the United Kingdom as an example, most FTSE-100 companies are multinational anyway?; (ii) whether to use past results as a proxy for future estimates (as is normally done for betas)—in other words, are we right to assume that the future will be like the past?; (iii) whether to use an arithmetic index or a geometric index (the former frequently produces results about 1.5–2.0 percentage points per year higher); (iv) whether to use very short-term or long-term risk-free bonds (using short-term bonds produces higher market risk premium because rates on short-term bonds are normally

[5] The KPMG Equity Market Risk Premium Research of July 2018, was conducted by Marcel Groenendijk, Herman Engelbrecht, Romy Marsal and Richard van Baardwijk. The Credit Suisse Global Investment Returns Yearbooks were written by Elroy Dimson, Paul Marsh and Mike Staunton.

lower than those on long-term bonds); (v) whether to use a one-year holding period or a longer period—possibly much longer; (vi) over what past time period should we calculate the actual 'achieved' risk premium? The last five years, the last twenty-five, or the last seventy-five years?

6. Is the market risk premium before-tax or (as is normally assumed) after-tax? Can we properly allow for a changing tax system over time?

General

7. Are we right to concentrate entirely on market risk in using CAPM? Can we really ignore specific risk? What about (a) managers and (b) family-company shareholders, neither of whom will probably be anything like fully diversified? And however large the company, there is likely to be an important difference of outlook between its managers and its shareholders. Managers are normally committed largely to a specific company and may therefore be concerned with its *total* risk (that is, both market risk and specific risk). Shareholders, on the other hand, are mobile and can normally hold diversified portfolios. So the theory says, if they do, they need care only about market risk. One important question is the extent to which market pressures force managers to act in the interests of shareholders (by worrying only about market risk, as opposed to total risk).
8. The Capital Asset Pricing Model also has implications with respect to profit-seeking. Is it really, as the theory implies, more rational for shareholders to hold diversified portfolios, in order to avoid risks for which they cannot expect to get any reward? Or is it, as some successful investors believe, better to 'put all one's eggs in one basket'—*and then watch the basket*?
9. Many aspects of capital investment projects and valuing assets are likely to be more important than refining the supposed accuracy of the discount rate. So might it make sense to limit one's use of CAPM to seeing whether the industry concerned seems to be low, average or high risk? Maybe one could then similarly distinguish between (a) cost reduction; (b) expansion; and (c) new product projects as low risk, average risk and high risk, respectively.

The point of the above questions is not to denigrate the Capital Asset Pricing Model. But it would be absurd to pretend its results can be precisely accurate in practice—there are just too many dubious assumptions. Use with caution! And, fortunately, there is an alternative way of estimating the cost of equity, to which we now turn.

7.5 Cost of Equity (Dividend Growth Model)

Valuing shares and companies is something we tackle in detail in Chapter 9. However, it is necessary for understanding what you will see is an entirely different way of trying to estimate the cost of equity, to look at one method of valuing shares at this point—the Dividend Growth Model. In principle we can value equity shares in the same way as any other cash-generating asset. Thus we discount the expected future cash receipts (dividends) from owning the shares, using the opportunity cost of equity capital—this should give the value of the shares, because if someone pays now the NPV of the dividend stream for the shares from the End of Year 1, the total transaction has a zero NPV. If that were not the case, then either the buyer would have a positive NPV and thus the seller an equal but *negative* NPV, or vice versa. Why would anyone buy or sell an asset that gives them a negative NPV? So the price will be the exact NPV of the future dividend stream. (Of course, if the buyer and seller require different returns on their investment or anticipate different dividend streams, there might be scope for a win–win situation where both have, or think they have, a positive NPV, but we will not elaborate further on this here.) You may be thinking to yourself at this point, surely there are *two* benefits to shareholders in owning shares—dividends and capital gains. So how can we value shares by just looking at the dividend flows?

To answer this, consider a company which, for simplicity's sake, has announced that it will pay dividends of $1 per year into the indefinite future. The average required return of its equity investors is 10 per cent per year. We know from our work on perpetuities that the value of this investment to someone who holds the shares for ever is the annual cash flow multiplied by 1/r, or

$$1 \times \frac{1}{0.1} = \$10$$

But what about someone who sells the share at the end of year 2, for example? We can calculate how much they should be able to sell the shares for—it is the NPV of the future dividend stream at the end of year 2, which is still

$$1 \times \frac{1}{0.1} = \$10$$

But don't forget that (i) they have received dividends in years 1 and 2, and (ii) the $10 they receive at the end of year 2 needs to be discounted back to its present value. Thus the cash flows are:

Year	0	1	2
Dividends		1	1
Sale of share			10
Total cash flows	0	1	11
		x	x
Discount factor at 10%		0.909	0.826
Present value		0.909	9.086
Net Present Value	**10.00**		

So, the value now is still \$10! It will be \$10 whether or not the shares are sold in the future—all we need to think about is the dividend stream.

In reality, instead of a regular fixed money annuity, we have to deal with dividends which can fluctuate. This does not negate the idea that the value of a share is the NPV of its dividend streams—it just makes the calculations more complicated. One way of adding *some* complexity, but not too much (!), is to assume that the latest annual net dividend per share will grow at a constant rate indefinitely into the future.

If the most recent annual net dividend per share paid is d_0, and the expected (assumed constant) annual rate of growth in future net dividends per share is g (which should be shown as a decimal, not a percentage, in the formula), and the required return of our shareholders is k_e (also shown as a decimal), then we find the present value per share (p for "price") by discounting the expected future dividends for ever. Fortunately, there is a simple formula for a valuing a growing perpetuity. It is as presented in Eq. 7.4:-

$$p = \frac{d_1}{k_e - g} \tag{7.4}$$

Note that the dividend in Eq. 7.4 is that received at the end of year 1, d_1. We may well only know the amount of dividend just paid (d_0), but we also know that the dividends are growing at a constant rate. So if g is 5 per cent (or 0.05) and the most recent dividend was 10 cents, the next dividend, d_1, will be 10.5 cents.

Algebraically,

$$d_1 = d_0 \times (1 + g)$$
$$\text{or } 10.5 = 10 \times (1.05)$$

So, if you are prepared to accept that a share might yield a dividend growing at a constant rate for ever, we have a formula to calculate its value. This formula might not be too fanciful, provided the growth rate is not unfeasibly high, given that, as we know, the further into the future the cash flows occur, the more they are discounted. Bear in mind, though, that both k_e and g are only rough estimates, so the difference between them (k_e—g) may be subject to a considerable margin of error.

Example 7.4

Burnham Ltd. has just paid a dividend of 10p for this year on its ordinary shares; the expected future growth rate in dividends per share is 10 per cent a year; and the opportunity cost of equity capital is reckoned to be 15 per cent a year.

$$p = \frac{d_1}{k_e - g}$$

$$p = \frac{10 \times 1.10}{.15 - .10}$$

$$p = 220$$

The dividend growth model would value Burnham Ltd's ordinary shares at 220p each.

This is all very well, but what we really want at this point is k_e, the cost of equity. However, in the case of public, quoted companies, we already have p, the share price. So the formula can be re-arranged to calculate k_e, thus from Eq. 7.4, we can derive Eq. 7.5 as follows:-

$$k_e = \frac{d_1}{p} + g \tag{7.5}$$

You can see from Eq. 7.5 that, in order to determine the (opportunity) cost of equity capital, k_e, we are in effect simply adding the assumed constant growth rate to the dividend yield, based on d_1—the end-of-current-year dividend.◄

Example 7.5

Gordon Inc's most recent dividend paid (d_0) was 20¢ per share, and the dividend is expected to grow at 3 per cent per year for the foreseeable future. Its current share price is $4.12. What is its cost of equity?

$$k_e = \frac{d_1}{p} + g$$

$$k_e = \frac{20.6}{412} + .03$$

$$= 0.05 + 0.03 = 0.08$$

The cost of equity is 0.08, or 8 per cent. Note the importance of working in decimals and converting back to a percentage only at the end. If you don't, you might well think of growth as 3 per cent, d_1/p as 0.05, and conclude that k_e is 3.05 per cent—which is wrong by a factor of nearly 3 times!◄

7.5.1 The Growth Rate, g

Where do we get the expected growth rate, g, which we use in Eqs. 7.4 and 7.5, from? There are essentially three possible sources. Firstly, if we are lucky, the company might actually have announced a dividend policy of increases of x per cent per year!

Secondly, we can analyse the company's historical increases in dividends to see if there is a consistent pattern.

Year	Dividend paid ($)	Annual increase
0	1.17	3.5%
−1	1.13	2.7%
−2	1.10	2.8%
−3	1.07	3.9%
−4	1.03	3.0%
−5	1.00	

Here, the annual increases don't vary by much, so the historical data is probably good enough for an estimate of g into the future. The average of the annual increases is 3.18 per cent. To be very accurate and work out the compound annual growth rate of dividends between 5 years ago and just now, the formula is:-

$$\sqrt[5]{\frac{1.17}{1.00}} - 1$$

Gives 1.0319 −1, that is .0319, or 3.19 per cent.

Note that the root to use in the formula is the number of years between the two dividend payments we are considering.

Finally, failing the above (and if you haven't studied any accounting, you may want to skip this section!), we could use a formula based on historic returns on equity and some data from the company's Balance Sheet, as stated in Eq. 7.6:

$$g = Retention\ Ratio\ x\ Return\ on\ Equity \tag{7.6}$$

This is best understood by way of an example:-

Example 7.6

Grayling SARL has Balance Sheet equity of €2,000m. Its profit for the year in 2021 was €400m, representing a Return on Equity of 20 per cent. Of that €400m, €300m was paid out in dividends, such that by definition €100m was retained within the business—its retention ratio is 100/400, or 25 per cent. The formula indicates its growth rate (in both profits and dividends, because the theory is based on the retention ratio staying constant) should be 25% × 20% = 5%. Let's now prove this:-

	2021	2022	Change
€m			
Equity	2000	2100	
Profit for the year*	400	420	5%
Dividend paid	300	315	5%
Retained profit	100	105	

*Representing a Return on Equity of 20%

Note that in 2022 the equity has increased by €100m—the retained profit from 2021. If the company continues to make a Return on Equity of 20 per cent, then in 2022 it will make €420m in profits—so if it pays out 75 per cent of them in dividends, as in 2021, the dividend payment will be €315m—an increase of 5 per cent, as shown in the formula.

Although the theory assumes a constant retention ratio and constant return on equity, we could relax the latter assumption by using the predicted return on the *reinvested* profits, if we think that will be different from the return on the equity earned or provided in previous years.◀

7.5.2 Which Ke?

It is highly likely that if you calculate the cost of equity using both the CAPM and the Dividend Growth Model, you will end up with different figures. So which do you choose? There are no hard and fast rules. You might just take the average of the two results—add them up and divide by two! You might, however, feel that the assumptions in one model are, in the specific case you are examining, more unrealistic than the other, in which case you should bias your answer towards the result from the other model. Whatever approach you take, it is important to remember that calculating k_e is more an art than a science, and a ballpark figure might have to do.

7.6 Weighted Average Cost of Capital (WACC)

7.6.1 Overall Cost of Capital

A firm's cost of capital is the minimum return its assets must produce to justify raising the funds to acquire them. We have discussed how to estimate a company's after-tax cost of debt; and we have seen that the cost of equity is largely an opportunity cost whether one uses the Capital Asset Pricing Model or the Dividend Growth Model. Combining the cost of debt and the cost of equity gives the company's overall weighted average cost of capital (WACC). *This is the basis for the discount rate to use as the hurdle rate in assessing capital investment projects.*

Equation 7.7 gives the formula for calculating the WACC:

$$\begin{aligned} \text{WACC} &= (\text{the proportion of debt} \times \text{the cost debt}) \\ &\quad + (\text{the proportion of equity} \times \text{the cost of equity}) \end{aligned} \tag{7.7}$$

As a rule, it is best to separate two questions: (a) whether a project is worth investing in or not; and (b) if it is, how to finance it. A company may plan to finance a project by borrowing; but it still bases the project's minimum rate of return (the discount rate for NPV purposes) on the overall weighted average cost of capital. In effect we think of using a pool of funds (both debt and equity) to finance all projects. After all, debt is almost always less costly to a company than equity (debt is less risky in the eyes of the lender than equity is in the eyes of the investor).

However, a company cannot go on indefinitely borrowing a greater and greater proportion of its total funding, as discussed in the next chapter. So, it would be "unfair" to judge a project using the company's cost of debt just because that is how that particular project is to be financed, when the next project, through no fault of its own, has to be financed by expensive equity and is thus subject to a higher discount rate! Consequently, the weighted average cost of capital (WACC) should be the basis of the discount rate whatever the funding method of the particular project.

We must remember that nearly all the numbers are only estimates: the amount and timing of the incremental cash flows from a capital project; and the costs of debt and of equity (as well as their respective weightings). For this reason, it is probably not worth distinguishing between two kinds of equity capital—retained earnings and new issues of equity shares—even though share issues would involve some extra costs. (Remember too that the WACC is a weighted average of the *marginal* costs of debt and of equity.)

7.6.2 Adjusting WACC for Risk

Rather than using the WACC itself as the hurdle rate for all capital projects (the horizontal 10 per cent line in the example shown in Fig. 7.4), a company may choose to use a higher figure than the WACC (= require a higher rate of return) for high-risk projects and a lower figure than the WACC (= accept a lower required rate of return) for low-risk projects. Otherwise, there would be a tendency to accept too many high-risk projects (such as H) and to reject too many low-risk projects (such as L).

How much to adjust the WACC for risk is a matter of judgement. The cash flows for capital projects usually involve such fallible estimates that a difference of one or two percentage points in the discount rate is unlikely to be critical (There is also a question about how to define—let alone measure—'risk').

For a project with zero risk (if there could be such a thing), the relevant required rate of return would be the risk-free rate of return—say, 2.0 per cent (Not 0 per

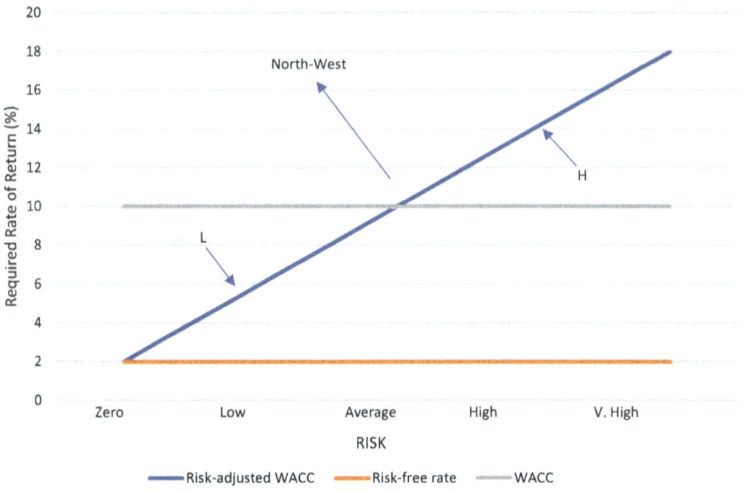

Fig. 7.4 Adjusting WACC for risk

cent, of course!). The WACC itself, say 10 per cent, would be a suitable required rate of return for a 'typical' project with 'average' risk.

A rough rule of thumb for other projects of varying risk might be as follows: for a project thought to have below-average risk, move halfway from 'average' to 'zero' risk (that is, to a required rate of return of 6 per cent—halfway between 10 per cent and 2 per cent); for a project with an above-average level of risk, move as much *above* the WACC (to 14 per cent); and for a very high-risk project, move as far again above the WACC (to 18 per cent).

Some commentators advise against adjusting the WACC at all, given that (a) the adjustments are somewhat arbitrary, and (b) doing so assumes each cash flow line on our project spreadsheet is equally risky. Instead, they advise using the WACC for all projects, but create several spreadsheets examining different scenarios (see the discussion on scenario analysis in Chapter 4). What happens if sales are 10 per cent above the best estimate; 20 per cent below; 40 per cent below? Maybe a deal has been done with the workforce that they will be paid the same amount for the first 3 years of the project regardless. This figure can be left the same in all scenarios, whereas if the WACC had been adjusted upwards because this is overall a 'risky' project, the higher WACC would have been applied to the salaries figure (along with all the other figures), when in fact it is a certainty and therefore not 'risky' as such.

Of course, managers are not merely trying to measure levels of risk and required return. They are also trying to manage the projects in order to 'move' them to the 'north-west' (on Fig. 7.4)—either to the 'west' (by reducing the risk) or to the 'north' (by increasing the expected return), or both.

We saw earlier (Chapter 5) how lenders may seek to reduce their risk (by personal guarantees, by taking security or by loan covenants). Company managers, too, may seek to reduce risk by various means, such as: extensive market research; arranging long-term sales contracts; or dual sourcing. Managers may also try to increase returns, for example, by expanding the volume of sales; increasing selling prices; or reducing costs without hurting quality (these may be easier said than done).

7.7 A Concluding Note: The WACC and Value Creation

Whether or not we adjust the WACC for the risk of the project before using it as the hurdle rate in capital investment appraisal, it should be obvious that the lower the WACC, the higher the NPV of the project (remember, the hurdle rate is the rate at which we discount expected future cash flows to arrive at their present value). Moreover, as discussed in Chapter 2, the NPV is the value created to shareholders over and above the minimum return (or compensation) they demand for investing in the firm. Thus, a firm that aims to maximize value to its shareholders should endeavour to reduce its WACC. The decision regarding the mix of debt and equity a firm uses to finance its activities is principally what determines the WACC (as well as investors' perception of the firm's risk, of course). It is thus to this decision that we turn in the next chapter.

7.7.1 Problems

Problem 7.1

a. ABC plc has a beta of 1.2. If the risk-free rate of return is 2.5 per cent and the market risk premium is 6.0 per cent, what is ABC's cost of equity capital?
b. DEF Inc has a beta of 0.75. If the market risk premium is 6.0 per cent and DEF's cost of equity capital is 8.0 per cent, what is the risk-free rate of return?
c. GHI plc has a cost of equity capital of 16.5 per cent. If the market risk premium is 8.0 per cent and the risk-free rate of return is 4.5 per cent, what is GHI's beta?
d. JKL Inc has a beta of 0.8, and a cost of equity capital of 8.8 per cent. The risk-free rate of return is 4.0 per cent. What is the market risk premium?
e. MNO plc has a beta of 0.75. The risk-free rate of return is 4.0 per cent and the cost of equity capital is 10.0 per cent. How much does the cost of equity increase if the beta doubles?

Problem 7.2

a. MD Enterprises plc expects to pay a net dividend at the end of this year of 6.0p per share; and the market expects the dividend to increase by 5 per cent a year. The company's cost of equity capital is estimated at 15 per cent a year. Using the dividend growth model, what would you expect the company's current market price per share to be?
b. MD Enterprises plc has run into trouble. The company's policy is to pay out a constant proportion of its earnings in dividends each year; but earnings per share are now expected to grow by only 2 per cent a year for the foreseeable future. Instead of 6.0p per share (as in part [a] above), the company is now planning a dividend of only 4.0p per share this year-end. The prospects for the industry look gloomy, and the risk premium applicable to the company has increased, so that the cost of equity capital is now reckoned to be 20 per cent a year. What combined effect will all these changes have on the company's market price per share?
c. PLQ Inc paid a dividend of 6.0¢ per share last year. The current dividend yield (based on next year's dividend) is 5.0 per cent and dividends are expected to grow in line with earnings at 8.0 per cent a year in future. What is the cost of equity capital?
d. RST has a cost of equity capital of 14.4 per cent. The current dividend yield (based on next year's dividend) is 10.0 per cent. What is the (constant) annual growth rate expected in future?
e. UVW GmbH expects to pay a dividend at the end of this year of 12.0¢ per share. The current share price is 240¢. The cost of equity capital is twice the expected growth rate in dividends. Using the assumptions of the dividend growth model, what is the expected (constant) annual growth rate in earnings?

Problem 7.3

a. XY plc has equity with a market value of £60 million and debt with a market value of £20 million. The cost of equity capital is 12.0 per cent and the cost of debt is 6.0 per cent. What is XY's weighted average cost of capital (WACC)?
b. ZA has a WACC of 12.0 per cent. The cost of debt is 6.0 per cent and the cost of equity is 15.0 per cent. What are the weights of debt and equity, respectively?
c. BC has a WACC of 12.0 per cent. The cost of debt is 5.0 per cent. The debt/equity weights are 30/70. What is the cost of equity capital?

Problem 7.4 DE Inc has book values of debt and equity of $200m and $400m, respectively. Assume the market value of debt is the same as the book value. The cost of debt is 6.0 per cent, and the cost of equity is 12.0 per cent. If the market value of equity is $600m, how much will the WACC be increased by using market value weights rather than book value weights?

References

Desmoulins-Lebeault, F., & Kharoubi-Rakotomalala, C. (2012). Non-Gaussian diversification: When *size* matters. *Journal of Banking & Finance, 36*(7), 1987–1996.

Dimson, E., Marsh, P., & Staunton, M. (2015). Equity premiums around the world. In B. Hammond, M. Leibowitz, & L. Siegel (Eds.), *Rethinking the equity risk premium*. Research Foundation of CFA Institute, 2011–1. Available at SSRN: https://ssrn.com/abstract=2616249

Hammond, P. B. Jr., & Leibowitz, M. L. (2015). Rethinking the equity risk premium: An overview and some new ideas. In B. Hammond, M. Leibowitz, & L. Siegel (Eds.), *Rethinking the equity risk premium*. Rethinking the Equity Premium, Research Foundation of CFA Institute, 2011–1. Available at SSRN: https://ssrn.com/abstract=2616249

Jacob, M. T., & Shivdasani, A. (2012, July–August). Do you know your cost of capital? *Harvard Business Review*, 118–124.

Capital Structure and Dividend Policy

8

8.1 Introduction

How a firm invests funds is probably far more important than its sources of finance. This is because most financial markets are more competitive, with better information, than most markets dealing in 'real' goods and services. So, in general, financing decisions provide fewer chances of large profits or losses. Nevertheless, the lower a company's financing costs, the lower will be the discount rate to apply to its projects, and thus the more profitable its projects—and indeed, the more likely it is that a project will have a positive NPV rather than a negative one—and thus the greater the value of the company and its return to shareholders. Likewise, how much of the firm's profit is distributed as dividends to shareholders, versus how much is retained to finance investment, is probably not so important because the firm should be able to raise more capital if it has good investment opportunities for which it needs funds. Similarly, investors can sell some of their shares to generate cash if the cash dividend paid by the firm does not satisfy their cash needs. Nonetheless, policies regarding capital structure and dividends vary greatly from company to company and appear to be important to investors. For example, in 2021, 90 per cent of all companies (globally) either raised their dividends or held them steady, and the third quarter of 2021 saw an all-time high in global dividend payouts of just over $400 billion.[1]

[1] Source: *The Global Dividend Index Report* by British asset manager Janus Henderson, dated November 2021 (Edition 32), available at: https://cdn.janushenderson.com/webdocs/Issue+32+Report+Global+%28English%29.pdf.

R. Manos et al., *Corporate Finance for Business*,
https://doi.org/10.1007/978-3-030-92419-5_8

This chapter is devoted to these two policy decisions. First, the capital structure decision, that is, the mix of debt and equity that the firm uses to finance its activities. Second, the dividend policy decision, that is, determining what part of profits to distribute to shareholders, with the remainder by definition being reinvested in the firm. We start in Sect. 8.2, by discussing the debt ratio (gearing) and its various implications. Section 8.3 focuses on the question of how a firm can choose between debt and equity, while Sect. 8.4 looks at dividend policy, share buybacks, and how these policies can impact the firm's capital structure. Section 8.5 reviews how the capital structure, or gearing, might change as the firm progresses through its life cycle. In Sect. 8.6 we provide an overview of empirical evidence on capital structure practices, followed by the concluding Sect. 8.7 and practice problems.

To reiterate, the main point of the capital structure decision is to find the optimal mix of debt and equity such that the overall return required by finance providers (equity and debt holders) is minimized. To the extent that the WACC is the discount rate used in investment appraisal tools such as the NPV (and to compare the IRR against), reducing the WACC has the potential to increase the NPV thereby creating value to shareholders (see Chapter 2).

8.2 Debt Ratio (Gearing)

We saw in the previous chapter that the company's financing cost, the Weighted Average Cost of Capital, is calculated by the formula:

$$(Proportion\,of\,debt \times the\,cost\,of\,debt) + (Proportion\,of\,equity \times the\,cost\,of\,equity)$$

Ultimately, the company's objective will therefore be to see if there is a gearing ratio (the proportion of debt in the formula) that minimizes the WACC.[2]

We have also seen in Chapter 7 that the cost of debt is almost always lower than the cost of equity. So, looking at the formula, does this not indicate that we should have more and more debt (gearing), because this will reduce the WACC (we get a higher and higher proportion of the cheaper element)?

Consider, for example, company A with a cost of debt of 5 per cent and a cost of equity of 11 per cent. If these costs stay constant regardless of the extent of the gearing, the WACC at different levels of gearing (ignoring tax for now) is shown in Table 8.1.

Ultimately, of course, in this scenario 100 per cent gearing would give the lowest WACC at 5 per cent. Unfortunately, the solution to the ideal gearing ratio conundrum is not so straightforward. Why not? Because the cost of both debt and equity are *dynamic* with respect to the proportion of debt. As the level of debt increases, the required return of both debtholders and shareholders changes. So the question becomes, is there an optimum gearing ratio that minimizes the WACC?

[2] Gearing is also referred to as leverage.

Table 8.1 WACC with no taxes

Equity	Debt	k_e	k_d	WACC
100%	0%	11%	5%	11.0%
90%	10%	11%	5%	10.4%
80%	20%	11%	5%	9.8%
70%	30%	11%	5%	9.2%
60%	40%	11%	5%	8.6%
50%	50%	11%	5%	8.0%
40%	60%	11%	5%	7.4%
30%	70%	11%	5%	6.8%
20%	80%	11%	5%	6.2%

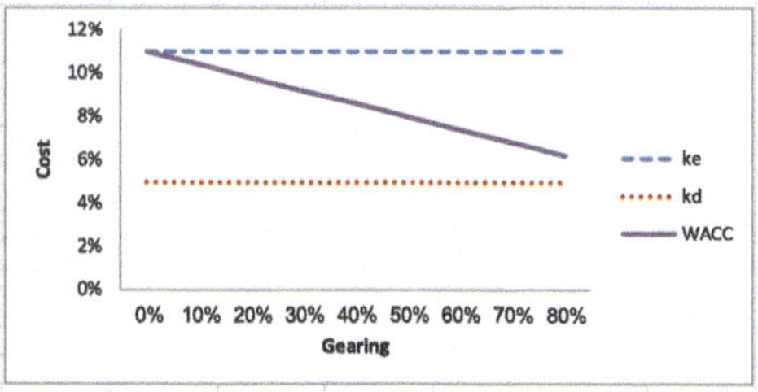

8.2.1 Gearing and the Volatility of Returns

The first thing we need to consider is that as the gearing increases, the potential volatility of returns to shareholders also increases. Consider the following example, Table 8.2, (which ignores taxes for now—they do not change the principle) of a high-geared and a low-geared company.

When the performance of the company is good, although the absolute level of profit of the low-geared company is higher because it pays less interest, it is the high-geared company that makes by far the best return on its shareholders' funds (equity), because it is sharing the lower profit between a much lower level of equity. However, the interest of course has to be paid whether the results are good or bad, and in the poor performance case, it can be seen that the Return on Equity of the high-geared company has fallen below that of the low-geared. Even more important is the much greater *volatility* of the returns on the high-geared

Table 8.2 Volatility of returns to shareholders

	High-geared (80%)	Low-geared (20%)
Debt @ 5%	800	200
Equity	200	800
	1000	1000
Good performance		
Profit before interest	150	150
Interest	40	10
Profit	110	140
Return on Equity (Profit ÷ Equity)	**55%**	**18%**
Poor performance		
Profit before interest	45	45
Interest	40	10
Profit	5	35
Return on Equity (Profit ÷ Equity)	**3%**	**4%**

Table 8.3 WACC with no taxes under Modigliani and Miller

Equity	Debt	k_e	k_d	WACC
100%	0%	11.00%	5%	11%
90%	10%	11.67%	5%	11%
80%	20%	12.50%	5%	11%
70%	30%	13.57%	5%	11%
60%	40%	15.00%	5%	11%
50%	50%	17.00%	5%	11%
40%	60%	20.00%	5%	11%
30%	70%	25.00%	5%	11%
20%	80%	35.00%	5%	11%

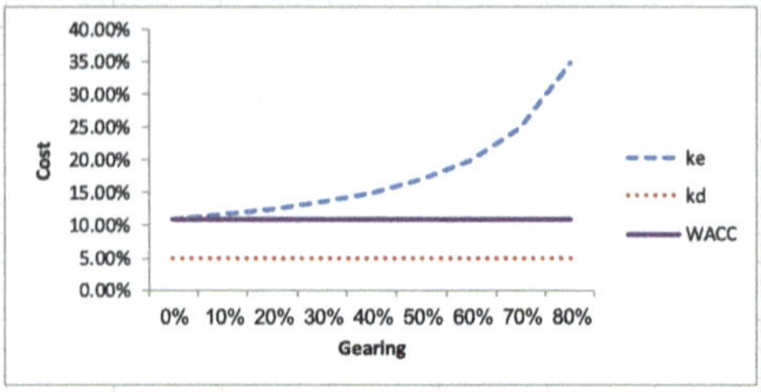

company's shareholders' funds—55 per cent down to 3 per cent as opposed to 18 per cent down to 4 per cent. This volatility will be seen by shareholders as representing a significant increase in the risk they are having to bear, and we have seen that investors require an increased return to compensate them for any increased risk. Consequently, shareholders will require a higher minimum return on their investment as the level of gearing increases—that is, the k_e will go up.

But by how much? One theory, put forward (and demonstrated mathematically) by Modigliani and Miller, is that the increased required return by shareholders goes up by exactly the amount that offsets the benefit of the greater proportion of cheaper-than-equity debt, as shown in Table 8.3.

The k_e in the table has been calculated so as to result in the WACC staying constant at 11 per cent—the cost of equity when there is no debt. In other words, the theory states that in a world without taxes, the WACC is independent of the level of gearing. Modigliani and Miller make several other assumptions in arriving at this conclusion, including the ability of individuals to borrow and lend at the same rate as the firm, the absence of distress costs (see below) and the availability of perfect knowledge. Whether or not their theory is true given those assumptions, life becomes more complicated when the assumptions get relaxed—and we start with the introduction of taxes.

8.2.2 Tax Relief on Interest

We saw in Chapter 7 that the interest on debt is normally tax deductible, and the easiest way to incorporate this into investment appraisal analysis is to simply deduct the corporate tax rate from the headline interest rate to arrive at the k_{dat} (the cost of debt after tax). So, in our example, if the interest rate is 5 per cent and the corporate tax rate is 40 per cent, then the cost of debt that we should use is 5 per cent minus (40 per cent of 5 per cent) = 3 per cent. But there is no reason why the cost of equity that we calculated in the previous table should change (or not by very much) just because the cost of debt has reduced solely due to the tax relief, so we only need to substitute 3 per cent for 5 per cent as the cost of debt into the table, Table 8.4.

Table 8.4 WACC with tax at 40%

Equity	Debt	k_e	k_{dat}	WACC
100%	0%	11.00%	3%	**11.0%**
90%	10%	11.67%	3%	**10.8%**
80%	20%	12.50%	3%	**10.6%**
70%	30%	13.57%	3%	**10.4%**
60%	40%	15.00%	3%	**10.2%**
50%	50%	17.00%	3%	**10.0%**
40%	60%	20.00%	3%	**9.8%**
30%	70%	25.00%	3%	**9.6%**
20%	80%	35.00%	3%	**9.4%**

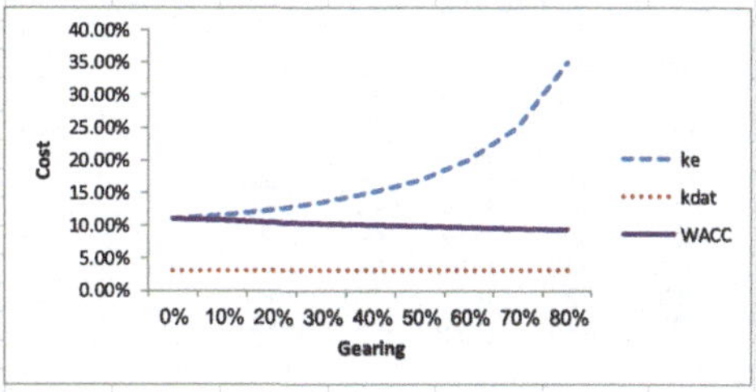

You can see that this new situation has restored the benefits of increasing levels of debt, as this reduces the WACC. However, a crucial point about debt is of course that the borrower must be able to service both the interest payments and the repayment schedule (remember this is a crucial difference between debt and equity—the company has no obligation to pay dividends, nor would it normally repay the equity). As the level of debt gets higher and higher, the interest and repayments will become harder and harder to meet.

8.2.3 Distress Costs

Distress costs refer to the costs, whether monetary or otherwise, of dealing with a situation where the company is having difficulty meeting its interest and repayment requirements on time. These might include liquidation costs, losses due to having to sell assets urgently at 'distress prices', diversion of management time, uncertainty about the firm's future affecting customers, current employees, potential employees, suppliers, and so on.

At what level of gearing is there 'too much' debt? It would vary for different industries. A company with high business risk (such as a car manufacturer) might not be able to bear much financial risk (gearing) on top; whereas a 'safe' company with low business risk (such as a utility) might be able to take on quite high levels of gearing without risking distress. Factors such as how fast assets could be realized in an emergency, predictability of cash flows, and exposure to fixed costs that by definition cannot rapidly be reduced, should also be taken into consideration. As gearing rises, and the likelihood of financial distress increases, so the required return of *both* lenders and equity investors will also start to rise—lenders because of the increasing chance of default; and equity investors because there is little chance of receiving a dividend if the company is having difficulty paying its interest bill, and because if the company *does* default on its debt terms the whole company might end up in liquidation, at which point the shareholders could lose all their investment. Consequently, the relationship between the gearing and the WACC might look something like Table 8.5.

Table 8.5 WACC with tax and distress costs

Equity	Debt	k_e	k_{dat}	WACC
100%	0%	10.0%	3.0%	10.0%
90%	10%	10.0%	3.0%	9.3%
80%	20%	10.0%	3.0%	8.6%
70%	30%	10.0%	3.0%	7.9%
60%	40%	11.0%	3.5%	8.0%
50%	50%	12.0%	4.5%	8.3%
40%	60%	13.0%	6.5%	9.1%
30%	70%	16.0%	9.0%	11.1%
20%	80%	21.0%	13.0%	14.6%

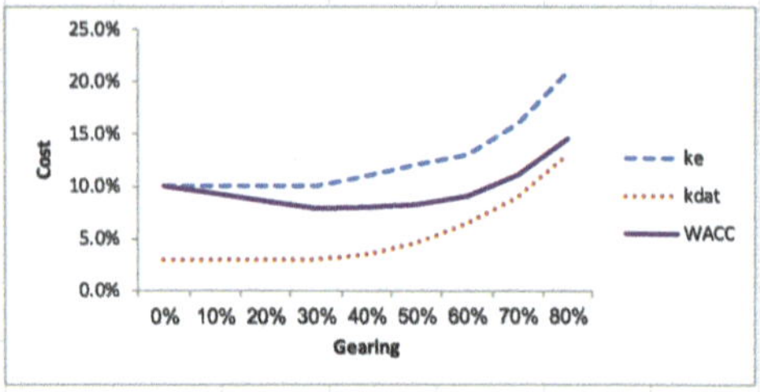

We can see that under this view of gearing, while there may technically be an absolute optimum gearing level, there is likely to be a *range* of capital structures that are close to the optimal. Over a wide range of moderate gearing, the overall average cost of capital is almost flat, because the benefit of an increasing proportion of debt, which is cheaper than equity, is offset by the increased cost of both debt and equity due to the increased riskiness of becoming more highly geared. Thus the WACC—and hence the firm's market value—is not very sensitive to small changes in gearing within that range. Outside the range, however, the company may have 'too much' debt or 'too little'. It can then increase its overall market value by adjusting its financial gearing (see below) and moving towards the optimal range. The problem for Finance Directors is to know where the company's gearing *is* on that range—for example, would a reduction in debt reduce market value because the company would then be under-geared, or an increase in debt reduce value because the company would then be over-geared?

Figure 8.1 shows this traditional view, both in terms of a U-shaped weighted average cost of capital and in terms of an inverted-U showing the firm's market value.

Note that if companies can borrow quite a lot before their WACC starts to rise, it may not make sense, from the shareholders' point of view, for firms to aim for the very highest credit rating.

8.3 Debt Versus Equity

8.3.1 Risk and Return

Borrowing is normally cheaper after tax than equity capital; but the risk to the borrowing company is higher. How then can firms choose between debt and equity? We have seen that, ideally, the firm should be seeking a combination of debt and equity that minimises its Weighted Average Cost of Capital, thus maximizing the value of each project and hence the firm itself. However, sometimes other factors are relevant, and we consider them in this section.

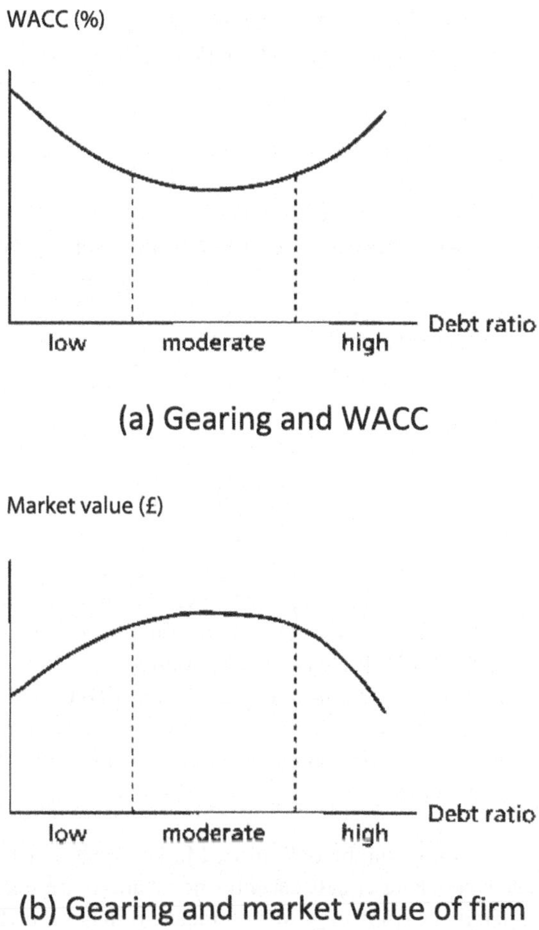

Fig. 8.1 The effect of gearing on (a) WACC and (b) market value

One such factor that companies might wish to take into consideration in deciding on the balance between debt and equity when raising *new* finance is the likely impact on the company's earnings per share (EPS) calculation. [Its EPS is its profit after tax divided by the number of shares in issue.]

Example 8.1

Rutherfords' current level of earnings before interest and tax (EBIT) is $20 million a year; current debt, with a market value of about $45 million, pays annual interest of $3 million a year; and 30 million ordinary shares are outstanding. The company now needs $30 million of new capital to finance investment projects which are expected to increase profits (before interest and tax) by $5 million a year.

The choice is between (a) issuing 6 million ordinary shares at $5 net (compared with the current market price of $5.60 per share), or borrowing $30 million through ten-year bonds at 8 per cent a year interest. On what basis should the company choose?

As a start, we can calculate what earnings per share (EPS) would amount to under each alternative. Table 8.6 shows that if EBIT really does increase by $5 million, the new EPS would rise to 42.8¢ if Rutherfords were to issue 6 million ordinary shares, and to 45.7¢ if the company borrows $30 million.

We can also see what is the 'cross-over' EBIT level ($x) at which EPS (in the first year) would be the same under the two methods of finance. For Rutherfords, simple algebra shows that the cross-over point comes at an EBIT level of $17.4 million:

$$(\text{debt})\frac{70\%(x-5.4)}{30}=\frac{70\%(x-3.0)}{36}(\text{equity})$$

$$36(x-5.4)=30(x-3.0)$$

$$x=17.4$$

Figure 8.2 shows that above the cross-over level of EBIT of $17.4 million, EPS will be higher with debt (due to the effect of gearing); whereas below it, EPS will be higher with the equity issue.

It is also worth noticing at what EBIT level in each case EPS is zero. $5.4 million for debt and $3.0 million for equity. These, of course, are the respective amounts of debt interest payable. Until EBIT exceeds that level, EPS will be negative.◀

We know that by definition: Market Value = EPS × (P/E). In words: the market price per share equals earnings per share multiplied by the price/earnings ratio (for a detailed explanation of the price/earnings ratio (P/E), see Sect. 9.2.2 in the next chapter). This equation is almost a tautology, because in E × (P/E) the E cancels

Table 8.6 Rutherfords earnings per share calculations

		Increased capital		Cross-over EBIT	
$ million	Now	Equity	Debt	Equity	Debt
EBIT	20.00	25.00	25.00	17.40	17.40
Debt Interest	3.00	3.00	5.40	3.00	5.40
Profit before tax	17.00	22.00	19.60	14.40	12.00
Tax @ 30%	5.10	6.60	5.88	4.32	3.60
Profit after tax	11.90	15.40	13.72	10.08	8.40
Ordinary shares (m)	30	36	30	36	30
EPS (cents)	**39.7**	**42.8**	**45.7**	**28.0**	**28.0**

Fig. 8.2 Rutherfords EPS cross-over chart

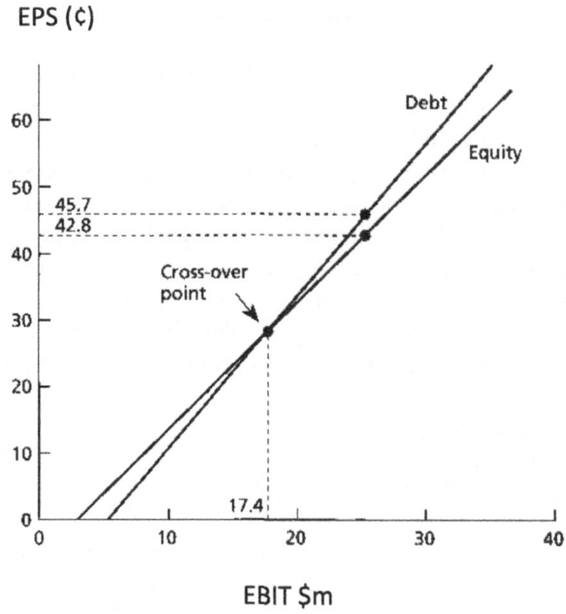

out leaving just P—so the market value equals the price! But sometimes the P/E ratio has a life of its own, as it were, such that if the EPS are increased, then EPS multiplied by the P/E will also increase if the P/E stays constant. Will it stay constant? We are in fact not entitled to assume that the market value of each ordinary share need be higher if Rutherfords goes for debt, merely because the EPS would (probably) be higher. That would imply the same price/earnings multiple if the company borrows as if it issues new equity shares. But debt, being riskier for the company, might result in a lower price/earnings multiple than the equity issue. Hence it is possible for the financing alternative which produces a lower EPS (i.e. equity), actually to result in a higher market price per share.

Just how risky is it for Rutherfords to borrow another $30 million? It would increase the debt ratio from about 21 per cent to about 31 per cent (based on market values); and it would reduce *interest cover* from 6.7 times to 4.6 times. (You may wish to check where these numbers come from.) The company's directors will have to decide whether these numbers are acceptable.

The main problem, however, is not about doing the calculations based on certain assumptions. It is about using commercial judgement to balance risks and returns. For example, how likely is EBIT in future to fall below the cross-over level of $17.4 million? How much would it matter if that did happen on occasion? What might be the impact of future inflation? What effect, in this case, might the increased risk from higher borrowing have on the price/earnings multiple (which is currently about 14)?

8.3.2 The Pecking Order Hypothesis

Another approach is the pecking order hypothesis on which we provide some empirical findings in Sect. 8.6. According to this view, companies do not have any 'optimum' or 'target' debt ratio in mind. Instead, when they need money to invest in profitable projects, managers prefer retained earnings (a type of equity, of course) to debt, and debt to *new* issues of equity.

Table 8.7 suggests that shareholders, in contrast, might prefer debt to retained earnings, as a rule. The implication is that often shareholders might prefer a company to have a higher debt ratio than managers are comfortable with. Under company law, though, shareholders cannot vote to increase dividends (and hence reduce retained earnings, which would increase the debt ratio).

Table 8.7 Managers and shareholders under the pecking order hypothesis

	Diversified shareholders	Managers
Order of preference		
First	Debt	Retained earnings
Second	Retained earnings	Debt
Third	New issue of equity	New issue of equity

This may explain why companies in the same industry (with, presumably, similar business risks) may often end up with very different debt ratios. It may simply be by chance. And the pecking order theory is probably not really inconsistent with the 'traditional' view of capital structure in the last section. Both views conclude that, over a wide range of moderate gearing, capital structure, or fine-tuning it, is really not an important issue.

8.3.3 Other Relevant Factors

Choices about long-term finance are by no means solely a matter of numbers (many of which one can only guess). Other aspects of long-term finance may be of paramount importance.

8.3.3.1 Term

The choice between short-term and long-term borrowing depends mainly on comparing the relative costs and risks. To avoid uncertainty, a firm might try to 'match' the period of its borrowing to the period for which it needed the money. Thus it would finance long-term needs (say for a new plant expected to last for fifteen years) by long-term money (either long-term debt or equity), and short-term needs (say to finance high seasonal raw material inventory) by short-term sources. As a rule one might expect longer-term money to have a somewhat higher cost. Of course equity is very long-term money.

But a company may not be sure how much money it requires, nor for how long. Estimates of the amount and timing of capital project cash flows can be subject to very wide margins of error. It may often make sense to think of a company's needs as consisting of a long-term 'base load' which it can forecast with fair certainty, and a varying balance of short-term needs, depending on the nature of the business.

8.3.3.2 Control

For small and medium-sized enterprises, the question of control of the equity capital is often critical. The controlling shareholders are often members of one or two families. They probably have limited surplus funds outside the business. Hence they may not wish their company to make a rights issue of new ordinary shares, since it might, if they don't take up their own rights, dilute their own equity interests and could mean them losing control.

'Control' may also refer to borrowing arrangements involving covenants or other restrictions (see Chapter 5) which owner/managers may dislike, especially if the restrictions become higher as the level of gearing gets higher. As a result, some companies may prefer to limit their rate of expansion to that which they can finance out of retained profits, even if that may mean shareholders foregoing larger potential profits from more aggressive financing.

8.3.3.3 Flexibility

Even in larger companies, managers will usually value flexibility—keeping their options open. Thus they may not choose to borrow all the way up to some supposed 'optimum' level of gearing if that would rule out more borrowing for a number of years, or if it would make debt too expensive in time of crisis (see the empirical evidence discussed in Sect. 8.6). Managers like to leave themselves elbow room to allow for the unexpected or even the unforeseeable. Even when the outlook seems fine, they often worry about rainy days ahead.

Making a loss, of course, reduces a company's total retained earnings and thus the amount of its balance sheet equity. Paying ordinary dividends has the same result. A seemingly adequate level of gearing can soon become uncomfortably high through one or two years' losses, combined with further borrowing to finance current operations. So it is perhaps not surprising if managers sometimes seem to the outside observer to be rather cautious. In practice, some company managements (both of large and of smaller firms) seem on occasion to prefer lower risks to themselves rather than higher returns for diversified shareholders. In other words, they prefer managers (themselves) to sleep well rather than shareholders to eat well!

8.3.3.4 Overall Risk

We mentioned earlier in this chapter that companies should avoid having too much high risk finance (debt) if the riskiness of its business is itself high. In fact, we can expand this into a more general principle—where possible, a company should have an inverse relationship between its business risk and its financial risk—the lower one is, the higher the other should be, and vice-versa.

But what is wrong with minimizing a company's overall riskiness by having a low business risk model combined with low financial risk (little debt)? Surely that would make the company an attractive proposition to risk-averse investors? The answer lies in Fig. 8.1. You can see there that if a company has too little debt, it does not maximize its market value. Check that you remember why—because it is failing to make the most of cheap debt and the tax-deductibility of interest, and therefore its WACC is higher than it could be, and therefore the NPV of its projects is lower. This is particularly the case if the business risk is low, and hence cash flow predictability is high, and thus a certain amount of debt is eminently sustainable. If the market value of the company is not being maximized, it might ultimately be liable to an unwanted takeover bid where the predator company injects debt into the target, thereby increasing its value by this action alone.

8.3.4 Adjusting Capital Structure

How a company invests funds determines its business risk; how it finances them determines its financial risk. A company can adjust its financial risk (gearing) by changing the proportions of debt and equity in its capital structure, as Fig. 8.3 shows.

Equity	(a) By retaining profits or paying out dividends;
	(b) By issuing new shares or buying back existing ones in issue.
Debt	By borrowing money or repaying existing debt.
Both	By converting debt into equity.

In addition to the above, which all involve real cash flows (except the conversion of debt into equity), under international accounting standards a company can change its balance sheet capital structure by revaluing fixed assets upwards. This has the effect of reducing gearing, calculated at book values, as it increases the book amount of equity (by increasing the 'revaluation reserve').

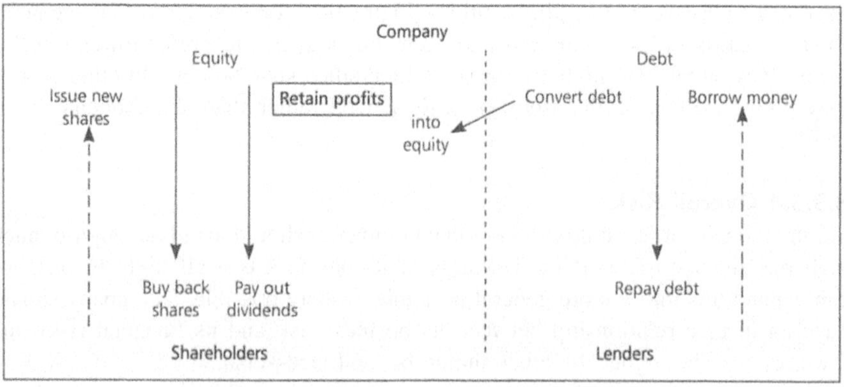

Fig. 8.3 Events that change capital structure

8.4 Dividend Policy, Share Buybacks and the Firm's Capital Structure

8.4.1 Do Dividends Matter?

Ordinary dividends are cash payments by a company to its shareholders out of after-tax profits. Do they matter to investors? As with the capital structure conundrum, it was Modigliani and Miller who suggested in the 1960s that in a 'perfect' capital market, with no taxes or transaction costs, dividend policy is irrelevant.

In reality, however, it appears that dividends do matter. For example, companies that were forced to cut their dividends during 2020 due to the COVID-19 pandemic and lockdowns were quick to reverse the trend during the following year. Australia and the UK displayed the strongest rebound, with companies from these countries achieving an underlying growth rate in dividend payouts of 97 and 59.9 per cent respectively in the third quarter of 2021. Similarly, the dividend payouts of US corporations rose in the third quarter of 2021 by 10.2 per cent on an underlying basis, to a record high of \$130.7bn. Moreover, 97 per cent of US companies in 2021 raised their dividends year-on-year or held them steady. Table 8.8 and Fig. 8.4 present the annual dividends across regions over time. Note that the percentage change in dividend payouts given in Table 8.8 (% change) is the headline growth rate, that is, the change in total gross dividends including, for instance, special dividends.

Table 8.8 Annual dividends by region (US\$ billions)[3]

Region	2017	%*	2018	%*	2019	%*	2020	%*	Q3 2020	%*	Q3 2021	%*
Emerging Markets	$105.8	19%	$127.6	20.6%	$139.7	9.5%	$127.7	-8.6%	$58.4	1.9%	$76.5	31.0%
Europe ex UK	$221.9	1%	$253.0	14.0%	$247.5	-2.2%	$168.5	-31.9%	$33.7	62.9%	$22.1	-34.4%
Japan	$70.0	8%	$79.1	13.0%	$85.1	7.6%	$80.7	-5.2%	$5.3	-11.2%	$6.7	25.9%
North America	$475.7	7%	$509.7	7.2%	$535.6	5.1%	$550.6	2.8%	$129.8	-4.2%	$143.4	10.5%
Asia Pacific ex Japan	$141.6	23%	$151.0	6.7%	$151.4	0.2%	$124.0	-18.1%	$53.5	-16.1%	$73.7	37.9%
UK	$98.4	3%	$102.7	4.4%	$108.8	6.0%	$65.2	-40.0%	$18.9	-46.2%	$35.5	88.6%
Total	$1,113.4	8%	$1,223.1	9.9%	$1,268.1	3.7%	$1,116.7	-11.9%	$299.6	-5.9%	$358.0	19.5%
Divs outside top 1,200	$141.3	8%	$155.2	9.9%	$160.9	3.7%	$141.7	-11.9%	$38.0	-5.9%	$45.4	19.5%
Grand total	$1,254.6	8%	$1,378.3	9.9%	$1,429.0	3.7%	$1,258.4	-11.9%	$337.6	-5.9%	$403.5	19.5%

* % change

Let's start with Miller and Modigliani's 1961 paper on dividend policy in which they argue that in a 'perfect' capital market dividend policy should not affect shareholders' wealth (Miller and Modigliani 1961). Dividends paid would transfer cash

---

[3] Source: Page 4 of *The Global Dividend Index Report* by Janus Henderson, dated November 2021 (Edition 32), available at: https://cdn.janushenderson.com/webdocs/Issue+32+Report+Global+%28English%29.pdf.

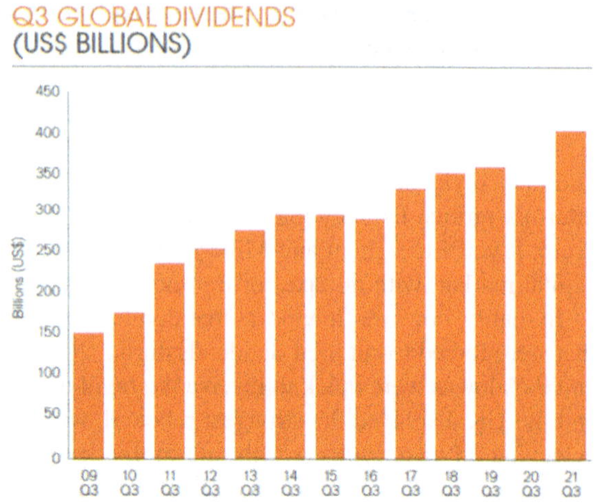

Fig. 8.4 The total amount of dividends paid globally in the 3rd quarter of each year from 2009 to 2021[4]

to shareholders, but the market value of the shares would fall to precisely reflect the dividend payment; dividend policy would not convey any information about future prospects; and any shareholders who wanted more cash than a company chose to pay in dividends could simply sell some of their shares: in effect, declaring their own dividends.

Example 8.2

To begin with, Jane Smith owned 25 per cent of the shares in two identical companies, Adam plc and Bede plc. Adam paid out all its profits each year in dividends, while Bede retained all its profits to reinvest. (Thus the companies do not remain identical; but we ignore this for the sake of the example.) Smith kept her 25 per cent shareholding in Adam, which (with no retained profits to generate growth) remained the same size. Each year Smith sold enough shares in Bede, which (by retaining all its profits) was growing larger, to provide the same amount of cash as Adam's dividends.

As Fig. 8.5 shows, after some years Bede was much larger than Adam, but Smith's reducing share in Bede was worth exactly the same (the areas shown) as her constant 25 per cent share in Adam. Since Smith had received the same amount of cash from her shareholding (either in dividends or from the sale of some shares), the companies' different dividend policies had (in theory) had exactly the same effect on Smith's wealth. (In this presumed perfect market there were no taxes or transaction costs.)◀

[4] Source: Page 5 of *The Global Dividend Index Report* by Janus Henderson, dated November 2021 (Edition 32), available at: https://cdn.janushenderson.com/webdocs/Issue+32+Report+Global+%28English%29.pdf.

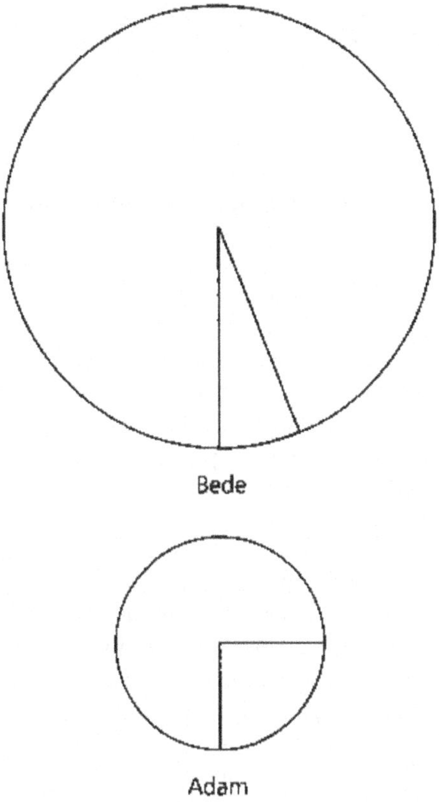

Fig. 8.5 Smith's shareholdings in Adam and Bede after some years

In the real world the tax position of different shareholders can vary, from pension funds to lower-rate or higher-rate individual taxpayers. So it can be hard for companies to tell what dividend policy might be best for 'shareholders as a whole'. Transaction costs, too, matter in practice. A company which paid out 'too much' dividend one year would find it expensive to make a rights issue (a negative dividend!) the next year to compensate—and there are brokers' fees to pay if you have to sell shares, rather than receive dividends, to get money from the company.

8.4.2 Taxes on Shareholders' Returns

A company aiming to maximize shareholders' wealth may well need to allow for the income tax that its shareholders might have to pay on dividends and the capital gains tax they might have to pay on any profit when shares are sold. It is quite possible that dividends and capital gains will attract different rates of tax both to one another and according to what level or tier of total income or capital gains the shareholder finds themselves in—and there might be different annual allowances before the tax kicks in. Moreover, there is some delay in incurring capital gains tax, since it is payable only on realized gains, not as gains accrue—and we know the timings of cash flows are important! Consequently, a company really needs to know as well as it can what the tax profiles of its shareholders (or at least its major ones) are.

8.4.3 Choosing a Dividend Policy

Although it is the company's *directors* who set the dividend policy of the firm, shareholders can have *some* say in the matter in that, at annual general meetings, they may vote to *reduce* a proposed final dividend (though they rarely do), thereby by definition increasing the amount of retained profits. But they cannot vote to *increase* dividends above those proposed by the directors, though they might *want* larger dividends to prevent managers from frittering away retained profits on unsuitable projects.

Most companies seem to decide on a dividend first, basing the current year's dividend on last year's payout. Dividends normally increase somewhat from year to year, partly to keep pace with inflation and also to reflect increased real earnings. Any profits left over (retained) are then available for investment by the company. A different approach would be first to choose how much to invest, and how to finance it, and then to treat dividends as the residual. Dividends often seem to follow a step-like pattern rather than varying in line with earnings (see Fig. 8.6, which compares dividends per share to earnings per share). Thus the absolute money amount of the dividend slightly increases each year, rather than the payout being a constant proportion of earnings.

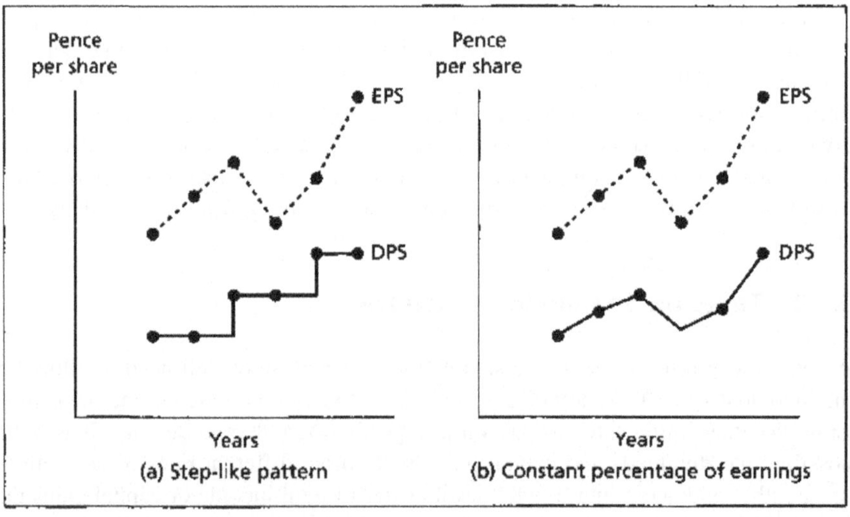

Fig. 8.6 Two patterns of dividend payout

Retained earnings for a period will be negative where there are losses or where dividends exceed profits. But companies need to have cumulative retained profits in order legally to distribute dividends to shareholders—they cannot pay out dividends that will lead to negative retained earnings.

If retained earnings represent a volatile source of funds, companies could vary their investment spending. Or they could finance all worthwhile projects by borrowing or issuing more equity capital. Most companies are reluctant either to increase gearing or to issue more equity shares. They may therefore prefer to restrict regular dividends to a level where they can expect to finance all worthwhile investment projects out of retained earnings (plus a pro rata increase in borrowing to maintain the gearing ratio). They might cover varying investment needs by surplus cash or by *short-term* changes in gearing.

Paying dividends reduces shareholders' funds, and hence increases gearing. Indeed, loan covenants may restrict maximum dividends payable in order not to let gearing increase too much. In principle a company which lacks cash could borrow to finance dividends, which would increase gearing even more (as debt replaced equity).

One can value shares on the basis of future dividends (Chapter 7), but in the end it is earnings that matter. Many companies *try* to keep their dividend payout ratio (or its reciprocal, the dividend cover) fairly constant. Dividends per share will then grow at much the same rate as earnings. (Indeed the so-called dividend growth model makes precisely this assumption.) If profits fluctuate from year to year, companies may have a dividend payout ratio target as an average over several years.

A loss-making company might choose not to omit or even reduce its dividend in a bad year. For managements can use dividend policy to communicate with shareholders about future prospects. This idea is often referred to as the 'signalling theory of dividends' and is based on the idea that managers normally know more than shareholders about their company's future prospects (this is called 'information asymmetry'). A loss-making company might maintain its dividend as a signal that earnings would soon recover. In contrast, cutting the dividend could signify that a decline in earnings might take some time to reverse. For a similar reason, managers may not want to increase dividends too much in a good year if that risks having to reduce dividends again later.

A company should tell shareholders clearly what its dividend policy actually is (and why) and stick to it. Any policy may suit some shareholders better than others from the point of view of tax. But shareholders can satisfy their own requirements in this respect by investing in companies that follow their preferences between generating dividends or capital gains. Changing the dividend policy without warning might both disappoint shareholders who relied on the old policy and create needless uncertainty about the future.

In deciding on dividend policy, directors should focus on the most important question: who can use the money best, company or shareholders? Thus 'mature' companies with few investment opportunities may tend to pay out a high proportion of their after-tax profits in dividends; while 'growth' companies with many good projects to invest in may prefer a much lower payout ratio.

8.4.4 Share Buybacks

Like dividend payments, share buybacks/repurchases have the effect of reducing equity and increasing gearing. They also, of course, reduce the size of the company. Possible reasons for a company buying back its own shares include the following:

1. Buying out the estates of deceased shareholders.
2. Buying back employee scheme shares when the employee leaves.
3. Buying out dissident shareholders.
4. Offering investors an option to sell their shares back after a time.
5. Reducing capital, possibly to increase financial gearing.
6. Supporting the market for the shares (keeping the share price high).
7. Returning to shareholders, funds which the company cannot use profitably.
8. Converting public companies back into private ones.

Only the last four reasons would be likely to apply to public companies. For private companies, the purchase price will normally be subject to capital gains tax in shareholders' hands, rather than income tax.

The exact treatment of bought-back shares varies from country to country. Sometimes the shares are simply cancelled and no longer exist. Sometimes they continue in existence in the company's 'ownership', but do not have voting rights, do not receive dividends and do not count towards the number of shares in issue when calculating the earnings per share.

'Special' dividends (often so-called in order to dissuade shareholders from expecting equally high levels of dividend in the future!) are one-off much higher than usual dividend payments, somewhat similar to share buybacks in many of their effects; but the tax consequences are different.

8.5 Capital Structure and the Corporate Life Cycle

This section explores the relationship between business risk and financial risk (use of debt) over a firm's life cycle. It also discusses changes in debt policy (capital structure) and in dividend policy over time. The approach is adapted from Ruth Bender, *Corporate Financial Strategy* (4th Edition, Routledge, 2014).

8.5.1 Start-up

Most business start-ups involve high risk. There may be difficult technical problems to overcome. Even if the product 'works', can the firm make it for a low enough cost? And will enough customers want to buy it? Such high business risks suggest that it would be a mistake to pile much (if any) financial risk on top. Indeed, most start-ups should probably finance themselves entirely with equity capital and have no interest-bearing debt at all. Remember, interest ***must*** be paid, but dividends are at the discretion of the directors.

In any event debt might be expensive because it would carry a high risk premium. Most new businesses make no taxable profit in the first year or two, implying they would have to pay any debt interest—with no tax shield—gross of tax (giving them a higher Weighted Average Cost of Capital). And since a start-up business probably has few tangible assets with much resale value if anything goes wrong, the costs of financial distress could be very high. Moreover, the high risk of complete failure means that a start-up business is quite likely to generate no net cash inflow from trading. In which case any debt at all, however little, could almost at once lead to severe financial distress.

Investors should not mind whether their returns come by way of dividends or capital gains. So it normally makes sense for a start-up business to pay no dividends in the first few years. (New companies may anyway often lack the post-tax profits legally needed to permit the payment of dividends.) Such a firm will probably have negative cash flows to begin with. Given a policy of zero borrowing, it might actually need to raise more equity capital to replace any cash dividends it did pay. And since transaction costs are mostly fixed, raising small amounts of equity capital is very expensive.

8.5.2 Growth

If a start-up business gets over the first hurdle and survives, the business risk will decline. But a successful new business will often be growing fast and be thirsty for cash. It will probably still be best to keep debt low, and to proceed to raise new equity capital in one of three ways: retention of most or all of the profits; a rights issue to existing shareholders; or a launch of the business to the public. The third method will also enable the founding venture capitalists to realize some or all of their investment.

Heavy discretionary investment in technical research and in promoting the new product may restrict profits at this stage. In any event, tax relief on investment in fixed assets (perhaps needed to expand production) may keep taxable profits very low or negative. Assuming that substantial business risks still remain, and possibly still lacking a tax shield on any debt interest, borrowing at this stage may continue to be expensive. But the costs of potential financial distress should be declining from their previous very high levels, as the business starts to acquire tangible fixed assets with some definite resale value.

Needing to finance rapid growth, the most obvious source of funds is internally generated cash. This implies that dividends should still be zero. But if the company is thinking of going public in the near future, it may wish to start paying a nominal dividend to build up a track record.

8.5.3 Maturity

Once the company reaches maturity, with the rapid growth period over, profits should become fairly steady. Dividends can now increase and represent a sizeable proportion of profits. Although the firm may need to replace existing fixed assets, in the absence of rapid inflation it should be able to do so mainly out of provisions for depreciation.

With the company now well established, business risk should be fairly low, enabling it to substitute debt for equity. This may even mean borrowing to increase dividend payments—in order to adjust the capital structure more quickly. (If there were no real growth, in principle the firm should be able to pay out all real profits in dividends.)

The potential conflict between managers and shareholders will be apparent. High dividends and fairly high debt ratios at this stage may help to maximize shareholders' wealth. But managers may be tempted to retain too much profit and use some of the funds to diversify in order to reduce their own personal risk from the company failing. But shareholders would probably prefer to achieve diversification for themselves by holding a portfolio of different shares. It is not easy in practice for shareholders to put pressure on managers to increase the level of dividend payout (or indeed the debt ratio).

8.5.4 Decline

It is unlikely that a company will actually plan its own decline, let alone demise, but, as mentioned above, it is possible that the shareholders will have dissuaded the managers away from the diversification of the business, and thus perhaps towards an approach of managed decline. In this declining phase, managers should prolong the company's life for as long as it can generate positive cash flows that exceed a reasonable rate of return on the net realizable value of the assets. *Whether or not* to replace fixed assets now becomes a genuine question, whereas earlier the main question may have been *when* to replace them (and with what modifications).

Internal cash flows will probably exceed reported profits, since depreciation expense may well exceed new investment in replacement fixed assets. (Thus the net book value of fixed assets will be falling.) Dividends paid may even exceed reported profits, thus running down the cumulative balance of profit retained in earlier years. (An offsetting influence may be the unwinding of deferred tax provisions from earlier years. These may have reduced reported profits in earlier years, but only now result in cash outflows.)

Levels of debt, too, should be high at this stage, since lenders may be able to assess accurately the realizable value of any assets against which they are lending. The main strategic problem towards the end of the company's life may be not with shareholders or lenders, but with the managers themselves. For managers are often reluctant to announce simply, 'Our work is done', and then retire gracefully!

8.6 Overview of Selected Empirical Evidence on the Financing Decision

Some readers might be interested in what the empirical evidence shows as to how companies go about making the financing decision. What follows in this section is more complex than the general tenor of the book, and those wishing to gain a more general overview of finance may wish to skip it, and can do so without interfering with their overall understanding of the subject.

Empirical research relating to the financing decision is vast and can be organized under the key theories, as we do now. Yet despite that vast empirical evidence of which we cover here only a tiny amount, most researchers agree that there are still many unresolved questions relating to this decision. For example, why do some firms issue equity while others use debt? Why do firms change their financing policies when they fear a financial crisis is looming? Why do firms often prefer to accumulate cash instead of distributing dividends, thereby avoiding the need to issue external finance?

8.6.1 Pecking Order Hypothesis

Agliardi et al. (2016) investigate those questions. They start by reporting that cash holdings of U.S. corporations increased greatly after the 2008 global financial crisis, growing at an annual rate of 11 per cent until 2014. The explanation offered is that in the face of great economic uncertainty, firms prefer to pile up cash as a cushion, thereby avoiding going to the market for additional debt or equity. This explanation is in line with the pecking order hypothesis of Myers and Majluf (1984) which suggests that firms prefer to finance their activities with internal funds (retained earnings). If external funds are needed, then debt is preferred to issuing new shares (external equity).

Note that the idea underlying this hypothesis is the existence of asymmetric information. That is, when one party to a transaction has more information about the quality of the underlying asset or service to be transacted than the other party. This can lead the less informed party to make adverse selection. For example, a firm will issue new shares when managers who are more informed about the true value of the shares know that the shares are currently overvalued by the market.

Potential investors who are less informed about the value of the firm than managers may buy the shares at an unreasonably high price, thereby making an adverse selection which is due to asymmetric information vis-à-vis the firm's managers.

Investors are aware of these problems and to avoid making adverse selection, mark down the share price as soon as the firm announces a new issue.

Asymmetric information and the adverse selection problem lead firms to prefer the source of finance which carries the smallest adverse selection cost. External equity is the least preferred means to raise capital because from the point of view of external investors the true value of the firm's shares is harder to estimate than its debt. Thus, debt dominates over external equity because it is less prone to mispricing, although it also has information problems, particularly when the risk of default is high. Internal finance (retained earnings) is the preferred source of finance because it is not susceptible to asymmetric information, adverse selection, and hence, mispricing.

The idea in Agliardi et al. (2016) is that periods of great uncertainty make these problems more severe, leading firms to hoard cash to avoid having to raise external finance. In line with this explanation, Chang et al. (2019) show that equity issuance increases during periods of economic recovery. They also show that relative to other firms, this effect is more significant for financially constrained firms. This is consistent with the notion that information asymmetries and adverse selection matter more for equity issuance by financially constrained firms which tend to be small, young, and high growth, with plenty of investment opportunities, but which are highly risky and difficult to value.

Moreover, according to Chang et al. (2019) macroeconomic conditions also have an impact on the choice of the maturity of debt raised. For example, financially constrained firms lengthen debt maturity when the economy peaks, and inflation increases, presumably to reduce refinancing risk should the economy go into recession.

Not all studies support the pecking order hypothesis. For example, according to this hypothesis, equity issuance should be infrequent. This is inconsistent with the findings of Huang and Ritter (2005), who report that equity issues are frequent in the case of publicly traded US firms. Similarly, Li and Mauer (2016) study how firms make financial decisions when investment opportunities arrive randomly and may disappear quickly because of competition or technological obsolescence. This issue is particularly true in high technology industries, or in industries with fierce competition. Because they arrive randomly, the firm may face an investment opportunity when it is short on cash. This makes the possibility of financing the investment opportunity with debt less appealing because the shortage of cash means that debt servicing will be more difficult. The problem is that the firm may be unable to wait for its cash flow state to improve due to fear of missing out on the investment opportunity. Consequently, Li and Mauer (2016) find that randomly arriving and short-lived investment opportunities are more likely to be financed with equity than with debt, a result which is inconsistent with the pecking order hypothesis.

8.6.2 Trade-Off Theory

A competing theory which seeks to explain the financing decision, is the trade-off theory. The idea is that the optimal capital structure is found by balancing the advantages and costs of using debt. The advantage of using debt is that it provides an interest tax shield. That is, debt is beneficial because, unlike dividends paid to equity holders, interest paid to lenders is tax deductible, thereby reducing the firm's tax liability.

The disadvantage of using debt is that it exposes the firm to financial distress and agency costs. The costs of financial distress include those related to bankruptcy, but also pre-bankruptcy costs such as staff seeking other employment, suppliers hardening the payment terms, customers leaving, etc. Agency costs refer to costs associated with the principal-agent relationship, where the agent is given authority to make decisions on behalf of the principal. Conflicts of interest between the two parties may give rise to agency costs. In the context of a corporation, agency costs arise due to conflicts of interest between shareholders who own the firm (the principals), and managers, who are the agents that manage the firm on behalf of the owners. Jensen and Meckling (1976) define three types of agency costs, namely monitoring, bonding and residual. Monitoring costs are costs related to monitoring the agent to mitigate agency behaviour. Bonding costs are those related to the establishment of trust and alignment of interests between the principal and the agent (e.g. bonus payments on good performance). Finally, the remaining costs that arise from agency behaviour that are not controlled by monitoring or bonding are referred to as residual costs.

Thus, the trade-off theory asserts that the financing decision is determined by balancing the marginal benefits of debt (interest tax shield) with costs related to financial distress, bankruptcy, or agency behaviour. Shyam-Sunder and Myers (1999) show that in line with the trade-off theory, a firm that aims to maximize its value would choose the proportion of debt it uses so as to position itself at the top of the curve in Fig. 8.7, where the market value of the firm is maximized. The firm would do so by equating the marginal present values of interest tax shields against the marginal costs of using debt.

The trade-off theory implies that there is an optimal debt ratio (mix of debt and equity) which firms seek and target. The dynamic version of the trade-off theory suggests that firms may make financial decisions that take them away from this target, but that they revert to it over long periods of adjustment.

Mahajan and Tartaroglu (2008) find that firms in G-7 countries fully rebalance their capital structure after equity issuance, suggesting that these firms behave in line with a dynamic version of the trade-off theory. In contrast, evidence reported by Shyam-Sunder and Myers (1999) does not support the idea that publicly traded, mature firms have optimal debt ratios. However, more recent evidence by Mc Namara et al. (2017) show that the debt level of privately held European small and medium-sized enterprises (SMEs) is higher in countries with a more efficient debt recovery environment. In other words, in countries where bankruptcy costs are lower due to higher recovery rates, firms tend to have higher debt ratios. These

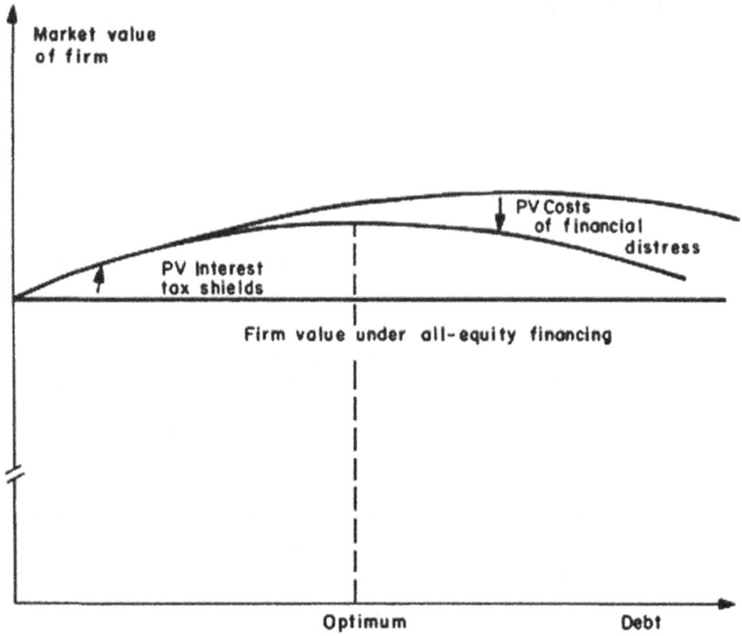

Fig. 8.7 The trade-off theory of optimal capital structure[5]

results are supportive of the trade-off theory. Ayyagari et al. (2021) arrive at similar conclusions from their study of the financing decisions of firms in emerging markets which are made following periods of economic downturns. Particularly, the authors find that low-risk firms tend to take on debt, presumably because of the low probability that they will enter a state of financial distress. In contrast, firms more likely to be short on cash following an economic shock have less debt, possibly because of the need to service it.

Other research also finds support for the trade-off theory and for the existence of an optimal debt ratio. This includes strong evidence of industry differences in debt ratios, suggesting that there is an optimal debt ratio that is common to firms in the same industry due to a similar structure of debt-related benefits and costs. For example, industries with high intangible assets (e.g., due to high research and development expenditures), are exposed to higher distress costs. These may result from the difficulty of using such assets as collateral and selling them in the case of distress. Moreover, intangible assets are exposed to higher distress costs because accounting rules often do not allow the recognition of such assets on the balance sheet, resulting in high valuation uncertainty. Consequently, firms in industries that are characterized by high intangible assets (e.g., in the knowledge economy)

[5] Source: Shyam-Sunder and Myers (1999).

tend to use less debt. Lim et al. (2020) show that the inverse relationship between intangible assets and debt ratio applies to certain intangible assets but not to all.

Likewise, firms in industries that facilitate the utilization of the interest tax shield (e.g. utilities) tend to issue more debt. In addition, some research finds that firms expand their use of debt following regulatory changes which increase the value of the interest tax shield. For example, Faccio and Xu (2015) use nearly 500 shifts in statutory corporate and personal income tax rates to show that firms increase their debt levels following an increase in corporate taxes (when the interest tax shield is more valuable). Moreover, firms increase their debt levels following a rise in personal taxes on dividend income, while they reduce their debt levels following a rise in personal taxes on interest income. These results are consistent with the trade-off theory.

8.6.3 Market Timing Hypothesis

Baker and Wurgler (2002) propose another theory to explain the corporate financing decision and the resultant mix of debt and equity (capital structure) on firms' balance sheets. The authors note that in their financing decisions, managers attempt to 'time' the equity market. They are more likely to issue equity when the firm's market value is high relative to past value, in order to take advantage of an 'overvalued' stock price. Similarly, firms tend to repurchase equity when the firm's market value is low, in order to take advantage of an undervalued stock price. This is because a share repurchase is the opposite of issuance, in that cash is exchanged for existing shares instead of new shares exchanged for cash. Consequently, the relative amount of debt and equity in the firm's capital structure is related to its historical market values. This is the market timing hypothesis of Baker and Wurgler (2002) which suggests that capital structure is the cumulative outcome of past financing decisions that aim to time the equity market.

Support for the market timing hypothesis comes from research which finds that raising equity coincides with high market valuations and that equity issues are followed by low returns. Huang and Ritter (2005) find that past security issues have a long-lasting effect on the firm's mix of debt and equity (capital structure) in the case of publicly traded US firms. Graham and Harvey (2001) report survey evidence which suggests that managers try to time the equity market.

There is, however, some evidence contradicting the predictions of the market timing hypothesis. For example, Dittmar and Dittmar (2008) find a positive correlation between repurchases and equity issues. This is inconsistent with the market timing hypothesis which suggests a negative correlation between share repurchases and equity issues, because the former tend to occur when firms are undervalued, while the latter tend to occur when firms are overvalued.

8.6.4 Other Explanations for the Financing Decision

Although empirical research on financing decisions is based primarily on pecking order, trade-off, and market timing theories, there are also some exceptions. For example, Keasey et al. (2015) use owners' willingness to dilute control to explain the financing decision. Using a European sample of listed firms for the period 2000–2009, the authors find that recently-formed family firms are less willing to dilute control by issuing equity, and therefore tend to rely more on debt.

Another example is the study by Datta et al. (2021) which investigates the impact of gender on the corporate financing decision. The authors find that women executives choose a significantly shorter debt maturity structure compared to their male counterparts. The authors also find that firms led by women benefit from higher corporate credit ratings which indicates that the arguably greater ethical approach of women executives compensates for the refinancing risk commonly associated with shorter-term debt.

Agrawal and Matsa (2013) relate the financing decision to the labour market. The authors show that firms choose conservative financial policies (that is, choose to use less debt which is considered riskier than equity from the firm's point of view) in order to mitigate worker exposure to unemployment risk. By so doing, firms decrease the risk of financial distress and costly layoffs. This, in turn, is likely to reduce the amount of compensation that workers require to offset unemployment risk. Agrawal and Matsa (2013) note that such considerations are particularly relevant for the financing decisions of firms in industries that tend to experience frequent layoffs and job losses. Moreover, in states where unemployment benefits are high, layoffs are less costly to workers thereby reducing their demands to be compensated by their employers for unemployment risk. Consequently, in states with high unemployment benefits, firms tend to use more debt which provides benefits to the firm such as the interest tax shield. Thus, one could think of the labour market explanation offered by Agrawal and Matsa (2013) for the corporate financing decision, as an extension of the trade-off theory.

8.7 A Concluding Note

This chapter discussed the capital structure and dividend policy decisions and how they impact each other. Additionally, we reviewed share buybacks which, like dividends, also have the impact of increasing the firm's debt ratio. We saw how the firm's capital structure might change as it matures, and provided some empirical evidence to link various capital structure explanations with what firms do in practice.

As we have stressed at the beginning of this chapter, the capital structure decision aims to find the optimal mix of debt and equity that minimizes the overall cost of capital to the firm. Minimizing the cost of capital is akin to maximizing the value of the firm, as we discuss in the next chapter.

8.7.1 Problems

Problem 8.1 Laurel plc and Hardy plc are similar companies except for their financial gearing. Each company's capital employed (debt plus equity) is £120 million and each pays out all profit after tax (PAT) in each year as dividends to shareholders. Laurel's debt ratio (debt/capital employed) is 15 per cent, Hardy's 60 per cent. The rate of debt interest is 10 per cent a year (before tax). The rate of corporate tax is 30 per cent. In Year 1, the Return on Capital Employed (EBIT divided by (debt plus equity)) for each company is 25 per cent; in Year 2 it is only 7.5 per cent.

a. Calculate the after-tax Return on Equity (PAT divided by equity) and the interest cover (EBIT divided by interest payable) for Laurel and Hardy for Year 1 and Year 2.
b. At what level of Return on Capital Employed will the Return on Equity for the two companies be the same?

Problem 8.2 Borg Inc and McEnroe Inc, two companies in the same industry, are of similar size but have different levels of gearing. In Year 1 each company made an operating profit of $90 million, increasing by 50% in Year 2. Each company has capital employed of $1000 million (with 1500 million ordinary shares in issue) and both pay out all profits after tax as dividends to equity holders. Borg has a debt ratio of 5 per cent, McEnroe of 20 per cent. In each case the rate of debt interest is 15 per cent a year. Assume a corporate tax rate of 40 per cent.
For each company in each year, calculate: (i) after-tax Return on Equity; (ii) earnings per share; and (iii) interest cover.

Problem 8.3 Travis Gmbh has an operating profit of €150 million. Currently debt interest payable is €20 million a year, the corporate tax rate stands at 40 per cent and there are 600 million ordinary shares in issue. Travis is planning to raise an extra €300 million of capital to finance expansion, which is expected to increase operating profit by €50 million a year. Two alternatives are being considered:

1. Issue 120 million new ordinary shares at €2.50 each (compared with the current market price of €3.00); or
2. Borrow €300 million @12 per cent a year interest

a. For each alternative calculate: (i) earnings per share; and (ii) interest cover.
b. At what level of current operating profit would earnings per share be the same under the alternative financing proposals?

Problem 8.4 Andover Equipment plc needs to raise £30 million of new capital to finance a major expansion which is expected to increase operating profit by £6.0 million a year. The company currently has 200 million ordinary shares in issue, and the current market price is 180p each. The balance sheet shows total debt of £90 million (with an average interest rate of 10 per cent a year) and shareholders' funds of £180 million. Andover is considering two alternative ways to raise the new money. One is a 1 for 10 rights issue at 150p. The other is to borrow £30 million at 8 per cent a year for 10 years (Ignore transaction costs.) Annual operating profit (EBIT) is currently £54 million. Assume a tax rate of 30 per cent on profits.

a. Calculate and compare the following ratios before expansion and after expansion under each of the financing alternatives:
   i. Earnings Per Share (EPS)
   ii. Interest cover
   iii. Debt ratio. i.e., Debt to (Debt plus Equity), using the market value of equity and the book value of debt (assuming the book value of debt is similar to its market value).
b. Calculate the level of earnings before interest and tax (EBIT) at which EPS under the two financing alternatives will be the same.

Problem 8.5 (Challenging!) In a perfect capital market, without taxes or transaction costs, lives a person who holds 1 per cent of the shares of company X which earns £1 million in profit before interest every year. Company X is financed with equity, currently trading at £8 million and debt, currently trading at its par value of £8 million. The debt bears an annual coupon rate of 5 per cent, and the company's dividend policy is to pay out all earnings after interest, as dividends. The weighted average cost of capital (WACC) of company X is 6.25 per cent.

a. The company is considering raising £8 million in new shares and using the proceeds to pay off the debt.
   i. Show that the WACC of the company remains the same when it becomes an all-equity firm.
   ii. Show how the investor can maintain the same stream of income and percentage of holdings in the firm's equity as they had before the change in the capital structure, by taking a personal loan at 5%. The investor wishes to keep the same level of risk (operational and financial) to which they are currently exposed.
b. Company X which is now an all-equity firm, is considering investing next year in a new project of the same risk profile as its existing projects. The idea is to retain next year's profits of £1 million, and instead of paying it out as dividends, to invest in equipment that costs £1 million. The project is expected to generate an annual net cash flow of £70,000 a year forever, starting in two years' time (end of year 2), at which time the firm will return to its 100 per cent dividend payout policy.
   i. Should the firm go ahead with the project?
   ii. Calculate the impact of the project on the value of the firm
   iii. Assuming the firm undertakes the project, what would be its annual dividends starting in year 2?

iv. Show how the investor can maintain the same level of net disposable funds next year as they have had in the past by selling some of their holdings. How much dividend will they be receiving from year 2 onwards? What will be their annual income, net of the interest on their personal loan?

References

Agliardi, E., Agliardi, R., & Spanjers, W. (2016). Corporate financing decisions under ambiguity: Pecking order and liquidity policy implications. *Journal of Business Research, 69*(12), 6012–6020.

Agrawal, A. K., & Matsa, D. A. (2013). Labor unemployment risk and corporate financing decisions. *Journal of Financial Economics, 108*(2), 449–470.

Ayyagari, M., Demirgüç-Kunt, A., & Maksimovic, V. (2021). How common are credit-less recoveries? Firm-level evidence on the role of financial markets in crisis recovery. *Journal of Corporate Finance, 69*, 102016.

Baker, M., & Wurgler, J. (2002). Market timing and capital structure. *The Journal of Finance, 57*(1), 1–32.

Chang, X., Chen, Y., & Dasgupta, S. (2019). Macroeconomic conditions, financial constraints, and firms' financing decisions. *Journal of Banking & Finance, 101*, 242–255.

Datta, S., Doan, T., & Toscano, F. (2021). Top executive gender, board gender diversity, and financing decisions: Evidence from debt structure choice. *Journal of Banking & Finance, 125*, 106070.

Dittmar, A. K., & Dittmar, R. F. (2008). The timing of financing decisions: An examination of the correlation in financing waves. *Journal of Financial Economics, 90*(1), 59–83.

Faccio, M., & Xu, J. (2015). Taxes and capital structure. *Journal of financial and Quantitative analysis, 50*(3), 277–300.

Graham, J. R., & Harvey, C. R. (2001). The theory and practice of corporate finance: Evidence from the field. *Journal of Financial Economics, 60*(2–3), 187–243.

Huang, R., & Ritter, J. R. (2005). Testing the market timing theory of capital structure. *Journal of Financial and Quantitative Analysis, 1*(2), 221–246.

Jensen, M. C., & Meckling, W. H. (1976). Theory of the firm: Managerial behavior, agency costs and ownership structure. *Journal of Financial Economics, 3*(4), 305–360.

Keasey, K., Martinez, B., & Pindado, J. (2015). Young family firms: Financing decisions and the willingness to dilute control. *Journal of Corporate Finance, 34*, 47–63.

Li, J. Y., & Mauer, D. C. (2016). Financing uncertain growth. *Journal of Corporate Finance, 41*, 241–261.

Lim, S. C., Macias, A. J., & Moeller, T. (2020). Intangible assets and capital structure. *Journal of Banking & Finance, 118*, 105873.

Mahajan, A., & Tartaroglu, S. (2008). Equity market timing and capital structure: International evidence. *Journal of Banking & Finance, 32*(5), 754–766.

Mc Namara, A., Murro, P., & O'Donohoe, S. (2017). Countries lending infrastructure and capital structure determination: The case of European SMEs. *Journal of Corporate Finance, 43*, 122–138.

Miller, M. H., & Modigliani, F. (1961). Dividend policy, growth, and the valuation of shares, *The Journal of Business, 34*(4), 411–433.

Myers, S. C., & Majluf, N. S. (1984). When firms have information that investors do not have. *Journal of Financial Economics, 13*, 187–221.

Shyam-Sunder, L., & Myers, S. C. (1999). Testing static tradeoff against pecking order models of capital structure. *Journal of Financial Economics, 51*(2), 219–244.

Valuing Companies 9

9.1 Introduction

There are a number of reasons why one might want to value a company. Obviously, it is important if a company is potentially being sold, that both the seller and the buyer have some (probably different!) idea of its value. Other situations might include the issuing of new shares to a new or even existing group of investors, valuation for tax purposes on a death or divorce, and so on.

Valuing a company is a complex exercise and definitely more of an art than a science. Ultimately a company is worth what someone is prepared to pay for it, but the buyer must have some basis for this calculation. This chapter gives an introduction to the valuation techniques that are frequently used (Sect. 9.2). Each is likely to yield a different result, such that a view must be taken as to the most accurate figure.

In Chapter 7 we looked at the valuation of shares (in the context of the Dividend Growth Model) when one is buying a non-controlling and non-influencing interest in a company (in other words, a fairly small percentage of the shares). This chapter will concentrate on valuing whole companies, then go on to look at aspects of acquisitions and mergers (Sect. 9.3). Concluding comments are offered in Sect. 9.4, followed by some practice problems.

9.2 The Three Main Techniques of Valuation

There are three main techniques for valuing companies, and we shall look at each in turn.

R. Manos et al., *Corporate Finance for Business*,
https://doi.org/10.1007/978-3-030-92419-5_9

9.2.1 Assets Basis

Looking at the net realizable value of the assets of the company, less the sum of its current and non-current liabilities, is going to give us the *minimum* value of its equity. After all, the current management could realize that amount by simply breaking up the company themselves. But at least this gives us a starting point. Considerable care has to be taken in arriving at this figure, though. Taking the figures from the latest Balance Sheet is unlikely to be sufficiently accurate—things will have moved on since the Balance Sheet date, non-current asset values are not necessarily accurately reflective of what those assets could be sold for right now, perhaps further provisions are needed against slow-moving inventories or doubtful receivables, and so on. Ideally the valuer/purchaser would want plenty of access to company information and the actual assets to verify what their true values are.

9.2.2 Price/Earnings Multiples

9.2.2.1 Definitions

Put simply, a price/earnings multiple (or P/E ratio) is the market price of an ordinary share divided by the earnings per share. In aggregate, this amounts to the market capitalization of the equity divided by the annual profit (=earnings) available for ordinary shareholders.

Thus:

$$\text{P/E ratio} = \text{Share Price/Earnings per Share}$$

Or, multiplying both the share price and the earnings per share by the number of shares,

$$\text{P/E ratio} = \text{Market Capitalisation/Earnings}$$

For listed companies, the market price per share is the current market price. Thus, the price/earnings ratio fluctuates from day to day. The 'earnings' for last year are fixed, but the market price changes. In the UK *last year's* earnings are used for the 'earnings per share'. (US analysts often use an estimate of current year ['prospective'] earnings.)

If one uses the bottom-line earnings figure, including some items which will not recur, the earnings figure—hence the price/earnings ratio too—can fluctuate quite sharply. One might prefer to use a 'normalized' earnings figure, which was more stable, based on earnings before exceptional items; but this does require subjective judgement.

9.2.2.2 Using Price/Earnings Multiples

With listed companies, we have a market price, so we already know their value. But if another company makes a bid for a listed company, we can calculate what P/E ratio that represents by simply dividing the sum bid by either the most recent, or the prospective, earnings. This can then be compared to the P/E ratios of similar quoted companies to get some idea as to whether the bidder has over-paid or perhaps got a bargain.

With unlisted companies, however, by definition we don't have a market price in the same way. (There may be records of recent share deals to indicate what recent market prices have been; but there may not.) We will, however, have an earnings figure. So it may be tempting to try to estimate the market value of the company by applying to the earnings figure an 'appropriate' price/earnings multiple, thus:

$$\text{Market value} = \text{P/E} \times \text{earnings}$$

But whose P/E do we base the valuation on? As a start, we might try to find a listed company in the same industry, and preferably with similar growth prospects. We might then note the listed company's price/earnings multiple, then reduce it somewhat, to allow for the 'extra risk' in the unlisted company; and use that as a rough guide to the possible value per share in the unlisted company.

For instance, suppose Lower is a listed company and Upper is an unlisted one. Lower's shares are quoted at 150¢, and last year's earnings per share was 10.0¢. So Lower's price/earnings ratio, on the usual basis, is 15.0. Let us suppose Upper has slightly worse growth prospects than Lower; so that if everything else was the same, we might look for a price/earnings multiple for Upper of around 13 (rather than Lower's 15).

But since Upper is unquoted, we might feel that this adds a good deal to its riskiness (from an ordinary shareholder's point of view). So we might want to downgrade the provisional price/earnings ratio of 13 even further, say to 11, to allow for this. Now suppose that Upper's earnings last year were \$5m. Then we might reckon that a value of about \$55m [\$5m × 11] for Upper would be about right.

It should be apparent how many rather crude assumptions we have had to make to get this far. But it is already clear that price/earnings ratios are hardly very scientific, in that if a company made a loss last year (but still, of course, has a positive share price), its price/earnings ratio will be *negative!*

9.2.3 Discounting Future Cash Flows

9.2.3.1 The Cash Flows

Certainly, the most sophisticated method of valuing a company is to use exactly the same techniques that one uses to value a capital project (see Chapters 2 and 3). That means estimating the amount and timing of the cash flows, and then discounting at a suitable discount rate.

The 'cash flows' will be the operating cash flows, together with tax effects, as well as any investments in (or disposals of) working capital or fixed assets. It is normally best, as with other capital projects, to *exclude* financing charges, such as interest payments.

Note that if we value a company as a whole (that is, debt capital plus equity capital), which will normally be the case with DCF valuation techniques, then in order to get to the value of the ***equity*** alone, which is usually what we want, we shall need to deduct the value of the company's debt (see Chapter 5) to arrive at this.

9.2.3.2 The Discount Rate

Suppose Company A is trying to value Company B with a view to acquiring it. People sometimes ask: should Company A discount Company B's expected future cash flows (a) at Company A's own cost of capital, or (b) should it use Company B's cost of capital? The answer is: to value Company B you should use Company B's cost of capital. The discount rate to use in valuing a business is a rate which reflects the risks of *that* business, not the risks of the company making the acquisition. What matters is the riskiness of the *use* of funds, not of their source. (If we are valuing the whole of the business to be acquired, in CAPM terms that means using the WACC, *not* the cost of equity capital alone.)

Unless the company to be acquired is a public quoted company, and thus has easily-available beta calculations, calculating its cost of equity can be difficult. The easiest way, using the CAPM approach, is to add a suitable risk premium to the risk-free rate of return. The risk premium should reflect the estimated riskiness of Company B, let us say with a beta of 1.25. Figure 9.1 shows this, resulting in a real discount rate of 12 per cent.

There is an alternative way, which comes to the same thing in the end, for Company A to value Company B. That is for Company A to *start* from its own WACC (cost of capital), and then make a 'risk-adjustment' to allow for the (possible) difference in riskiness of the asset it is planning to acquire (and therefore needing to value). Figure 9.2 illustrates.

9.2.3.3 Terminal Values

Horizon Period

How many years' cash flows should we consider in valuing a company (F)? If we want to assume that F has an infinite life, the obvious answer is to make the valuation in two stages: (1) look at a number of years (perhaps ten) in some detail; and then (2) try to assess its value at that point (called the "terminal value"), then discount it back to its present value. For evaluating the terminal value, we can use any one of the same three methods as we can use for valuing the whole company: the assets basis, a P/E ratio and DCF.

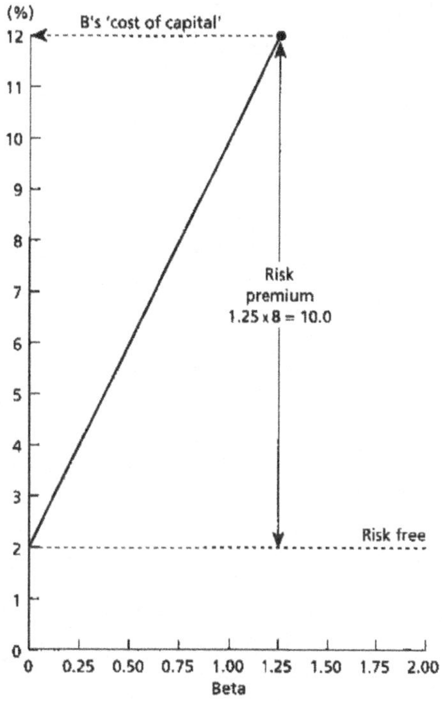

Fig. 9.1 B's cost of capital: risk-free rate plus a suitable risk premium for Company B

Valuation Methods

The assets basis would simply try to estimate the value of the net assets of the business at the end of the period of detailed calculation—this would obviously be a minimum value of the business and hence give a conservative estimate of the acquired company as a whole.

The P/E ratio method would look at the net earnings of the final year of the detailed calculations and apply an appropriate P/E ratio to those earnings to work out the terminal value. As we have already seen, the choice of *what* P/E ratio to use can be problematic—but we also know that, at best, valuation techniques can only give us a ballpark figure, so an approximate P/E will usually suffice.

DCF techniques will revolve around annuities or perpetuities. We might, for example, assume that beyond Year 10 F's cash flows amount to a 'perpetuity'—that is, the cash flows achieved in year 10 continue indefinitely in real terms into the future (having checked, of course, that there was nothing 'unusual' about the cash flows of year 10). We saw how to value perpetuities in Chapter 2.

If we expect a constant level of growth beyond year 10, we could use the growing perpetuities formula from Chapter 7.

$$terminal\ value = \frac{cash\ flow_{11}}{k_e - g}$$

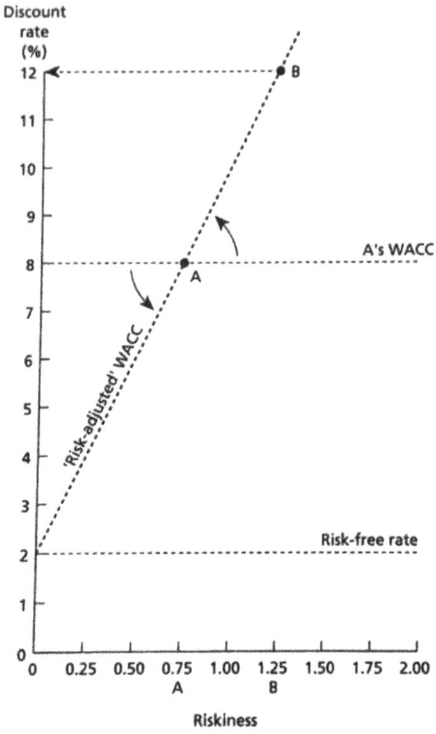

Fig. 9.2 B's cost of capital: risk-adjustment to A's cost of capital

Note that the formula still works if growth is negative (the denominator will be k_e plus the rate of decline), which could be a useful way of allowing for an expected gradual *decline* in earnings after year 10.

If we were *not* to assume that Company F will last for ever, we will use annuities (see Chapter 2) instead of perpetuities and we must decide when it is to 'die'. At high discount rates this may not matter much. Table 9.1 shows the extra present value as one extends an annuity from 10 to 25 years (and then to 40 years and to infinity) at three real discount rates: 5 per cent, 10 per cent and 15 per cent.

Table 9.1 Present value of annuities (10, 25, 40 years) and a perpetuity at various discount rates

Years	10	25	40	Perpetuity
5%	7.722	14.094	17.159	20.000
Change from previous PV		*6.372*	*3.065*	*2.841*
10%	6.145	9.077	9.779	10.000
Change from previous PV		*2.932*	*0.702*	*0.221*
15%	5.019	6.464	6.642	6.667
Change from previous PV		*1.445*	*0.178*	*0.025*

Discounting the Terminal Value

When we have in one way or another managed to produce a terminal value as at the horizon date (let us now suppose that this is at the end of Year 5, to simplify the details), we still have one remaining point to bear in mind. Given that we want to establish the value (that is, the *present*—end of Year 0—value) of the company, we must remember to *discount* the terminal value back from the horizon date into end of year (EOY) 0 terms.

The discount rate to use for this exercise, of course, may well be different from the rate used to establish the EOY 5 terminal value itself (even if we used DCF—see above). For instance, suppose we can estimate specific cash inflows for Company G for the first five years in money terms (that is, including any expected inflation), whereas the annuities beyond the horizon date may well be in 'real' terms. The discount rate needed to establish the *present value* of the terminal value will then need to be a *money* discount rate, not a real one, as Table 9.2 shows.

Table 9.2 Discounting terminal value back to EOY 0

EOY 0 present value	EOY 1-5	EOY 5	EOY 6-horizon
	Money cashflows		Real cashflows
←	Discount to EOY 0 at money rate	←	Discount to EOY 5 at real rate
		=Terminal Value	
←	←	Discount to EOY 0 at money rate	

There is no doubt there exists some danger of confusion unless one is very careful. One way to overcome this may be to 'label' the money amounts to denote whether they are, for example, current dollars (c$) or Year 5 dollars (5$).

9.3 Mergers and Acquisitions

9.3.1 Reasons for Acquisitions

9.3.1.1 Reasons for Buying

'Mergers' and 'acquisitions' both combine two or more separate businesses into one enterprise, with a single top management and common ownership. The term 'merger' often covers both. Strictly in a merger two companies M and N pool all their assets and liabilities; and shareholders exchange their shares in M or in N for shares in a new holding company MN. In an acquisition, A buys all (or most) of the equity shares, or the (net) assets, in B. The purchase price may comprise cash, which buys out the previous ownership interests in B, or shares in A. *Thus, an acquisition is simply an example of a capital investment project* (from A's point of view). It may involve a larger amount than most normal 'projects'; and the strategic implications may be very important.

The main arguments for mergers are economies of scale and transferring control of resources to better managers. The main arguments against this are the dangers of monopoly, or less competition, leading to waste and/or excessively high prices. It is not clear a priori whether higher concentration in an industry will increase or reduce competition. One needs to look at relevant markets, including imports, not merely at 'domestic' production; and one must also consider the impact of *potential* competition.

Most mergers are horizontal, combining firms in the same business: for example, a daily newspaper merging with a Sunday newspaper. They are most likely to lead to economies of scale, but they may also tend towards monopoly. Economies of scale vary between industries. They need not apply only to production: there may be savings in marketing, research and even finance. Size can also bring important drawbacks ('diseconomies of scale'): remoteness of management control; extra layers of overhead cost; and rigid bureaucracy.

Vertical mergers combine firms at different stages of production in the same industry. They may aim to control quality, or to ensure sources of supply or retail outlets. Thus, a producer of soft drinks might combine 'upstream' with fruit growers or a company making containers, or 'downstream' with a firm running ice cream vans.

Conglomerate mergers combine firms in different industries, perhaps with no obvious connection: for example, a cigarette maker and an insurance company, or a drinks producer and a chain of opticians. Such mergers are fairly rare (they are out of fashion these days). Benefits might stem from tax savings, management skills in the centre, or financial efficiencies. It can be hard to interpret group accounts (consolidated accounts) which add together numbers from different industries. Hence group accounts disclose separately the merged company's sales, profits and assets in the various different industry segments in which they operate.

The acquiring company may want to achieve expansion more quickly than by internal growth. In some industries size may be essential to compete globally. There may be a desire to avoid outside control: it is much harder for governments to interfere with transactions within a group than with 'visible' market deals between separate companies. (This may be an important reason for some global mergers.) Table 9.3 sets out a number of possible reasons for one business to acquire another, some of which may overlap.

9.3.1.2 Reasons for Selling

Many commercial assets are for sale 'if the price is right', even if the owners were not planning to sell. People who have founded a business, or inherited it, may want either to retire or to spread their investment risk. They can often defer any capital gains tax bill by receiving shares rather than cash; and if they accept shares in a listed company, they can dispose of them whenever they choose.

Another reason for selling a business may be management problems: either succession or lack of ability to manage a larger business following a period of growth. The death, retirement, or departure, of one or two key people can often reveal a need for new management. Sometimes selling an ailing business may

Table 9.3 Reasons for acquisition

Production
1. Expanding capacity
2. Economies of scale
3. Acquiring technology
4. Vertical integration, for quality control or supply reasons
Marketing
5. Expanding market share
6. Extending product range
7. Gaining entry to new markets
8. Eliminating competition
9. Vertical integration, for distribution reasons
Miscellaneous
10. Target company's shares or assets 'under-priced'
11. Acquirer's shares 'over-valued'
12. Applying superior management skills to the acquiree's business
13. Acquiring management skills to apply to the acquirer's business
14. Preventing a competitor from acquiring the target company
15. Making the acquiring company itself less attractive to a predator
16. Tax benefits
17. Avoiding government interference
18. Diversifying business risk
19. Empire building

simply be 'a civilized alternative to bankruptcy'. Sale as a going concern will normally produce a better price than winding a firm up; and it will avoid many human and legal problems. Selling a *division* of a group of companies may make strategic sense if it no longer fits with the 'core' business, or if the group needs extra finance for the rest of its business. It may also make the vendor company less attractive to a predator (by selling the 'crown jewels'). Table 9.4 lists reasons for selling a company.

9.3.2 Management Versus Shareholders

Managers are likely to have all their eggs in one basket (their job, and possible share options in the company), so they may be keen to merge to reduce their company's total risk. In theory this makes no sense for the company's owners if they hold a portfolio of shares and can thus diversify away for themselves most of any company's 'unique risk' (see Chapter 7). But owners of family companies

Table 9.4 Reasons for selling (part of) a business

Ownership
1. Owner wants to diversify risk
2. Owner wants to reduce tax problems on death
Management
3. Manager(s) about to retire, with no obvious successor
4. Poor business prospects under control of present management, possibly following expansion or a change of direction
Part of a group
5. Needs extra source of finance
6. No longer fits with core business or strategy of vendor group
7. Make *vendor* less attractive to a predator
Miscellaneous
8. Needs economies of scale (might justify *acquisition* rather than sale!)
9. Vendor's shares or assets 'over valued'

may not be in this position; hence they too may be quite keen on their company diversifying.

Getting into new areas of business may be exciting for managers, but it may also involve big risks. A famous economist once said: 'People want an interesting life'. On average acquiring groups have to pay a bid premium of about 25–30 per cent on the vendor's (pre-bid) share price. This may absorb nearly all of the economic gains from the merger, leaving little if any reward for shareholders in the acquiring group.

Managers may welcome size for its own sake if their pay partly depends on it, whereas shareholders want a good rate of return on equity. That is why shareholders would often prefer a higher dividend payout ratio than the top managers (see Chapter 8). Merging may also improve a group's credit rating, which may make life more comfortable for managers.

Poor quality managers, who fail to maximize shareholder wealth, ought in the end to be vulnerable to a takeover bid for control of their company. This could yield large profits for those who organize such a bid. They could either run the business better themselves, or hire other managers to do so, or split it up and sell parts of it off. Private companies, however, may not be easy to take over, hence they are high-risk investments, certainly for minority shareholders. In practice, though, even for listed companies, the short-term pressure on incompetent or unlucky managers may be less than the theory suggests.

9.3.3 Joint ventures and Minority Interests

So far we have been discussing mergers and acquisitions on the basis that they involve purchasing 100 per cent of a company's equity shares. But share deals between 'partners' may involve less than 100 per cent of the equity, especially in international transactions. Taking a minority interest in a foreign company is often an early stage in learning about operating in a different country.

For example, if a company wishes to expand into a foreign country, it may make sense to proceed by way of a strategic alliance (joint venture or minority interest). In a joint venture, each of two partners owns 50 per cent of the equity. Under the so-called 'equity basis', the accounts of both companies normally show the investment at cost plus any share of post-acquisition retained profits, while the income statement reports the share of profits or losses (not just dividends received, if any). Where the investing company holds only a minority interest in the equity, it will still normally use the equity basis of accounting if the share of equity held is at least 20 per cent (in an associated company or 'related company').

Why would a company choose not to own 100 per cent of the equity? It does, of course, reduce the amount it needs to invest in the enterprise. More important, however, is probably the benefit to be gained from the foreign partner's local knowhow and connections, at least for a time.

In one sense, a minority interest, or investment in a joint venture, may resemble an option (see Chapter 4). It may provide an investing company with a springboard for developing 100 per cent interests in the country or industry concerned, when it has learned enough (and also when it has begun to establish a local reputation of its own). On the other hand, the local partner may be gaining access to foreign technology. On this view, such arrangements may often turn out not to be long term, but more opportunistic.

9.3.4 The Process of Merging

9.3.4.1 Valuation

As discussed above, an acquiring company may regard an acquisition as a capital investment project. The amount of the investment is the purchase price, plus any extra amount which the acquirer plans to invest in the business (including restructuring costs), less the expected disposal proceeds of any surplus assets. The assets being acquired may be equity shares in the acquired company, the assets of the group, or the assets of part of a group. Specified liabilities may also be taken over.

To work out the value of the acquisition from the acquiring company's point of view, estimates of the project's future cash flows and terminal value should allow for synergies, or other expected changes, as well as for any further investment. As a check it may be useful to employ the other valuation methods too: price/earnings multiples or even book values of assets.

9.3.4.2 Bargaining

In a 'friendly' deal, an acquirer (A) will try to find out why the seller (S) wants to sell. Is S aware of adverse future factors which A does not know about? Or are there personal reasons for selling? And S will try to discover A's motives. Does A

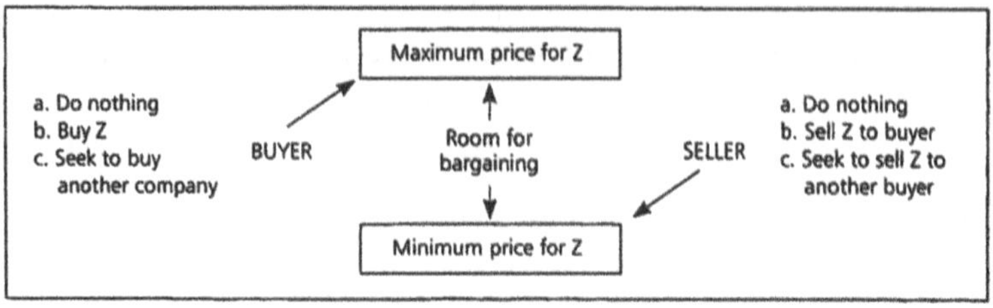

Fig. 9.3 Buyer and seller alternatives

value some aspect of the business more highly than S? If so, why? And how much is it worth to A?

Both A and S should take care throughout to keep an eye on other possible choices, as Fig. 9.3 shows. A will be comparing S with other possible purchases, or with internal growth. S will be looking around for other possible partners or thinking of continuing ownership. If there seems to be no feasible alternative for one party to the deal, that party may find it hard to drive much of a bargain.

Both buyer and seller should really have done a valuation exercise firstly with the seller company as is. That is, how much it is worth under current plans and management; and secondly under the potential new management, with possible synergies, other expected changes, etc. This should give the parties a maximum and minimum price to negotiate between. The larger the gap between the buyer's maximum price and the seller's minimum price, the more the scope for bargaining. Of course, the range may alter during the bargaining. In the excitement of an auction, a 'successful' buyer can easily end up paying far more than they planned; or this may be the price of keeping a deal friendly.

As stated earlier, for listed companies it has been common for the purchase price to average some 25–30 per cent more than the acquiree's pre-bid market price per share. This may often leave a demanding task for the acquirer's management to earn a profit on top of that premium. In other words, shareholders in companies being acquired often receive a significant premium; but shareholders in acquirer companies may often not do so well—most of the value of the hoped-for synergies has been given upfront to the acquired company's shareholders! Thus, the ability to walk away from a deal that is costing too much may not win much glory, but perhaps it serves the interests of shareholders better than expensive 'triumphs'.

Making the size of the purchase price partly conditional on the delivery of future profits (called "earn-outs") defers some of the cost and reduces the risk, because under the agreement the buyer will pay less if promised future profits fail to occur. This may also act as an incentive for the former owner-managers to continue working well. That is for stand-alone businesses. On the other hand, this kind of arrangement can turn out very messy if the buyer reorganizes the acquired business or combines it with existing business units.

In hostile takeover bids, the interests of the top management of the victim (V) may not coincide with those of its shareholders. The management may prefer continuing independence at almost any price. Regulations governing takeover practice normally requires V's directors to provide full details of any offer to enable V's shareholders to make an informed decision.

9.3.4.3 Financing

There are several ways in which a company can finance the acquisition of another company:

1. Use cash balances it already has;
2. Borrow the money;
3. Issue new shares (often to its existing shareholders in the form of a rights issue) and use the cash thus raised;
4. Issue new shares in itself, directly to the shareholders of the acquired company (a share-for-share swap). Thus a shareholder in the acquired company will now own shares in the acquiring company.
5. Some combination of the above.

Combining two formerly separate companies is likely to increase the total equity 'cushion', and thus to reduce the risk for existing creditors. Indeed, by reducing an enterprise's total risk, merging may encourage management to increase financial gearing (leverage).

The method of payment will affect the financial structure. For instance, a company with a 35 per cent debt ratio which acquires another company half its size could end up with a debt ratio varying from 23 per cent to 57 per cent, depending on whether it borrowed none or all of the purchase price. (The price might be paid by issuing loan stock in the acquiring group to the shareholders of the selling group; or the acquiring group might itself borrow in order to finance a purchase for cash.)

As mentioned, a well-known advantage of paying in equity shares is to delay any capital gains tax bill for the vendors, and to spread any such liability out over time if they sell their shares in more than one tranche.

9.3.4.4 Human Consequences

Over time most companies develop a style of their own; and it can be difficult to combine two firms with different cultures. Making a merger work takes a great deal of management time and effort. Depending on the nature of the merger (is it horizontal, vertical or conglomerate?), the new group's top management may wish to look in some detail at every significant aspect of the new business: each major product line, every plant, the main markets, all senior personnel.

Human problems often arise among the workforce as a result of a merger. 'Economies of scale' may be an abstract way of saying that one person can do two people's jobs. So the other person may have to go. Other employees may be demoted or have to move to a new office or factory, perhaps far away from their present home and friends. Such redeployment may often make good business sense, but to implement it requires great skill and tact on management's part. To avoid uncertainty it is usually a good idea to tell the workers in a newly acquired business as much as possible about future plans as soon as possible.

9.3.5 Why Some Mergers Fail

Measuring success or failure in the context of mergers and acquisitions is somewhat tricky. Whose point of view is one adopting? Is it the shareholders'? If so, the shareholders of the acquired company or of the acquiring company or both? Or is it the managers' point of view, the employees', the customers' or the 'national interest'?

We have stated that there is a fair amount of evidence that shareholders in companies being acquired receive a significant premium over the pre-bid share price—on average around 25–30 per cent. It seems, though, that shareholders in acquiring companies often get no measurable benefit at all. If this is correct, it suggests that there is a degree of success for mergers overall, but with the acquiree shareholders getting nearly all the resulting benefit.

However, in general terms it seems that—in the opinion of the managers concerned—about half of all large mergers are judged not to have been successful; to have failed. They may not be too worried about the impact on shareholders. What are the main reasons for failure? Significant reasons appear to be:

1. Cultural differences between the two companies.
2. Lack of post-merger integration planning
3. Lack of knowledge of the industry or target company.

The implication seems to be that some acquisitions are undertaken with too little thought.

9.4 A Concluding Note

In this chapter we introduced you to the main techniques for valuing whole companies and discussed aspects of acquisitions and mergers. Each of these topics is often the subject of a whole book, but here we were aiming to provide an overview of these issues and to link them to the concept of valuation and discounted cash flow methods which are at the heart of corporate finance. The following chapter concludes the book.

9.4.1 Problems

Problem 9.1 Hollyhock plc is proposing to acquire all the equity capital of Snapdragon Ltd. Future cash inflows for Snapdragon as a separate company are estimated at £4 million a year after tax. In addition, Hollyhock's management reckons that economies of scale can add a further £2 million a year after tax under their ownership. The move to acquire Snapdragon requires an immediate capital investment of £5 million (which is stated net of the effect of taxation).

Regular fixed capital investments needed to maintain Snapdragon's profits are to be taken as equal to the company's current depreciation expense of £2.5 million a year. Surplus Snapdragon assets to be sold immediately after the acquisition (without significantly affecting profits) are expected to realize £1 million net.

If the appropriate after-tax discount rate is 12 per cent a year, what is the maximum purchase price that Hollyhock plc should be prepared to pay for the equity in Snapdragon Ltd:

a. using a horizon period of 10 years?
b. using a horizon period of 15 years?

Problem 9.2 Beach Products Inc is planning a major acquisition costing $50 million. The company's present capital consists of 100 million 50¢ issued ordinary shares, $40 million retained earnings and $30 million 10 per cent secured debentures. The group's current profit before interest and tax (PBIT) is $25 million a year, which is expected to rise by $10 million a year (to $35 million a year) as a result of the acquisition.

Beach Products can pay for its new acquisition in two ways:

1. issuing 40 million ordinary shares at $1.25 each; or
2. issuing $50 million 12 per cent loan stock.

For each of the alternative methods of financing the acquisition, calculate and compare the:

a. ratio of debt to (debt plus equity) based on book values.
b. interest cover
c. earnings per share

after the acquisition with Beach Products Inc's present position. Assume a tax rate of 30 per cent.

Problem 9.3 Peverill Plastics plc is considering making a bid for control of Middlesex Mouldings Ltd. The company's directors have taken a five-year view. Middlesex's predicted cash flow for the first year is a net inflow of £8 million, and it is expected that this will increase by £1 million a year for each of the next four years (until and including year 5). If Peverill's bid is successful, it is believed that the cash inflow can be increased by a further £4 million a year; but only if £10 million is invested at once and a further £3 million invested at the end of each year for the next four years (until and including year 4) to maintain the plant.

a. Set out Middlesex's expected cash flows for each of the next five years if acquired by Peverill.
b. What is the maximum price that Peverill should offer for Middlesex? Assume a discount rate of 10 per cent and a five-year time horizon for the acquisition.
c. How else might Peverill try to value Middlesex Mouldings?

Problem 9.4 The following information is from Yahoo finance as of August 2021:

Company	Coca-Cola	PepsiCo
Earnings per share (based on most recent earnings)	$1.87	$5.92
Earnings per share (based on analysts' expectations for next year)	$2.36	$6.58
Market price per share	$56.80	$154.43
Market capitalization (billion $)	245.184	213.439

a. How many outstanding shares does each company have?
b. For each company, calculate the forward and historic price to earnings ratio and comment on the results.

Putting It All Together 10

10.1 Introduction

The aim of this concluding chapter is to summarize the main points of the textbook and to show how the financing and investment decisions interact. We start in Sect. 10.2 by summarizing the steps involved in determining the discount rate that the firm should use when considering investment in projects that are of the same risk class as its average existing project. Once we establish the discount rate (WACC), we move to Sect. 10.3 where we use it to make investment decisions. Section 10.4 summarizes this chapter and the key issues of the book as a whole through an encompassing example.

10.2 Estimating the Weighted Average Cost of Capital (WACC)

We start with the second part of the book which dealt with the financing decision, and how to estimate the firm's weighted average cost of capital. This is the discount rate that the firm should use to discount an average-risk project. Figure 10.1 illustrates the components of the WACC.

(a) **Cost of debt** is the marginal cost of debt—that is, the cost of new debt (YTM), post corporate tax.
Example If the YTM is 10 per cent, and corporation tax is 30 per cent, the post-tax cost of debt, k_{dat}, is: $k_{dat} = 0.10 \times (1 - 0.30) = 0.07$ or 7 per cent.

(b) **Proportions of debt and equity** are calculated as in Eqs. 10.1 and 10.2:

$$Weight_{debt} = \frac{Debt}{Debt + Equity} \tag{10.1}$$

$$Weight_{equity} = \frac{Equity}{Debt + Equity} \tag{10.2}$$

R. Manos et al., *Corporate Finance for Business*,
https://doi.org/10.1007/978-3-030-92419-5_10

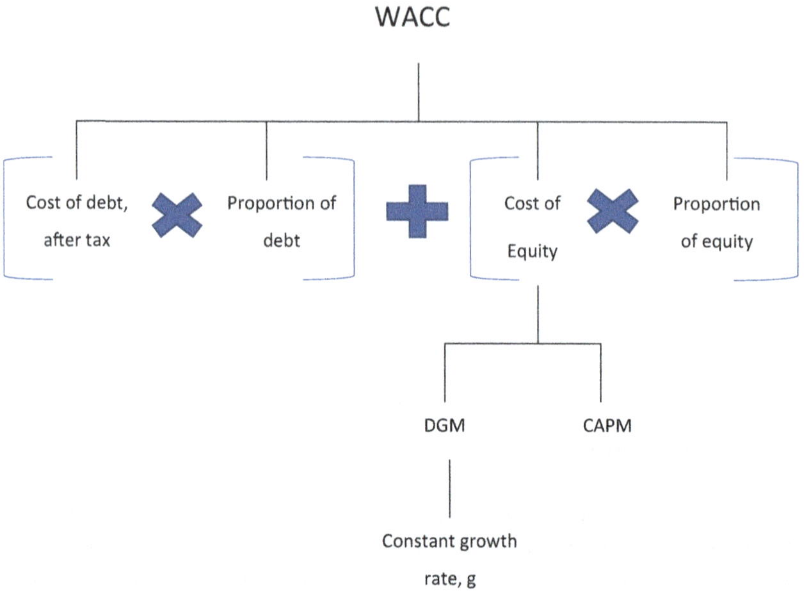

Fig. 10.1 Estimating the weighted average cost of capital (WACC)

and the sum of the weights is 1. Weighting can be based on:

a. **Book values**—use the figures for debt and equity from the Balance Sheet.
b. **Market values**—Often this is the preferred method:
   i. Debt: market value of bonds, or, if debt is not traded, then use the book value of debt.
   ii. Equity: $market\ capitalisation = number\ of\ shares \times share\ price$
c. **Target values**—may reflect, better than market values, the long-term capital structure of the firm. Still, a remaining challenge is to establish the firm's optimum debt/gearing ratio (if there is one). This in essence is the capital structure debate and there are a number of theories that aim to explain the capital structure decision including the *pecking order hypothesis*, the *trade-off theory* and the *market timing theory*.

(c) **The cost of equity** can be estimated using the dividend growth model (DGM) or the capital asset pricing model (CAPM).

(d) **The dividend growth model (DGM)** is of the form presented in Eq. 10.4, derived from Eq. 10.3:

$$P_0 = \frac{Div_1}{(k_e - g)} \tag{10.3}$$

where P_0 is the market price of the share today (the present value of the share), Div_1 is the expected dividend per share to be paid next year, k_e is the cost of equity and g is the constant rate of growth in dividends. Given that we know

P_0, because the share is traded in the market, we can manipulate Eq. 10.3 to find out k_e, as shown in Eq. 10.4:

$$k_e = \frac{Div_1}{P_0} + g \tag{10.4}$$

Note that:

a. Div_1 can be estimated using the most recent dividend and the constant rate of growth: $Div_1 = Div_0 \times (1 + g)$.
b. The ratio $\frac{Div_1}{P_0}$ is the forward looking dividend yield.

(e) **The constant rate of growth, *g*** can be estimated in two ways at least:

a. **The geometric average rate of change** in past dividends or in past earnings per share.

Example: if the dividend in 2018 was 100 per share, and two years later, in 2020, it was 121, then the average yearly rate of growth would be found by taking the nth root (in this case $n = 2$) of the ratio of the dividends and subtracting 1: $g = \sqrt[2]{\frac{121}{100}} - 1 = 10\%$. If the dividends per share in 2021 was 133, then we would use: $g = \sqrt[3]{\frac{133}{100}} - 1 = 10\%$.

b. **Using an equation** of the form presented by Eq. 10.5:

$$g = Retention\,ratio \times RoE \tag{10.5}$$

where the retention ratio is the percentage of retained earnings out of total earnings (or you could calculate it as 100 per cent minus the dividend payout ratio). RoE is the return on equity, calculated as the ratio of profit after tax to shareholders' equity.

Example A firm generated \$20 million profits on equity of \$100 million. It paid out dividends of \$15 million to its shareholders. The payout ratio is: $\frac{\$15m}{\$20m} = 75\%$. Therefore, the retention ratio is: $100\% - 75\% = 25\%$. Return on equity is: $\frac{\$20m}{\$100m} = 20\%$. So, the rate of growth is: $g = 0.25 \times 0.20 = 0.05$, or 5 per cent.

(f) **The capital asset pricing model (CAPM)** is an alternative to the DGM for estimating the cost of equity. The model asserts that the cost of equity is made up of two components:

a. Compensation for the time value of money (reflected in the risk free, r_f rate).
b. Compensation for risk that cannot be diversified away.

Note that the assumption underlying the CAPM is that investors hold diversified portfolios and hence do not demand compensation for specific risk (e.g. a change in management or fire breaking out in one of the firm's factories) because it is diversified away. Splitting total risk into diversifiable and non-diversifiable is one of the most important insights of modern portfolio theory and can be represented by Fig. 10.2.

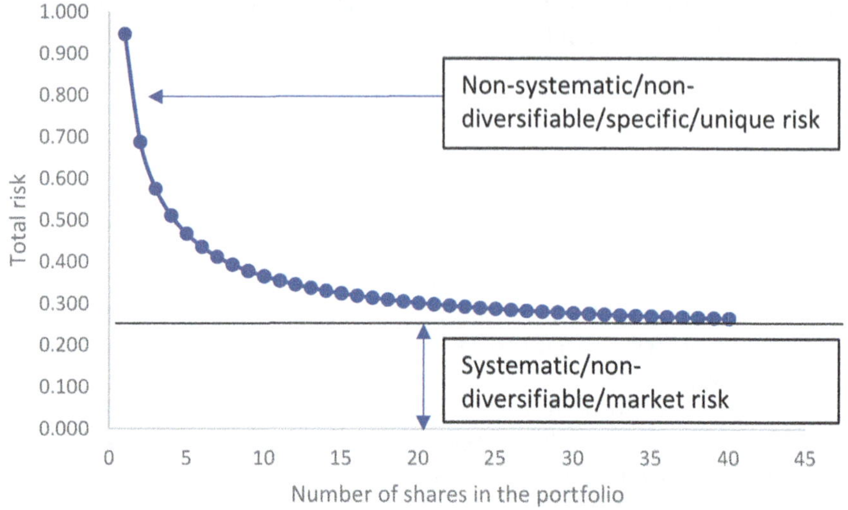

Fig. 10.2 Modern portfolio theory

Thus, the CAPM can be generally represented as in Eq. 10.6:

$$k_e = r_f + \beta(r_m - r_f) \tag{10.6}$$

where $r_m - r_f$ is the market risk premium and is equal to the difference between the return on the market (r_m) and the risk-free rate (r_f). Beta (β) is a measurement of the extent to which the share price of the specific share varies with the movement of the market as a whole. By definition the beta of the market is 1. A share with a beta of less than 1.0 is less risky than the whole market, while a share with a beta of more than 1.0 is riskier. This is illustrated in Fig. 10.3.

Fig. 10.3 The beta coefficient

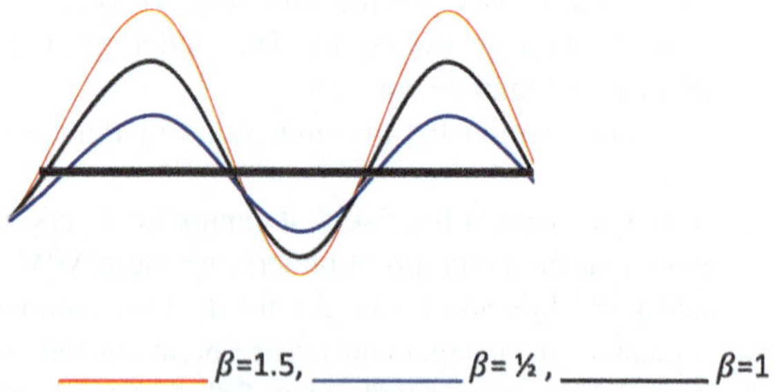

Using the CAPM is intuitive and practical. However, there are a number of challenges/debates surrounding its usage:

(a) What is the right figure for the *MRP*? Is it between 7 and 8 per cent? Some say it is less. Others say it depends on location.
(b) What is the risk-free rate? Is the rate on T-bills appropriate? Should we use the yield on government bonds?
(c) How stable is the beta coefficient?

10.3 Project Appraisal Tools: Discounting Future Cash Flows

Once the firm establishes its WACC it can use it in capital investment decisions, providing the investment being considered is of the same risk class as the average risk of the firm's existing projects. For example, assume a firm uses the net present value (NPV) rule. Once it has established an appropriate WACC, it may apply it as the discount rate to the cash flow forecast of the proposed project.

Preparing a cash flow forecast and discounting it to find the NPV of the project being considered was the topic of the first part of the book. The main points to remember are as follows:

1. **Time value of money principle**—record cash inflows and outflows at the time that they are expected to arise. This accounts for the opportunity cost of having the money earning a return in an alternative endeavour. It means that in preparing a cash flow forecast, one needs to ignore the accounting principle of matching revenue to the costs incurred in generating it.
2. **Depreciation**—the best example of point 1 is that of depreciation which is not a cash flow item (although it may have cash flow implications on tax payments).
3. **Incremental cash flows**—include all incremental cash flows. An incremental cash flow is one that is changed by the decision to undertake the project. An incremental cost may be difficult to identify if it is not directly related to the project. Think, for example, of the impact a new project will have on the demand for a competing product which the company is currently selling. Sales of the existing competitor product may decline, and the net margin on these sales should be included as a notional cash 'outflow' in the cash flow forecast prepared for the new proposal.
4. **Non-relevant cash flows**—include only relevant cash flows in the cash flow forecast. For example, a *sunk cost* is not relevant to the decision as to whether to undertake a project, as it is a cost that was already incurred and will not change if we decide to go ahead with the project. Think of the cost of market research carried out in preparation for a meeting to determine whether or not to execute a new project. Whatever the decision regarding the project, that cost has already been incurred and is thus not relevant to the decision at hand.

5. **Double counting**—financing costs, such as interest paid on a loan that was raised to finance the project, should not be included in the cash flow forecast. Although interest payments may directly relate to the loan taken out to finance the project, and are thus incremental to the project, they should nonetheless not be included in the cash flow forecast. The reason is that interest is compensation paid to providers of part of our total financing and as such is included in the WACC. Including it as a cash outflow in the cash flow forecast would mean that interest was double counted. The story for dividends paid to shareholders is the same.
6. **Opportunity costs**—cash flows that do not arise because of the decision to undertake the project are also relevant and should be included in the cash flow forecast. For example, if undertaking the project means that we cannot sell the old machine or rent out factory space which are needed for the production process of the new project, then these lost cash flows should be included as cash 'outflows', reducing the NPV of the project.
7. **Working capital adjustments**—the time value of money might require us to also make an adjustment for investment in working capital. This is in spite of the fact that investment in working capital is likely to be recovered by the end of the project—as you know, the timing of cash flows matters!
8. **Allocation of overheads**—this is the process of apportioning overhead costs to the various projects the company is undertaking. However, to the extent that the overheads are not incremental to the project being considered, they should be ignored.

Once a cash flow forecast for the project being considered is prepared, the firm should use the WACC to discount the future cash flows. Discounting takes care of the time value of money and can be used to estimate the present value of a proposed single project, or to ascertain the fair value of a financial security (e.g. a share or a bond), as well as to estimate the value of a whole firm (e.g. in mergers and acquisitions).

Discounting the proposed project's expected cash flows by using the WACC (or an appropriate risk-adjusted discount rate) amounts to calculating the net present value (NPV) of the project. If the NPV is positive, the project is a value creating investment, and should be accepted. Alternatively, the firm can find the IRR of the cash flows and compare it to the WACC which represents the current cost of capital. If the IRR is greater than the cost of capital, the project is worth undertaking.

Thus, the NPV and IRR rules are common methods for project appraisal which consider both the time value of money and the compensation that providers of corporate finance demand for the risk to which the project exposes them (reflected in the WACC). The main challenge is to estimate future cash flows and to select an appropriate discount rate to use. The discounting process itself, in contrast, is merely a technical exercise which can easily be performed in Excel®. Moreover, it often makes sense to assume future cash flows follow specific patterns, making discounting very distant cash flows much easier. Examples include annuities, perpetuities, and growing perpetuities.

The important thing to remember is that when dealing with future cash flows, uncertainty is inevitable. Managers may endeavour to reduce it by supplementing the use of project appraisal tools (e.g. NPV and the IRR) with risk analyses including such techniques as sensitivity analysis or scenario analysis.

Those, in essence, are the topics we covered in this book. Let us now demonstrate the key issues with an encompassing example.

10.4 Concluding Example

A food processing company is considering investing in new technology to boost energy efficiency and meet green goals. In particular, it is considering spending today \$1.5 million on a heat transformer that is expected to lower its energy bills by \$200,000 a year net of tax, starting next year and continuing forever.

In order to decide whether to go ahead with the project, the management convened a meeting to establish investment appraisal rules and review relevant data. Here are some important points to emerge from the meeting:

- If the payback (PB) rule is used, then the cutoff period for all projects is 10 years.
- The company has 14 million shares currently trading at \$100 per share.
- The company pays dividends on an annual basis. A dividend of \$8 has just been paid, and the next dividend is due next year. The rate of growth in the yearly dividend is 2 per cent.
- The company has 1 million bonds with a face value of \$1,000 per bond, currently trading at \$973 per bond. Interest of 4 per cent is paid annually and the next payment is due now. The bonds have 3 years to maturity.
- The company pays corporate tax at the rate of 25 per cent.

Calculate:

(a) **The payback period in years, on the proposed investment**
The payback is the amount of time it takes the cash inflows from the project to return the initial investment. To find the payback, we can divide the initial cost by the annual savings:
$\frac{\$1,500,000}{\$200,000} = 7.5 years$. Thus, in 7 and a half years, the project will 'break even'. This is within the cut off period of ten years, set by the firm.

(b) **The Internal Rate of Return (IRR) on the proposed investment**
The IRR is the discount rate which equates the NPV of the project to zero. In this case, the cash flow pattern is that of a perpetuity, so we have:

$$0 = -\$1,500,000 + \frac{\$200,000}{IRR} \rightarrow IRR = \frac{\$200,000}{\$1,500,000} \approx 13\%$$

(c) **The company's weighted average cost of capital (WACC)**
The cost of equity, using the Dividend Growth Model (DGM) is:

$$k_e = \frac{\$8 \times (1 + 0.02)}{100} + 0.02 = 0.102 = 10.2\%$$

The cost of debt is the internal rate of return (yield to maturity, YTM) of the following cash flows:

Year	0	1	2	3
Price/Principal	-$973.00			$1,000.00
Coupon	$40.00	$40.00	$40.00	$40.00
Total cashflow	-$933.00	$40.00	$40.00	$1,040.00
IRR	6.53%			

Using the formula $= IRR$ in Excel®,[1] we can find the cost of debt as:

$$k_d = 6.53\%$$

The after-tax cost of debt is:

$$0.0653 \times (1 - 0.25) = 4.90\%$$

The firm's value of equity (V_E), value of debt V_D, and the weights of equity and debt in its capital structure (W_E, W_D) are as follows:

$$V_E = \$100 \times 14{,}000{,}000 = \$1{,}400{,}000{,}000$$

$$V_D = \$973 \times 1{,}000{,}000 = \$973{,}000{,}000$$

$$W_E = \frac{\$1{,}400{,}000{,}000}{\$1{,}400{,}000{,}000 + \$973{,}000{,}000} = 59\% \rightarrow W_D = 1 - 59\% = 41\%$$

$$WACC = (0.102 \times 59\%) + (0.0490 \times 41\%) = 8\%$$

(d) **The net present value (NPV) of the proposed investment**
The NPV of the project is positive, and hence it should be accepted based on the NPV rule:

$$NPV = -\$1{,}500{,}000 + \frac{\$200{,}000}{0.08} = 1{,}000{,}000$$

[1] $= \mathrm{irr}(-933,40,40,1040) = 6.53\%$

Likewise, since the IRR of the project, at 13 per cent, is higher than the WACC (8 per cent), the IRR rule also suggests that the project should be accepted.

(e) **The amount by which the net of tax annual cash saving on the energy bills could drop, before the decision on the project is reversed (assuming the decision rule used by the firm is the NPV rule)**
We can solve this by equating the NPV to zero, and finding the yearly cash flow (CF) which solves the equation:

$$0 = -\$1{,}500{,}000 + \frac{CF}{0.08} \rightarrow CF = \$120{,}000$$

So, the annual cash flow (net of tax) could reduce by: \$200,000 – \$120,000 = \$80,000 before the decision on the project would change. This is a reduction of 40 per cent. This appears to be a safe margin, but is the firm confident that this is not going to happen?

10.5 Problems

10.5.1 Data for Problems 10.1–10.4

ROOT, a cricket ball manufacturer, has an investment appraisal policy that involves estimating as accurately as possible the cash flows of the first four years of the project, followed by the assumption of a fixed, constant level of cash flows per year from years 5–10. Any cash flows that might be received after year 10 are ignored, including the sale of any fixed assets, buildings and land and the recovery of working capital. It is now considering investment in a new factory to produce a new line of cricket balls. The site is already owned by the company, but existing buildings would need to be demolished immediately, at a cost of \$3 million, to allow for construction to begin. This amount is fully tax-deductible at the end of year one of the project. The current market value of the site and existing buildings is \$7 million. If the project does not go ahead, the site would be sold. The site itself is not relevant for tax purposes.

At the same time as clearing the site, the company would need to invest \$4 million to build the new factory. The manufacturing of the new line is based on new technology without which the project would not have been possible. The technology was purchased by the company six months ago, at a cost of \$2 million, but is currently of no value to any other potential manufacturers. Also, the company has already spent \$1 million on a marketing survey, relating to the demand for the new line of cricket balls in different countries.

The investment in the new factory would be depreciated for tax purposes on a straight-line basis over four years to a value of zero. The factory will actually last at least 12 years if repairs and maintenance, which are tax-deductible, costing \$1.5 million are carried out at the end of year 4. The company believes that working capital (mainly inventory) of 10 per cent of sales value is needed from the start of each year of the project for the four years of accurate calculations. After that it can be ignored. Fixed costs are $2.2 million per year. This excludes depreciation and existing Head Office overheads of $200,000 that would be allocated to the project. Variable production costs (excluding depreciation) are estimated at $180 per pack of balls for all four years, and the packs of balls would be sold for $400 each in years 1 and 2, and $410 each in years 3 and 4. Sales volumes, in packs, are estimated as follows:-

Year 1	Year 2	Year 3	Year 4
25,000	30,000	60,000	50,000

Profits are taxed at the rate of 25 per cent, with the tax payable in the year that profits were made. If the project shows a loss for tax purposes in a particular year, this loss can be offset against the taxable profits of other parts of the Company, such that a *positive* tax cash flow will be shown for the project in that year.

The net after-tax cash flows for years 5–10 are estimated by the company to be $6 million per year, and you should use these figures.

All figures, including years 5–10, are in nominal (that is, inflation-inclusive) terms.

ROOT is financed by debt and equity. The debt is in the form of bonds that are due for redemption at the end of ten years from now. There are 100,000 of these bonds of $1,000 face value in issue, which pay an annual coupon rate of 5 per cent. The next payment of interest is expected in one year's time. The current yield to maturity of other bonds of similar duration and risk is currently 6 per cent.

The beta of ROOT's equity is 1.5 and the expected return on the market portfolio is 12 per cent. This is 8 percentage points above the risk-free rate of return. There are 1 million shares in issue, with a current market price of $160.00 per share. Last week ROOT paid a dividend of $16.20 per share, and the dividend (paid annually) is expected to grow by 3.5 per cent per year indefinitely.

Problem 10.1 Set out the year-by-year cash flow forecast for the first four years of the project (years 0–4) if Root goes ahead with the project. If you make any assumptions, please state them. (Note that at this point, we ignore the cash flows that arise from year 5 to year 10.)

Problem 10.2

(a) Calculate the current market value of one of the company's bonds with a face value of $1,000, showing your workings. Briefly explain why the company's bond is traded at a different value to its face value.

(b) Calculate the company's gearing ratio [shown as a percentage] as defined by debt divided by (debt plus equity), based on market values.

Problem 10.3 Name two alternative approaches to calculating ROOT's cost of equity and use both of them to calculate its cost of equity. Assume that the company's actual cost of equity is the average of your two results and calculate this.

Problem 10.4

(a) Use your answers to problems 10.2 and 10.3 to calculate the WACC of the company.
(b) Calculate the Present Value (PV) as of year 4, of the net cash flows for the six years from year 5 to year 10, and insert the figure into the cash flow forecast you prepared in problem 10.1.
(c) Use the updated cash flow forecast (10.4b) and the WACC (10.4a) to calculate the NPV and the IRR of the project. Should ROOT go ahead with the project? Explain your answer.

Appendix: Discount Tables

Tables A1 and A2.

R. Manos et al., *Corporate Finance for Business*,
https://doi.org/10.1007/978-3-030-92419-5

Table A1 Discount factors for a lump sum to be received in t years, given a discount rate of r%: $DF_r^t = \frac{1}{(1+r)^t}$

Yr	1%	2%	3%	4%	5%	6%	7%	8%	9%	10%	11%	12%	13%	14%	15%	16%	17%	18%	19%	20%	21%	22%	23%	24%	25%
1	0.990	0.980	0.971	0.962	0.952	0.943	0.935	0.926	0.917	0.909	0.901	0.893	0.885	0.877	0.870	0.862	0.855	0.847	0.840	0.833	0.826	0.820	0.813	0.806	0.800
2	0.980	0.961	0.943	0.925	0.907	0.890	0.873	0.857	0.842	0.826	0.812	0.797	0.783	0.769	0.756	0.743	0.731	0.718	0.706	0.694	0.683	0.672	0.661	0.650	0.640
3	0.971	0.942	0.915	0.889	0.864	0.840	0.816	0.794	0.772	0.751	0.731	0.712	0.693	0.675	0.658	0.641	0.624	0.609	0.593	0.579	0.564	0.551	0.537	0.524	0.512
4	0.961	0.924	0.888	0.855	0.823	0.792	0.763	0.735	0.708	0.683	0.659	0.636	0.613	0.592	0.572	0.552	0.534	0.516	0.499	0.482	0.467	0.451	0.437	0.423	0.410
5	0.951	0.906	0.863	0.822	0.784	0.747	0.713	0.681	0.650	0.621	0.593	0.567	0.543	0.519	0.497	0.476	0.456	0.437	0.419	0.402	0.386	0.370	0.355	0.341	0.328
6	0.942	0.888	0.837	0.790	0.746	0.705	0.666	0.630	0.596	0.564	0.535	0.507	0.480	0.456	0.432	0.410	0.390	0.370	0.352	0.335	0.319	0.303	0.289	0.275	0.262
7	0.933	0.871	0.813	0.760	0.711	0.665	0.623	0.583	0.547	0.513	0.482	0.452	0.425	0.400	0.376	0.354	0.333	0.314	0.296	0.279	0.263	0.249	0.235	0.222	0.210
8	0.923	0.853	0.789	0.731	0.677	0.627	0.582	0.540	0.502	0.467	0.434	0.404	0.376	0.351	0.327	0.305	0.285	0.266	0.249	0.233	0.218	0.204	0.191	0.179	0.168
9	0.914	0.837	0.766	0.703	0.645	0.592	0.544	0.500	0.460	0.424	0.391	0.361	0.333	0.308	0.284	0.263	0.243	0.225	0.209	0.194	0.180	0.167	0.155	0.144	0.134
10	0.905	0.820	0.744	0.676	0.614	0.558	0.508	0.463	0.422	0.386	0.352	0.322	0.295	0.270	0.247	0.227	0.208	0.191	0.176	0.162	0.149	0.137	0.126	0.116	0.107
11	0.896	0.804	0.722	0.650	0.585	0.527	0.475	0.429	0.388	0.350	0.317	0.287	0.261	0.237	0.215	0.195	0.178	0.162	0.148	0.135	0.123	0.112	0.103	0.094	0.086
12	0.887	0.788	0.701	0.625	0.557	0.497	0.444	0.397	0.356	0.319	0.286	0.257	0.231	0.208	0.187	0.168	0.152	0.137	0.124	0.112	0.102	0.092	0.083	0.076	0.069
13	0.879	0.773	0.681	0.601	0.530	0.469	0.415	0.368	0.326	0.290	0.258	0.229	0.204	0.182	0.163	0.145	0.130	0.116	0.104	0.093	0.084	0.075	0.068	0.061	0.055
14	0.870	0.758	0.661	0.577	0.505	0.442	0.388	0.340	0.299	0.263	0.232	0.205	0.181	0.160	0.141	0.125	0.111	0.099	0.088	0.078	0.069	0.062	0.055	0.049	0.044
15	0.861	0.743	0.642	0.555	0.481	0.417	0.362	0.315	0.275	0.239	0.209	0.183	0.160	0.140	0.123	0.108	0.095	0.084	0.074	0.065	0.057	0.051	0.045	0.040	0.035
16	0.853	0.728	0.623	0.534	0.458	0.394	0.339	0.292	0.252	0.218	0.188	0.163	0.141	0.123	0.107	0.093	0.081	0.071	0.062	0.054	0.047	0.042	0.036	0.032	0.028
17	0.844	0.714	0.605	0.513	0.436	0.371	0.317	0.270	0.231	0.198	0.170	0.146	0.125	0.108	0.093	0.080	0.069	0.060	0.052	0.045	0.039	0.034	0.030	0.026	0.023
18	0.836	0.700	0.587	0.494	0.416	0.350	0.296	0.250	0.212	0.180	0.153	0.130	0.111	0.095	0.081	0.069	0.059	0.051	0.044	0.038	0.032	0.028	0.024	0.021	0.018
19	0.828	0.686	0.570	0.475	0.396	0.331	0.277	0.232	0.194	0.164	0.138	0.116	0.098	0.083	0.070	0.060	0.051	0.043	0.037	0.031	0.027	0.023	0.020	0.017	0.014
20	0.820	0.673	0.554	0.456	0.377	0.312	0.258	0.215	0.178	0.149	0.124	0.104	0.087	0.073	0.061	0.051	0.043	0.037	0.031	0.026	0.022	0.019	0.016	0.014	0.012
21	0.811	0.660	0.538	0.439	0.359	0.294	0.242	0.199	0.164	0.135	0.112	0.093	0.077	0.064	0.053	0.044	0.037	0.031	0.026	0.022	0.018	0.015	0.013	0.011	0.009
22	0.803	0.647	0.522	0.422	0.342	0.278	0.226	0.184	0.150	0.123	0.101	0.083	0.068	0.056	0.046	0.038	0.032	0.026	0.022	0.018	0.015	0.013	0.011	0.009	0.007
23	0.795	0.634	0.507	0.406	0.326	0.262	0.211	0.170	0.138	0.112	0.091	0.074	0.060	0.049	0.040	0.033	0.027	0.022	0.018	0.015	0.012	0.010	0.009	0.007	0.006
24	0.788	0.622	0.492	0.390	0.310	0.247	0.197	0.158	0.126	0.102	0.082	0.066	0.053	0.043	0.035	0.028	0.023	0.019	0.015	0.013	0.010	0.008	0.007	0.006	0.005
25	0.780	0.610	0.478	0.375	0.295	0.233	0.184	0.146	0.116	0.092	0.074	0.059	0.047	0.038	0.030	0.024	0.020	0.016	0.013	0.010	0.009	0.007	0.006	0.005	0.004

Note that the discount factor, DF_r^t, gives the present value of $1 to be received in t years at a discount rate r%

(continued)

Table A1 (continued)

Yr	1%	2%	3%	4%	5%	6%	7%	8%	9%	10%	11%	12%	13%	14%	15%	16%	17%	18%	19%	20%	21%	22%	23%	24%	25%
26	0.772	0.598	0.464	0.361	0.281	0.220	0.172	0.135	0.106	0.084	0.066	0.053	0.042	0.033	0.026	0.021	0.017	0.014	0.011	0.009	0.007	0.006	0.005	0.004	0.003
27	0.764	0.586	0.450	0.347	0.268	0.207	0.161	0.125	0.098	0.076	0.060	0.047	0.037	0.029	0.023	0.018	0.014	0.011	0.009	0.007	0.006	0.005	0.004	0.003	0.002
28	0.757	0.574	0.437	0.333	0.255	0.196	0.150	0.116	0.090	0.069	0.054	0.042	0.033	0.026	0.020	0.016	0.012	0.010	0.008	0.006	0.005	0.004	0.003	0.002	0.002
29	0.749	0.563	0.424	0.321	0.243	0.185	0.141	0.107	0.082	0.063	0.048	0.037	0.029	0.022	0.017	0.014	0.011	0.008	0.006	0.005	0.004	0.003	0.002	0.002	0.002
30	0.742	0.552	0.412	0.308	0.231	0.174	0.131	0.099	0.075	0.057	0.044	0.033	0.026	0.020	0.015	0.012	0.009	0.007	0.005	0.004	0.003	0.003	0.002	0.002	0.001
31	0.735	0.541	0.400	0.296	0.220	0.164	0.123	0.092	0.069	0.052	0.039	0.030	0.023	0.017	0.013	0.010	0.008	0.006	0.005	0.004	0.003	0.002	0.002	0.001	0.001
32	0.727	0.531	0.388	0.285	0.210	0.155	0.115	0.085	0.063	0.047	0.035	0.027	0.020	0.015	0.011	0.009	0.007	0.005	0.004	0.003	0.002	0.002	0.001	0.001	0.001
33	0.720	0.520	0.377	0.274	0.200	0.146	0.107	0.079	0.058	0.043	0.032	0.024	0.018	0.013	0.010	0.007	0.006	0.004	0.003	0.002	0.002	0.001	0.001	0.001	0.001
34	0.713	0.510	0.366	0.264	0.190	0.138	0.100	0.073	0.053	0.039	0.029	0.021	0.016	0.012	0.009	0.006	0.005	0.004	0.003	0.002	0.002	0.001	0.001	0.001	0.001
35	0.706	0.500	0.355	0.253	0.181	0.130	0.094	0.068	0.049	0.036	0.026	0.019	0.014	0.010	0.008	0.006	0.004	0.003	0.002	0.002	0.001	0.001	0.001	0.001	0.000
36	0.699	0.490	0.345	0.244	0.173	0.123	0.088	0.063	0.045	0.032	0.023	0.017	0.012	0.009	0.007	0.005	0.004	0.003	0.002	0.001	0.001	0.001	0.001	0.000	0.000
37	0.692	0.481	0.335	0.234	0.164	0.116	0.082	0.058	0.041	0.029	0.021	0.015	0.011	0.008	0.006	0.004	0.003	0.002	0.002	0.001	0.001	0.001	0.000	0.000	0.000
38	0.685	0.471	0.325	0.225	0.157	0.109	0.076	0.054	0.038	0.027	0.019	0.013	0.010	0.007	0.005	0.004	0.003	0.002	0.001	0.001	0.001	0.001	0.000	0.000	0.000
39	0.678	0.462	0.316	0.217	0.149	0.103	0.071	0.050	0.035	0.024	0.017	0.012	0.009	0.006	0.004	0.003	0.002	0.002	0.001	0.001	0.001	0.000	0.000	0.000	0.000
40	0.672	0.453	0.307	0.208	0.142	0.097	0.067	0.046	0.032	0.022	0.015	0.011	0.008	0.005	0.004	0.003	0.002	0.001	0.001	0.001	0.000	0.000	0.000	0.000	0.000
41	0.665	0.444	0.298	0.200	0.135	0.092	0.062	0.043	0.029	0.020	0.014	0.010	0.007	0.005	0.003	0.002	0.002	0.001	0.001	0.001	0.000	0.000	0.000	0.000	0.000
42	0.658	0.435	0.289	0.193	0.129	0.087	0.058	0.039	0.027	0.018	0.012	0.009	0.006	0.004	0.003	0.002	0.001	0.001	0.001	0.000	0.000	0.000	0.000	0.000	0.000
43	0.652	0.427	0.281	0.185	0.123	0.082	0.055	0.037	0.025	0.017	0.011	0.008	0.005	0.004	0.002	0.002	0.001	0.001	0.001	0.000	0.000	0.000	0.000	0.000	0.000
44	0.645	0.418	0.272	0.178	0.117	0.077	0.051	0.034	0.023	0.015	0.010	0.007	0.005	0.003	0.002	0.001	0.001	0.001	0.000	0.000	0.000	0.000	0.000	0.000	0.000
45	0.639	0.410	0.264	0.171	0.111	0.073	0.048	0.031	0.021	0.014	0.009	0.006	0.004	0.003	0.002	0.001	0.001	0.001	0.000	0.000	0.000	0.000	0.000	0.000	0.000
46	0.633	0.402	0.257	0.165	0.106	0.069	0.044	0.029	0.019	0.012	0.008	0.005	0.004	0.002	0.002	0.001	0.001	0.000	0.000	0.000	0.000	0.000	0.000	0.000	0.000
47	0.626	0.394	0.249	0.158	0.101	0.065	0.042	0.027	0.017	0.011	0.007	0.005	0.003	0.002	0.001	0.001	0.001	0.000	0.000	0.000	0.000	0.000	0.000	0.000	0.000
48	0.620	0.387	0.242	0.152	0.096	0.061	0.039	0.025	0.016	0.010	0.007	0.004	0.003	0.002	0.001	0.001	0.001	0.000	0.000	0.000	0.000	0.000	0.000	0.000	0.000
49	0.614	0.379	0.235	0.146	0.092	0.058	0.036	0.023	0.015	0.009	0.006	0.004	0.003	0.002	0.001	0.001	0.000	0.000	0.000	0.000	0.000	0.000	0.000	0.000	0.000
50	0.608	0.372	0.228	0.141	0.087	0.054	0.034	0.021	0.013	0.009	0.005	0.003	0.002	0.001	0.001	0.001	0.000	0.000	0.000	0.000	0.000	0.000	0.000	0.000	0.000

Note that the discount factor, DF_r^t, gives the present value of $1 to be received in t years at a discount rate r%

Table A2 Annuity factors for a series of constant amount to be received in each of t years, given a discount rate of r%: $AF_r^t = \frac{1}{r} - \frac{1}{r \times (1+r)^t}$

Yr	1%	2%	3%	4%	5%	6%	7%	8%	9%	10%	11%	12%	13%	14%	15%	16%	17%	18%	19%	20%	21%	22%	23%	24%	25%
1	0.990	0.980	0.971	0.962	0.952	0.943	0.935	0.926	0.917	0.909	0.901	0.893	0.885	0.877	0.870	0.862	0.855	0.847	0.840	0.833	0.826	0.820	0.813	0.806	0.800
2	1.970	1.942	1.913	1.886	1.859	1.833	1.808	1.783	1.759	1.736	1.713	1.690	1.668	1.647	1.626	1.605	1.585	1.566	1.547	1.528	1.509	1.492	1.474	1.457	1.440
3	2.941	2.884	2.829	2.775	2.723	2.673	2.624	2.577	2.531	2.487	2.444	2.402	2.361	2.322	2.283	2.246	2.210	2.174	2.140	2.106	2.074	2.042	2.011	1.981	1.952
4	3.902	3.808	3.717	3.630	3.546	3.465	3.387	3.312	3.240	3.170	3.102	3.037	2.974	2.914	2.855	2.798	2.743	2.690	2.639	2.589	2.540	2.494	2.448	2.404	2.362
5	4.853	4.713	4.580	4.452	4.329	4.212	4.100	3.993	3.890	3.791	3.696	3.605	3.517	3.433	3.352	3.274	3.199	3.127	3.058	2.991	2.926	2.864	2.803	2.745	2.689
6	5.795	5.601	5.417	5.242	5.076	4.917	4.767	4.623	4.486	4.355	4.231	4.111	3.998	3.889	3.784	3.685	3.589	3.498	3.410	3.326	3.245	3.167	3.092	3.020	2.951
7	6.728	6.472	6.230	6.002	5.786	5.582	5.389	5.206	5.033	4.868	4.712	4.564	4.423	4.288	4.160	4.039	3.922	3.812	3.706	3.605	3.508	3.416	3.327	3.242	3.161
8	7.652	7.325	7.020	6.733	6.463	6.210	5.971	5.747	5.535	5.335	5.146	4.968	4.799	4.639	4.487	4.344	4.207	4.078	3.954	3.837	3.726	3.619	3.518	3.421	3.329
9	8.566	8.162	7.786	7.435	7.108	6.802	6.515	6.247	5.995	5.759	5.537	5.328	5.132	4.946	4.772	4.607	4.451	4.303	4.163	4.031	3.905	3.786	3.673	3.566	3.463
10	9.471	8.983	8.530	8.111	7.722	7.360	7.024	6.710	6.418	6.145	5.889	5.650	5.426	5.216	5.019	4.833	4.659	4.494	4.339	4.192	4.054	3.923	3.799	3.682	3.571
11	10.368	9.787	9.253	8.760	8.306	7.887	7.499	7.139	6.805	6.495	6.207	5.938	5.687	5.453	5.234	5.029	4.836	4.656	4.486	4.327	4.177	4.035	3.902	3.776	3.656
12	11.255	10.575	9.954	9.385	8.863	8.384	7.943	7.536	7.161	6.814	6.492	6.194	5.918	5.660	5.421	5.197	4.988	4.793	4.611	4.439	4.278	4.127	3.985	3.851	3.725
13	12.134	11.348	10.635	9.986	9.394	8.853	8.358	7.904	7.487	7.103	6.750	6.424	6.122	5.842	5.583	5.342	5.118	4.910	4.715	4.533	4.362	4.203	4.053	3.912	3.780
14	13.004	12.106	11.296	10.563	9.899	9.295	8.745	8.244	7.786	7.367	6.982	6.628	6.302	6.002	5.724	5.468	5.229	5.008	4.802	4.611	4.432	4.265	4.108	3.962	3.824
15	13.865	12.849	11.938	11.118	10.380	9.712	9.108	8.559	8.061	7.606	7.191	6.811	6.462	6.142	5.847	5.575	5.324	5.092	4.876	4.675	4.489	4.315	4.153	4.001	3.859
16	14.718	13.578	12.561	11.652	10.838	10.106	9.447	8.851	8.313	7.824	7.379	6.974	6.604	6.265	5.954	5.668	5.405	5.162	4.938	4.730	4.536	4.357	4.189	4.033	3.887
17	15.562	14.292	13.166	12.166	11.274	10.477	9.763	9.122	8.544	8.022	7.549	7.120	6.729	6.373	6.047	5.749	5.475	5.222	4.990	4.775	4.576	4.391	4.219	4.059	3.910
18	16.398	14.992	13.754	12.659	11.690	10.828	10.059	9.372	8.756	8.201	7.702	7.250	6.840	6.467	6.128	5.818	5.534	5.273	5.033	4.812	4.608	4.419	4.243	4.080	3.928
19	17.226	15.678	14.324	13.134	12.085	11.158	10.336	9.604	8.950	8.365	7.839	7.366	6.938	6.550	6.198	5.877	5.584	5.316	5.070	4.843	4.635	4.442	4.263	4.097	3.942
20	18.046	16.351	14.877	13.590	12.462	11.470	10.594	9.818	9.129	8.514	7.963	7.469	7.025	6.623	6.259	5.929	5.628	5.353	5.101	4.870	4.657	4.460	4.279	4.110	3.954
21	18.857	17.011	15.415	14.029	12.821	11.764	10.836	10.017	9.292	8.649	8.075	7.562	7.102	6.687	6.312	5.973	5.665	5.384	5.127	4.891	4.675	4.476	4.292	4.121	3.963
22	19.660	17.658	15.937	14.451	13.163	12.042	11.061	10.201	9.442	8.772	8.176	7.645	7.170	6.743	6.359	6.011	5.696	5.410	5.149	4.909	4.690	4.488	4.302	4.130	3.970
23	20.456	18.292	16.444	14.857	13.489	12.303	11.272	10.371	9.580	8.883	8.266	7.718	7.230	6.792	6.399	6.044	5.723	5.432	5.167	4.925	4.703	4.499	4.311	4.137	3.976
24	21.243	18.914	16.936	15.247	13.799	12.550	11.469	10.529	9.707	8.985	8.348	7.784	7.283	6.835	6.434	6.073	5.746	5.451	5.182	4.937	4.713	4.507	4.318	4.143	3.981
25	22.023	19.523	17.413	15.622	14.094	12.783	11.654	10.675	9.823	9.077	8.422	7.843	7.330	6.873	6.464	6.097	5.766	5.467	5.195	4.948	4.721	4.514	4.323	4.147	3.985

Note that the annuity factor, AF_r^t, (for short, *a*) gives the present value of series of $1 to be received at the end of each of t years at a discount rate r%

(continued)

Table A2 (continued)

Yr	1%	2%	3%	4%	5%	6%	7%	8%	9%	10%	11%	12%	13%	14%	15%	16%	17%	18%	19%	20%	21%	22%	23%	24%	25%
26	22.795	20.121	17.877	15.983	14.375	13.003	11.826	10.810	9.929	9.161	8.488	7.896	7.372	6.906	6.491	6.118	5.783	5.480	5.206	4.956	4.728	4.520	4.328	4.151	3.988
27	23.560	20.707	18.327	16.330	14.643	13.211	11.987	10.935	10.027	9.237	8.548	7.943	7.409	6.935	6.514	6.136	5.798	5.492	5.215	4.964	4.734	4.524	4.332	4.154	3.990
28	24.316	21.281	18.764	16.663	14.898	13.406	12.137	11.051	10.116	9.307	8.602	7.984	7.441	6.961	6.534	6.152	5.810	5.502	5.223	4.970	4.739	4.528	4.335	4.157	3.992
29	25.066	21.844	19.188	16.984	15.141	13.591	12.278	11.158	10.198	9.370	8.650	8.022	7.470	6.983	6.551	6.166	5.820	5.510	5.229	4.975	4.743	4.531	4.337	4.159	3.994
30	25.808	22.396	19.600	17.292	15.372	13.765	12.409	11.258	10.274	9.427	8.694	8.055	7.496	7.003	6.566	6.177	5.829	5.517	5.235	4.979	4.746	4.534	4.339	4.160	3.995
31	26.542	22.938	20.000	17.588	15.593	13.929	12.532	11.350	10.343	9.479	8.733	8.085	7.518	7.020	6.579	6.187	5.837	5.523	5.239	4.982	4.749	4.536	4.341	4.161	3.996
32	27.270	23.468	20.389	17.874	15.803	14.084	12.647	11.435	10.406	9.526	8.769	8.112	7.538	7.035	6.591	6.196	5.844	5.528	5.243	4.985	4.751	4.538	4.342	4.162	3.997
33	27.990	23.989	20.766	18.148	16.003	14.230	12.754	11.514	10.464	9.569	8.801	8.135	7.556	7.048	6.600	6.203	5.849	5.532	5.246	4.988	4.753	4.539	4.343	4.163	3.997
34	28.703	24.499	21.132	18.411	16.193	14.368	12.854	11.587	10.518	9.609	8.829	8.157	7.572	7.060	6.609	6.210	5.854	5.536	5.249	4.990	4.755	4.540	4.344	4.164	3.998
35	29.409	24.999	21.487	18.665	16.374	14.498	12.948	11.655	10.567	9.644	8.855	8.176	7.586	7.070	6.617	6.215	5.858	5.539	5.251	4.992	4.756	4.541	4.345	4.164	3.998
36	30.108	25.489	21.832	18.908	16.547	14.621	13.035	11.717	10.612	9.677	8.879	8.192	7.598	7.079	6.623	6.220	5.862	5.541	5.253	4.993	4.757	4.542	4.345	4.165	3.999
37	30.800	25.969	22.167	19.143	16.711	14.737	13.117	11.775	10.653	9.706	8.900	8.208	7.609	7.087	6.629	6.224	5.865	5.543	5.255	4.994	4.758	4.543	4.346	4.165	3.999
38	31.485	26.441	22.492	19.368	16.868	14.846	13.193	11.829	10.691	9.733	8.919	8.221	7.618	7.094	6.634	6.228	5.867	5.545	5.256	4.995	4.759	4.543	4.346	4.165	3.999
39	32.163	26.903	22.808	19.584	17.017	14.949	13.265	11.879	10.726	9.757	8.936	8.233	7.627	7.100	6.638	6.231	5.869	5.547	5.257	4.996	4.759	4.544	4.346	4.166	3.999
40	32.835	27.355	23.115	19.793	17.159	15.046	13.332	11.925	10.757	9.779	8.951	8.244	7.634	7.105	6.642	6.233	5.871	5.548	5.258	4.997	4.760	4.544	4.347	4.166	3.999
41	33.500	27.799	23.412	19.993	17.294	15.138	13.394	11.967	10.787	9.799	8.965	8.253	7.641	7.110	6.645	6.236	5.873	5.549	5.259	4.997	4.760	4.544	4.347	4.166	4.000
42	34.158	28.235	23.701	20.186	17.423	15.225	13.452	12.007	10.813	9.817	8.977	8.262	7.647	7.114	6.648	6.238	5.874	5.550	5.260	4.998	4.760	4.544	4.347	4.166	4.000
43	34.810	28.662	23.982	20.371	17.546	15.306	13.507	12.043	10.838	9.834	8.989	8.270	7.652	7.117	6.650	6.239	5.875	5.551	5.260	4.998	4.761	4.545	4.347	4.166	4.000
44	35.455	29.080	24.254	20.549	17.663	15.383	13.558	12.077	10.861	9.849	8.999	8.276	7.657	7.120	6.652	6.241	5.876	5.552	5.261	4.998	4.761	4.545	4.347	4.166	4.000
45	36.095	29.490	24.519	20.720	17.774	15.456	13.606	12.108	10.881	9.863	9.008	8.283	7.661	7.123	6.654	6.242	5.877	5.552	5.261	4.999	4.761	4.545	4.347	4.166	4.000
46	36.727	29.892	24.775	20.885	17.880	15.524	13.650	12.137	10.900	9.875	9.016	8.288	7.664	7.126	6.656	6.243	5.878	5.553	5.261	4.999	4.761	4.545	4.348	4.166	4.000
47	37.354	30.287	25.025	21.043	17.981	15.589	13.692	12.164	10.918	9.887	9.024	8.293	7.668	7.128	6.657	6.244	5.879	5.553	5.262	4.999	4.761	4.545	4.348	4.166	4.000
48	37.974	30.673	25.267	21.195	18.077	15.650	13.730	12.189	10.934	9.897	9.030	8.297	7.671	7.130	6.659	6.245	5.879	5.554	5.262	4.999	4.761	4.545	4.348	4.167	4.000
49	38.588	31.052	25.502	21.341	18.169	15.708	13.767	12.212	10.948	9.906	9.036	8.301	7.673	7.131	6.660	6.246	5.880	5.554	5.262	4.999	4.761	4.545	4.348	4.167	4.000
50	39.196	31.424	25.730	21.482	18.256	15.762	13.801	12.233	10.962	9.915	9.042	8.304	7.675	7.133	6.661	6.246	5.880	5.554	5.262	4.999	4.762	4.545	4.348	4.167	4.000

Note that the annuity factor, AF_r^t, (for short, *a*) gives the present value of series of $1 tc be received at the end of each of t years at a discount rate r%

Solutions by Chapter

Chapter 1: Cash and Working Capital

Solution 1.1

Cashflow schedule

	Jan	Feb	March	April	May	June	July	Total
Purchase machine	−100,000							−100,000
Purchase goods		−50,000		−200,000				−250,000
Selling goods			150,000				300,000	450,000

Yearly depreciation:	**$**
Starting value of machine	100,000
Ending value of machine	80,000
Total depreciation	**20,000**

a. Profit:	**$**
Sales	450,000
Cost of sales	-250,000
Gross profit	200,000
Depreciation	-20,000
Net profit	**180,000**

R. Manos et al., *Corporate Finance for Business*,
https://doi.org/10.1007/978-3-030-92419-5

b. Cash flow:	$
Profit	180,000
Add back depreciation	20,000
Cash flow from operations	**200,000**

c. Cash balance @ end of June	$
Starting cash balance	200,000
Purchase machine for cash in Jan.	-100,000
Purchase inventory for cash in Feb & Apr	-250,000
Selling goods for cash in March	150,000
Cash balance at end of June	**0**

Solution 1.2

(a) Providing the machine has no end-of-life salvage value, and that the straight-line method is used, yearly depreciation is £200,000/10 = £20,000.
(b) If annual pre-depreciation profits amount to £50,000, then annual post-depreciation profit is £50,000 – £20,000 = £30,000.
(c) If annual pre-depreciation profits amount to £15,000, then annual post-depreciation profit is £15,000 – £20,000 = –£5,000. The calculation for the yearly depreciation would not change merely because the profit expected per year is lower. Rather, the depreciation should reflect the spreading of the cost of the machine over its useful economic life.
(d) If the useful economic life of the machine was estimated as 5 years, instead of 10, while profits would continue for 10 years, the impact on depreciation, post-depreciation profits and cash flow would be as follows:

Straight line basis	£	
Cost of machine:	200,000	
Useful economic life in years:	5	
(i) Yearly depreciation (years 1–5):	40,000	

(ii) Post depreciation profits	**Years 1–5**	**Years 6–10**
Yearly profit before depreciation:	50,000	50,000
Yearly depreciation:	-40,000	0
Post depreciation profits:	10,000	50,000

(iii) There would be no effect on cash flow

Solution 1.3

	£	£	£
Current liabilities			120,000
Accounts receivable	60,000		
Cash	40,000		
Quick assets		100,000	
Inventory	80,000		
Current assets			180,000
a. Current ratio	**1.50**		
b. Acid-test ratio	**0.83**		
c. Working capital	**60,000**		

Solution 1.4

	$	Days	Months	Comments
Sales	5,000,000			
Cost of goods sold	3,000,000			Direct costs of labour and materials
Inventory	400,000	49	1.6	Divide by Cost of goods sold*
Receivables	300,000	22	0.7	Divide by Sales*
Payables	280,000	34	1.1	Divide by Cost of goods sold*
Gross profit	2,000,000			Sales less Cost of goods sold
Working capital	420,000			Inventory + Receivables – Payables
Working capital cycle		37	1.2	Inventory days + Receivable days – Payable days
Gross profit margin ratio	40%			Sale less Cost of goods sold as percentage of Sales
Cost of goods sold ratio	60%			Cost of goods sold as percentage of Sales
	100%			
Current ratio	2.50	times		(Inventory + Receivables)/Payables
Acid test ratio	1.07	times		Receivables/Payables
Working capital to sales ratio	8.40%			Working capital / Sales

* multiplied by 365 to give number of days

Chapter 2: Basic Capital Project Appraisal

Solution 2.1

(a) Calculating the present value (PV) of a future sum, CF, to be received t years from now, given a rate of interest, r (Please note that the problems here can also be solved with the help of the discount table, A1):

(i)

$$PV = \frac{550}{(1+0.10)^1} = 500$$

(ii)

$$PV = \frac{1,728}{(1+0.20)^3} = 1{,}000$$

(iii)

$$PV = \frac{251}{(1+0.12)^2} = 200$$

(iv)

$$PV = \frac{2,000}{(1+0.08)^9} = 1{,}000$$

(b) Calculating the present value (PV) of an annuity:

Sum	For how many years	Starting in year	Discount rate (%)	Annuity factor	Discount factor	PV = Sum × Annuity factor × Discount factor
200	8	1	12	4.968		993.60
200	20	1	12	7.469		1,493.80
200	50	1	12	8.304		1,660.80
200	30	21	12	8.055	0.104	167.54
200	perpetuity	1	12	8.333		1,666.60

(c) Option (ii) of £2,000 a year for the next 20 years, discounted at 12 per cent a year yields the highest present value:

Cashflow	Number of years	Discount rate (%)	Annuity factor	PV = Sum*Annuity factor
3,000.00	20	20	4.870	14,610
2,000.00	20	12	7.469	14,938
1,000.00	20	3	14.877	14,877

(d) Option (ii) of $700 for 5 years yields higher present value than option (i) of $500 for 7 years:

Sum	Number of years	Discount rate (%)	Annuity factor	PV = Sum*Annuity factor
500.00	7	12	4.564	2,282
700.00	5	12	3.605	2,524

Solution 2.2

(a) The IRR on the project is the discount rate at which the NPV is equal to zero:

year	**0**	**10**
	-463	1000
factor	1	X
	-463	1000X

$-463 + 1000X = 0.$
$X = 0.463.$

Now go to discount factors (Table A1) and go along the year ten row until you find the figure 0.463. This is 8%, which is the IRR. Alternatively, use Excel® with 0 for years 1–9.

(b) Outlay of £5,400 will yield returns of £1,000 a year for 10 years:

(i)

year	**0**	**1-10**
	-5400	1000
factor	1	X
	-5400	1000X

$-5400 + 1000X = 0.$
$X = 5.4.$

Now go to annuity factors (Table A2) and go along the year ten row until you find the figure 5.4. This is approximately 13%, which is the IRR. Alternatively, use Excel® with 1000 for every year 1–10.

(ii)

year	**0**	**1-10**
	-5400	X
Factor at 20%	1	4.192
	-5400	4.192X

$-5400 + 4.192X = 0.$
$X = 1288.$
The annual money returns needed to yield a 20% IRR are 1288.

(c) Finding the present values of various delayed annuities:

Sum	First CF @ EOY	Last CF @ EOY	# Years	Discount rate (%)	Annuity factor	Discount factor	PV = Sum*Annuity factor*Discount factor
1,200.00	3	7	5	20	2.991	0.694	2,491
4,000.00	5	10	6	15	3.784	0.572	8,658
800.00	3	8	6	12	4.111	0.797	2,621
5,000.00	20	40	21	15	6.312	0.07	2,209

(d) Evaluating the NPV of four projects with IRR of 6 per cent:

Initial	Annuity	#Years	Annuity factor			NPV at a discount rate of:		
outlay		of annuity	4%	6%	8%	4%	6%	8%
−4,200.00	997	5	4.452	4.212	3.993	239	−1	−219
−4,200.00	571	10	8.111	7.36	6.71	431	3	−369
−4,200.00	366	20	13.59	11.47	9.818	774	−2	−607

- Using a discount rate lower than 6 per cent (in this case, 4 per cent) increases the NPV of all the projects (to a positive NPV). However, the change in interest rates affect the long-life project most.
- Using a discount rate higher than 6 per cent (in this case, 8 per cent) reduces the NPV of all the projects to a negative figure.

Solution 2.3

End of year	0	1	2	3	4	NPV	Difference in NPV
H cash flows (€)	−1,000	500	400	350	300	139	
J cash flows (€)	−1,000	400	400	400	400	142	3
Payback period						**Payback period**	
H	Accumulated	500	900	1,250		2.29	2 yrs, 4 months

End of year		0	1	2	3	4	NPV	Difference in NPV
J	cashflows (CFs)	400	800	1,200			2.50	2 yrs, 6 months
Discounted PB							**Discounted payback period**	
H discounted cashflows		−1000	435	302	230	172		
J discounted cashflows		−1000	348	302	263	229		
H	Accumulated		435	737	967	1139	3.19	3 yrs, 2 months
J	discounted CFs		348	650	913	1142	3.38	3 yrs, 5 months

Solution 2.4

(a) The NPV of project T is positive and its IRR is greater than the firm's opportunity cost of capital. Both rules, therefore, indicate that the firm should go ahead with it:

End of year	0	1	2	3	4	5
15%	-200,000	70,000	70,000	70,000	70,000	70,000
Discount factor	1.000	0.870	0.756	0.658	0.572	0.497
Present value	**-200,000**	**60,900**	**52,920**	**46,060**	**40,040**	**34,790**
NPV	34,710					
IRR	22.11%					

(b) To obtain the profit from the investment, we need to deduct depreciation. This is calculated on a straight-line basis over the useful economic life of the asset, assumed 5 years:

End of year	0	1	2	3	4	5
Net cashflows	-50,000	20,000	20,000	20,000	20,000	20,000
Depreciation		-10,000	-10,000	-10,000	-10,000	-10,000
Annual increase in profits		**10,000**	**10,000**	**10,000**	**10,000**	**10,000**
Average Accounting Rate of Return	**20%**	(Average yearly profit / Initial investment). Alternatively divide by average value of investment				
Payback period		20,000	40,000	60,000	**2.50**	**2 yrs, 6 months**
Annuity Factor	15%	3.352				
NPV	**17,040**	(– Initial investment + Annual cashflow × Annuity factor)				
IRR (using Excel =irr function)	**28.65%**					

Chapter 3: More on Capital Projects

Solution 3.1

At 20 per cent the NPV is positive, thus the company should go ahead with the project:

	0	1	2	3	4	5
1) Initial investment in fixed assets	-50,000					
2) Initial investment in inventory	-12,000					12,000
3) Sales		80,000	80,000	80,000	80,000	80,000
4) Running costs (depreciation is not a cash item)		-50,000	-50,000	-50,000	-50,000	-50,000
5) Net Cashflow	**-62,000**	**30,000**	**30,000**	**30,000**	**30,000**	**42,000**
6) Discount factor at 20%	1.000	0.833	0.694	0.579	0.482	0.402
7) Present value	-62,000	24,990	20,820	17,370	14,460	16,884
8) NPV	32,524					
9) IRR	41.18%					

Solution 3.2

At 20% the NPV is positive, thus the company should go ahead with the project:

$ Year	0	1	2	3	4	5
Fixed assets	-50,000					
Inventory	-12,000					12,000
After tax sale of asset	1,400					
Sales		80,000	80,000	80,000	80,000	80,000
Running costs		-50,000	-50,000	-50,000	-50,000	-50,000
Tax		-6,000	-6,000	-6,000	-6,000	-6,000
Net cash flow	-60,600	24,000	24,000	24,000	24,000	36,000
Discount factor at 20%	1	0.833	0.694	0.579	0.482	0.402
Present value	-60,600	19,992	16,656	13,896	11,568	14,472
Net Present Value	**15,984**					
IRR	**31%**					

Tax calculation					
"Profit"	30,000	30,000	30,000	30,000	30,000
Depreciation	-10,000	-10,000	-10,000	-10,000	-10,000
Taxable	20,000	20,000	20,000	20,000	20,000
Tax at 30%	**6,000**	**6,000**	**6,000**	**6,000**	**6,000**

To find the figure to which annual pre-tax operating cash inflows could fall before the project is no longer acceptable, we need to find the figure of pre-tax operating cash inflows at which the NPV = 0.

If the exercise is set up in Excel®, this can easily be done automatically, by using the function under '*Data*', '*what if analysis*', '*Goal Seek*'. The answer is 22,363.

Solution 3.3

€000

Year	0	1	2	3	4	5
Machine	-60.0					5.0
Saving		20.0	20.0	20.0	20.0	20.0
Tax		-2.4	-2.4	-2.4	-2.4	-2.4
Net cash flow	-60.0	17.6	17.6	17.6	17.6	22.6
Discount factor at 12%	1	0.893	0.797	0.712	0.636	0.567
Present value	-60	15.7	14.0	12.5	11.2	12.8
Net Present Value	**6.2**					

Tax calculation					
"Profit"	20.0	20.0	20.0	20.0	20.0
Depreciation	-12.0	-12.0	-12.0	-12.0	-12.0
Taxable	8.0	8.0	8.0	8.0	8.0
Tax at 30%	**2.4**	**2.4**	**2.4**	**2.4**	**2.4**

The NPV is positive, so the project should be accepted.

Chapter 4: Risk and Uncertainty

Solution 4.1

(a) The NPV is positive, thus the company should go ahead with the project:

Year	0	1	2	3	4
Initial outlay	-2,000,000				
Yearly rent		-1,400,000	-1,540,000	-1,694,000	-1,863,400
Yearly cost savings		3,000,000	2,850,000	2,707,500	2,572,125
Tax (30%)		-480,000	-393,000	-304,050	-212,618
Cash Flow	-2,000,000	1,120,000	917,000	709,450	496,107
Discount rate (20%)	1.000	0.833	0.694	0.579	0.482
Present value	-2,000,000	932,960	636,398	410,772	239,124
NPV	**219,254**				
IRR	**26.59%**				

(b) Using *'Goal Seek'* under *'What-if-analysis'* in Excel®, the maximum percentage change in each item before the NPV turns negative, yields the following results:

Item	Original value	NPV = 0 value	Change	% change
Initial outlay	−2,000,000	−2,219,254	−219,254	11.0
Rent in first year	−1,400,000	−1,506,900	−106,900	7.6
Percentage yearly reduction in cost savings	−5.00%	−8.45%	−3.45%	69.1
Tax rate	30%	36.94%	6.94%	23.1
Discount rate	20%	26.59%	6.59%	32.9

Solution 4.2

Year	%	0	1	2	3	4
Initial outlay		-2,000,000				
Yearly rent	12.00		-1,800,000	-2,016,000	-2,257,920	-2,528,870
Yearly cost savings	0.00		3,000,000	3,000,000	3,000,000	3,000,000
Tax	25.00		- 300,000	-246,000	-185,520	-117,782
Cash Flow		**-2,000,000**	**900,000**	**738,000**	**556,560**	**353,348**
Discount rate	20.00	1.000	0.833	0.694	0.579	0.482
Present value		-2,000,000	749,700	512,172	322,248	170,314
NPV		**-245,566**				
IRR		**12.35%**				

Solution 4.3

(a) Bloomingdale's can enter a forward agreement to buy €500,000 in three-months' time which it will then use to pay for the contract with Officine Générale. Under the forward agreement, it will buy €500,000 in three months at the forward rate of \$1.21/€. In Bloomingdale's local currency this amounts to €500,000*\$1.21/€ = \$605,000, which is known today and will not change regardless of what happens to the EUR/USD spot exchange rate by the time the payment is due.

Alternatively, Bloomingdale's may purchase a Call option. In that case there are two payments to be made and the actual cost in local currency is not certain (although the company knows the maximum cost). Specifically, Bloomingdale's will pay immediately the premium on the option, €500,000*\$0.01/€ = \$5,000. In addition, in three-months' time, the firm would exercise the option if the spot exchange rate is above the exercise price of \$1.22/€. In that case, the cost to Bloomingdale's in local currency terms would be: €500,000*\$1.22/€ = \$610,000. While this is clearly more expensive than the forward hedge, it is important to note that if the EUR decreases in value versus the USD (as reflected in the forward rate), then the option would not be exercised. In that case it would be cheaper to buy euros on the market. For example, if the spot exchange rate between the EUR and the USD in three-months' time is \$1.19/€, then the local cost of purchasing €500,000 is: €500,000*\$1.19/€ = \$595,000.

(b) There may be several reasons for a European fashion house to establish operations in the United States rather than selling its top brands via American outlets such as Bloomingdale's. For example, it is a way to get a solid handle on the US market for the company's products. In particular, if the firm wants to expand its sales in the United States, it should recruit American people who understand the American culture. Furthermore, by establishing an office in the United States, not only can this be good for understanding the culture, but it can also serve practical needs like housing excess inventory and samples.

Chapter 5: Corporate Borrowing

Solution 5.1

	a	b	c
Perpetuity	6	6	6
Discount rate	12%	10%	15%
Present value = payment/(discount rate)	50	60	40

Solution 5.2

$$PV = \frac{100 \times 4\%}{\text{interest rate}}$$

	a	b(i)	b(ii)
Coupon rate on government bonds	4%	4%	4%
Current/Present value of government bonds	60.00	80.00	133.33
Interest rate/yield to maturity	6.67%	5%	3%

Solution 5.3

a) Using Excel® and writing 0 for years 1–9:

year	0	10
	-853	1000

The IRR, and therefore the YTM, is 1.6%

b)

year	0	5
Current price/redemption value	-X	1000
factor at 1.5%	1	0.928
	-X	928

$-X + 928 = 0$
$X = 928$
Price = 928

Solution 5.4

a)

year	0	1	2	3
Interest		5	5	5
Current price/redemption value	-105			100
Total cash flows	-105	5	5	105

IRR from Excel® = 3.22%
The discount rate at which the current price is equal to the present value of future payments.

b) (i)

year	0	1	2
Interest		5	5
Current price/redemption value	-X		100
Total cash flows	-X	5	105
factor at 3%	1	0.971	0.943
	-X	4.86	99.02

$-X + 4.86 + 99.02 = 0$
$X = 103.88$
Market Price = £103.88

b) (ii) The current yield is 5/103.88 = 4.8%

Chapter 6: Ordinary Share Capital

Solution 6.1

(a) The Dow Jones Industrial Average (DJIA) is a stock market index of leading companies that are listed on stock exchanges in the United States. The DJIA is a narrow index which includes only 30 companies. This can be contrasted with the S&P500 index, another popular stock market index, which tracks 500 large companies listed on US stock exchanges. The DJIA is a price-weighted index, which means that the weight of each component in the index is based on the price of its stock. Again, this can be contrasted with the S&P500 index which is a value-weighted index where the weight of each component in the index is based on its market value. Three companies in the DJIA, as of 2021 include Coca-Cola, Intel and 3M (see https://www.cnbc.com/dow-30/ for a current list of components).

(b) Market capitalization is the total value of the shares of the company and is arrived at by multiplying the stock price by the total number of outstanding shares. For example, if the company has 10 million shares, currently trading at \$20 a share, then its market capitalization would be 10m × \$ 20 = \$ 200m. Market capitalization facilitates comparisons between companies and reflects the market's perception regarding the value of the company. While market capitalization is based on the value of all the company's shares, free-float market capitalization is based on the number of shares available for trading by the public, excluding shares not readily available for trading such as those held by the company's executives.

Solution 6.2

(a) Dividend yield: \$2/\$20 = 10%
(b) Capital gain yield: (\$25 − \$20)/\$20 = 25%
(c) Total return: 10% + 25% = 35%

Solution 6.3

(a) The profit on the short position is: (20*\$300) − (20*250) = \$1000
(b) The loss on the short position is: (20*\$300) − (20*330) = −\$600

Solution 6.4

(a) For each alternative, calculate the total number of shares after the issue, the market price per share and the value of the rights.

	(a) 3 for 2	(b) 1 for 4
Current market capitalization	240m × £3.30 = £792m	240m × £3.30 = £792m
Number of new shares	240m ÷ 2 × 3 = 360 m	240m ÷ 4 × 1 = 60m
Total raised	360m × £0.50 = £180m	60m × £3 = £180m
i. Total number of shares after issue	240m + 360m = 600m	240m + 60m = 300m
ii. New market price per share	(£792m + £180m) ÷ 600m = £1.62	(£792m + £180m) ÷ 300m = £3.24
iii. Value of rights (per new share)	£1.62 – £0.50 = £1.12	£3.24 – £3 = £0.24

(b) Calculate the position of Olivia Knox and Colin Berry.

Olivia Knox, taking up the rights	(a) 3 for 2	(b) 1 for 4
Holding pre-issue	2,000 × £3.30 = £6,600	2,000 × £3.30 = £6,600
Number of new shares	2,000 ÷ 2 × 3 = 3,000	2,000 ÷ 4 × 1 = 500
Cost of taking up rights	3,000 × £0.50 = £1,500	500 × £3 = £1,500
Total number of shares after issue	2,000 + 3,000 = 5,000	2,000 + 500 = 2,500
Total value of holding after issue	5,000 × £1.62 = £8,100	2,500 × £3.24 = £8,100
Net increase in wealth	£8,100 – £6,600 – £1,500 = £0	£8,100 – £6,600 – £1,500 = £0

Colin Berry, selling the rights	(a) 3 for 2	(b) 1 for 4
Holding pre-issue	2,000 × £3.30 = £6,600	2,000 × £3.30 = £6,600
Number of new shares	2,000 ÷ 2 × 3 = 3,000	2,000 ÷ 4 × 1 = 500
Income from selling the rights	3,000 × £1.12 = £3,360	500 × £0.24 = £120
Total number of shares after issue	2,000	2,000
Total value of holding after issue	2,000 × £1.62 = £3,240	2,000 × £3.24 = £6,480
Net increase/decrease in wealth	£3,240 – £6,600 + £3,360 = 0	£6,480 – £6,600 + £120 = 0

Chapter 7: Cost of Capital

Solution 7.1

(a) ABC: $k_e = 2.5\% + 1.2 \times 6\% = 9.7\%$
(b) DEF: $8\% = r_f + 0.75 \times 6\% \rightarrow r_f = 8\% - 4.5\% = 3.5\%$
(c) GHI: $16.5\% = 4.5\% + \beta_{GHI} \times 8\% \rightarrow \beta_{GHI} = (16.5\% - 4.5\%) \div 8\% = 1.5$
(d) JKL: $8.8\% = 4\% + 0.8 \times MRP\% \rightarrow MRP\% = (8.8\% - 4\%) \div 0.8 = 6\%$
(e) MNO: $10\% = 4\% + 0.75 \times MRP\% \rightarrow MRP\% = (10\% - 4\%) \div 0.75 = 8\%$

$4\% + (2 \times 0.75) \times 8\% = 16\%$, an increase of $16\% - 10\% =$ 6 percentage points

Solution 7.2

(a) MD Enterprises: Price today $= \frac{6p}{0.15-0.05} = 60p$
(b) MD Enterprises: Price today $= \frac{4p}{0.20-0.02} = 22p$
(c) PLQ: $k_e = \frac{Div_1}{Price} + g = 0.05 + 0.08 = 0.13 = 13\%$
(d) RST: $g = k_e - \frac{Div_1}{\text{price today}} = 0.144 - 0.10 = 0.044 = 4.4\%$
(e) UVW: price today $= \frac{Div_1}{k_e - g} = \frac{Div_1}{2 \times g - g} = \frac{Div_1}{g}$

$$g = \frac{Div_1}{\text{price today}} = \frac{12c}{240c} = 5.00\%$$

Solution 7.3

(a) XY: $WACC = \frac{E}{E+D} \times k_e + \frac{D}{E+D} \times k_d = \frac{60}{60+20} \times 12\% + \frac{20}{60+20} \times 6\% = 10.5\%$
(b) ZA: $12\% = 15\% \times W_E + 6\% \times (1 - W_E) \rightarrow W_E = \frac{12\% - 6\%}{15\% - 6\%} = 67\%,\ W_D = 33\%$
(c) BC: $12\% = \frac{70}{70+30} \times k_e + \frac{30}{70+30} \times 5\% \rightarrow k_e = \frac{12\% - 5\% \times 0.3}{0.7} = 15\%$

Solution 7.4

Based on book values: $WACC = \frac{400}{400+200} \times 12\% + \frac{200}{400+200} \times 6\% = 0.67 \times 12\% + 0.33 \times 6\% = 10\%$.

Based on market values: $WACC = \frac{600}{600+200} \times 12\% + \frac{200}{600+200} \times 6\% = 0.75 \times 12\% + 0.25 \times 6\% = 10.5\%$.

Chapter 8: Capital Structure

Solution 8.1

(a) The Return on Equity (RoE) and the interest cover for Laurel & Hardy for Year 1 & Year 2:

(in millions of £, unless otherwise indicated)	Year 1			Year 2		
	%	Laurel	Hardy	%	Laurel	Hardy
Capital		120	120		120	120
Debt Ratio		15%	60%		15%	60%
Debt		18	72		18	72
Equity		102	48		102	48
RoCE (Return on Capital Employed)		25%	25%		7.50%	7.50%
PBIT (Profit before interest & tax= Capital * RoCE)	25	**30**	**30**	7.50	**9**	**9**
Interest	10	1.8	7.2	10	1.8	7.2
PBT (Profit before tax)		**28.20**	**22.80**		**7.20**	**1.80**
Tax	30	8.46	6.84	30	2.16	0.54
PAT (Profit after tax)		**19.74**	**15.96**		**5.04**	**1.26**
Return on Equity (PAT/Equity)		19.35%	33.25%		4.94%	2.63%
Interest Cover (PBIT/Interest)		16.67	4.17		5.00	1.25

(b) $\frac{0.7(x-1.8)}{102} = \frac{0.7(x-7.2)}{48}$

$x = 12.$

so PBIT $= 12.$

So ROCE is $\frac{12}{120} = 10\%$

An alternative way to find the level of Return on Capital Employed at which the Return on Equity for the two companies is the same, is to use the function 'goal seek' in Excel®. For this purpose, you need to pursue the following steps:

1. Set the table of calculations in Excel® as shown here:

	A	B	C	D	E	F	G
1	(in millions of £, unless otherwise indicated)		Year1			Year2	
2			**Laurel**	**Hardy**		**Laurel**	**Hardy**
3	Capital		120	=C3		=C3	=D3
4	Debt Ratio		0.15	0.6		0.15	0.6
5	Debt		=C3*C4	=D3*D4		=F3*F4	=G3*G4
6	Equity		=C3-C5	=D3-D5		=F3-F5	=G3-G5
7							
8	RoCE (Return on Capital Employed)		0.25	=C8		0.075	=F8
9							
10	**PBIT (Profit before interest & tax = Capital * RoCE)**	=C8	**=C3*B10**	**=D3*B10**	=F8	**=F3*E10**	**=G3*E10**
11	Interest	0.1	=C5*B11	=D5*B11	0.1	=F5*E11	=G5*E11
12	**PBT (Profit before tax)**		**=C10-C11**	**=D10-D11**		**=F10-F11**	**=G10-G11**
13	Tax	0.3	=C12*B13	=D12*B13	0.3	=F12*E13	=G12*E13
14	**PAT (Profit after tax)**		**=C12-C13**	**=D12-D13**		**=F12-F13**	**=G12-G13**
15	Return on Equity (PAT/Equity)	=C15-D15	=C14/C6	=D14/D6	=F15-G15	=F14/F6	=G14/G6
16	Interest Cover (PBIT/Interest)		=C10/C11	=D10/D11		=F10/F11	=G10/G11

2. Once this is set, go to '*Data*', '*What-if-analysis*', '*Goal seek*' and set the cell B15 (difference in RoE for year 1) and E15 (difference in RoE for year 2) to *Zero*, by changing the value in cell C8 (RoCE for year 1) and F8 (RoCE for year 2).

The answer is RoCE of 10 per cent:

(in millions of £, unless otherwise indicated)	Year 1			Year 2		
		Laurel	Hardy		Laurel	Hardy
Capital		120	120		120	120
Debt Ratio		15%	60%		15%	60%
Debt		18	72		18	72
Equity		102	48		102	48
RoCE (Return on Capital Employed)		10%	10%		10%	10%
PBIT (Profit before interest & tax = Capital * RoCE)	10%	**12**	**12**	10%	**12**	**12**
Interest	10%	1.8	7.2	10%	1.8	7.2
PBT (Profit before tax)		**10.20**	**4.80**		**10.20**	**4.80**
Tax	30%	3.06	1.44	30%	3.06	1.44
PAT (Profit after tax)		**7.14**	**3.36**		**7.14**	**3.36**
RoE (Return on Equity = PAT/Equity)	0%	7.00%	7.00%	0%	7.00%	7.00%
Interest Cover (PBIT/Interest)		6.67	1.67		6.67	1.67

Solution 8.2

(in millions of $, unless otherwise indicated)		Year 1			Year 2	
	%	Borg	McEnroe	%	Borg	McEnroe
Capital		1000	1000		1000	1000
Number of shares		1500	1500		1500	1500
Debt Ratio		5%	20%		5%	20%
Debt (Capital*Debt Ratio)		50	200		50	200
Equity		950	800		950	800
Book value per share (Equity/Number of shares)		0.633	0.533		0.633	0.533
Operating Profit		**90**	**90**		**135**	**135**
Interest (Debt*interest rate)	15	7.5	30	15	7.5	30
PBT (Profit before tax)		**82.50**	**60.00**		**127.50**	**105.00**
Tax (PBT*tax rate)	40	33	24	40	51	42
PAT (Profit after tax)		**49.50**	**36.00**		**76.50**	**63.00**
(i) Return on Equity (PAT/Equity)		5.21%	4.50%		8.05%	7.88%
(ii) Earnings per share (PAT/number of shares), in cents		3.3	2.4		5.1	4.2
(iii) Interest Cover (PBIT/Interest)		12.00	3.00		18.00	4.50

Solution 8.3

(a) For each alternative calculate earnings per share and interest cover.

(in millions of €, unless otherwise indicated)		Now	Alternative 1	Alternative 2
Operating profit		150	200	200
Interest (under alternative 2, debt of 300 is raised at 12% interest)		20	20	56
Profit after interest		**130**	**180**	**144**
Tax (the tax rate of 40% is applied to profit after interest to arrive at tax liability)		52	72	57.6
Profit after tax (PAT)		**78**	**108**	**86.4**
Number of shares (under alternative 1, 120 new shares are issued)		600	720	600
Current share price		3		
(i)	**Earnings per share (PAT/number of shares), in cents**	**13**	**15**	**14.4**
(ii)	**Interest cover (operating profit / interest)**	**7.5**	**10**	**3.57**

(b) $\frac{0.6(x-20)}{720} = \frac{0.6(x-56)}{600}$.

$x =$ €236 m. This is the operating profit.

Alternatively, to find the level of operating profit at which earnings per share would be the same under the alternative financing proposals, one can use the function 'goal seek' in Excel®. For this purpose, you need to pursue the following steps:

i. Set the table of calculations in Excel® as shown here:

	A	B	C	D	E	F
1.	(in millions of €, unless otherwise indicated)			**Now**	**alternative 1**	**alternative 2**
2.	Operating profit			150	200	= E2
3.	Interest	300	0.12	20	= D3	= D3 + B3*C3
4.	**Profit after interest**			**= D2 – D3**	**= E2 – E3**	**= F2 – F3**
5.	Tax	0.4		= D4*B5	= E4*B5	= F4*B5
6.	**Profit after tax (PAT)**			**= D4 – D5**	**= E4 – E5**	**= F4 – F5**
7.	Number of shares	120		600	= D7 + B7	= D7
8.	Current share price			3	2.5	= D8
9.	**(i) Earnings per share (PAT/number of shares)**	**= E9 – F9**		**= D6/D7**	**= E6/E7**	**= F6/F7**
10.	**(ii) Interest cover (operating profit / interest)**			**= D2/D3**	**= E2/E3**	**= F2/F3**

ii. Once this is set, go to '*Data*', '*What-if-analysis*', '*Goal Seek*' and set the cell B9 (the difference between earnings per share under the two alternatives) to *Zero*, by changing the value in cell D2 (current operating profit).

The answer is €236m operating profit:

(in millions of €, unless otherwise indicated)	**Now**	**alternative 1**	**alternative 2**
Operating profit	150	236	236
Interest	20	20	56
Profit after interest	**130**	**216**	**180**
Tax	52	86.4	72
Profit after tax (PAT)	**78**	**129.6**	**108**
Number of shares	600	720	600
Current share price	3	2.5	3
(i) Earnings per share, in Euro cents (PAT/number of shares)	**13**	**18**	**18**
(ii) Interest cover (operating profit / interest)	**7.5**	**11.8**	**4.21**

Solution 8.4

a. Here are the calculations for the comparison of the two-alternative financing:

(in millions £, unless otherwise indicated)	Now	After expansion Rights	Borrow
Annual operating profit (EBIT)	54.00	60.00	60.00
Interest (debt*interest rate)	9.00	9.00	11.40
Profit Before Tax (PBT)	45.00	51.00	48.60
Tax	13.50	15.30	14.58
Profit After Tax (PAT)	31.50	35.70	34.02
i. Earnings per Share in p(EPS) = PAT/number of shares	15.75	16.23	17.01
ii. Interest cover = EBIT/interest payment	6.00	6.67	5.26
iii. Debt ratio = Debt / (Debt + Equity)	20.00%	18.75%	25.00%

b. To find the level of profit before interest and tax (EBIT) at which EPS would be the same under the alternative financing proposals, solve the following equation:

$\frac{0.7(x-9)}{220} = \frac{0.7(x-11.4)}{200}$.

$x = 35.40$. This is the EBIT.

Solution 8.5

From the dividend growth model:

$$k_e = \frac{d_1}{p} + g$$

but because the dividend payout is 100%, g = 0 (Remember, g = Retention Ratio * Return on Equity. The retention ratio is zero – all profits are paid out as dividends).

So, in this case:

$$k_e = \frac{d_1}{p}$$

Note that d_1 and p can stand for the dividend per share and the price per share respectively, or for the total dividends and the market capitalisation of the firm, respectively.

	With debt	All equity
Profit before interest	1,000,000	1,000,000
Interest @ 5%	(400,000)	0
Profit after interest	600,000	1,000,000
Dividend	(600,000)	(1,000,000)
Retained	0	0

k_e with all equity = 1,000,000/16,000,000 = 6.25% [The market capitalisation is now the original £8m plus the new share capital of £8m.]

As there is no debt, the WACC must also be equal to 6.25% - the same as when the debt ratio was 50%.

(a) (ii)

	Now	All equity
Dividend received	6,000	10,000
Interest on £80,000* @ 5%	(0)	(4,000)
Net Income	6,000	6,000

* The investor buys 1% of the new shares issued (£8m) by taking out a loan at 5%. They now have "personal gearing" of 50%, and therefore the same level of risk as when the company itself was geared.

(b) (i)

The value of a perpetuity is the annual cash flow divided by the discount rate: 70,000/0.0625 = 1,120,000.

However, it is received from the end of year 2 onwards, so we have:-

Year	1
Investment	(1,000,000)
Perpetuity value	1,120,000
Net	120,000
Factor at 6.25%	0.941
NPV	112,920

The NPV is positive so the project should be accepted.

(b) (ii)

The value of the firm should theoretically increase by the NPV of the project: £16,000,000 plus £112,920 = £16,112,920. In reality, many factors influence the value of the firm, possibly including, here, the temporary change of dividend policy.

(b) (iii)

Dividend payments from Year 2 onwards are £1,000,000 plus £70,000 = £1,070,000.

(b) (iv)

Market value of investor's equity (1%)	161,129
Sale of shares in Yr 1 to equal "normal" dividend	(10,000)
Remaining value	151,129
% holding remaining (151,129/16,112,920)	0.938%
Annual dividends received from year 2 onwards (0.938%)	10,037
Less interest on loan	(4,000)
Net income from year 2 onwards	6,037

By selling some of their shares and decreasing their holdings in the firm's equity from 1% to 0.938%, the investor generated 'home made dividends'. But despite the reduction in the percentage of holdings, their yearly net income from year 2 onwards has increased from 6,000 to 6,037. This is of course due to the firm investing in a positive NPV project.

Chapter 9: Valuing Companies: Acquisitions and Mergers

Solution 9.1

in £ million	Year 0
Immediate capital investment	-5
Sell Snapdragon assets	1
Net initial investment	**-4**

		Years 1–10/15
Cash inflow on Snapdragon		4
Cash inflow arising from economies of scale		2
Less regular fixed capital investments per year		-2.5
Net yearly cashflow		**3.5**
Discount rate	12%	

	#Years	Discount factor	NPV (£ million)
a. horizon period (in years) of:	10	5.650	15.78
b. horizon period (in years) of:	15	6.811	19.84

Solution 9.2

(in millions, unless otherwise stated)	Now	Equity financing	Debt financing
Current debt	30	30	30
Current Equity (#shares*Book Value per share + Retained Earnings)	90	90	90
New Debt raised			50
New Equity raised (#new shares * issue price)		50	
i. Debt to debt plus capital ratio (debt to capital ratio)	**25.00%**	**17.65%**	**47.06%**
Current interest payment (debt*interest rate)	3	3	3
Additional interest payment (new debt * interest rate)			6
Current PBIT	25	25	25
Additional PBIT		10	10
ii. Interest cover (PBIT/Interest)	**8.33**	**11.67**	**3.89**
Current number of shares	100	100	100
Additional shares		40	
Profit before tax (PBT = PBIT - interest)	22	32	26
Tax (PBT-tax)	6.6	9.6	7.8
Profit after tax (PAT = PBT-tax)	15.4	22.4	18.20
iii. Earnings per share, in $ (PAT/#shares)	**0.154**	**0.160**	**0.182**

Solution 9.3

Year	**0**	**1**	**2**	**3**	**4**	**5**
Cashflow		8	9	10	11	12
Increase in cashflow		4	4	4	4	4
Investment	-10	-3	-3	-3	-3	
Net cashflow	**-10**	**9**	**10**	**11**	**12**	**16**
Discount factor at 10%	1.000	0.909	0.826	0.751	0.683	0.621
Present value	**-10.00**	**8.18**	**8.26**	**8.26**	**8.20**	**9.93**
NPV	**32.84**					

Figures in £ million, unless otherwise indicated.

Other possible methods of valuation include price/earnings multiple or asset values.

Solution 9.4

Company	Coca-Cola	PepsiCo
Earnings per share (based on most recent earnings)	1.870	5.920
Earnings per share (based on analysts' expectations for next year)	2.360	6.580
Market price per share	56.800	154.430
Market capitalization (billion $)	245.184	213.439
Number of shares, billion (market capitalization / market price per share)	**4.317**	**1.382**
Historic price to earnings ratio (market price/ historic EPS)	**30.374**	**26.086**
Forward price to earnings ratio (market price/ anticipated EPS)	**24.068**	**23.470**

It appears that the two companies have more or less the same PE ratio, but that the PE of Coca-Cola is slightly higher. If the difference was greater, an investor considering buying one of these companies would have been facing the task of determining the reason for that. One possibility is that Coca-Cola was too expensive (over-valued), while PepsiCo was a bargain (under-valued) to be invested in. Alternatively, maybe the low PE of Pepsi was an indication of an increased risk for the company, while the high PE of Coca-Cola was an indication of high prospects for growth.

Chapter 10: Putting It All Together

Year	0	1	2	3	4
Cost of demolishing existing buildings	-3,000,000				
Opportunity cost of not selling site	-7,000,000				
Cost of building the new factory	-4,000,000				
Cost of repair and maintenance					-1,500,000
Sales (selling price*volume)		10,000,000	12,000,000	24,600,000	20,500,000
Variable costs (cost per unit*volume)		-4,500,000	-5,400,000	-10,800,000	-9,000,000
Fixed costs		-2,200,000	-2,200,000	-2,200,000	-2,200,000
Working capital	-1,000,000	-200,000	-1,260,000	410,000	0
Less tax		175,000	-850,000	-2,650,000	-1,700,000
Total	**-15,000,000**	**3,275,000**	**2,290,000**	**9,360,000**	**6,100,000**

Note that the $200,000 overheads should not be included as these are not incremental.

Workings:	0	1	2	3	4
Change in working capital:					
Working capital (paid at start of year)		1,000,000	1,200,000	2,460,000	2,050,000
Change in working capital	**-1,000,000**	**-200,000**	**-1,260,000**	**410,000**	
Tax:					
Profit (sales – variable & fixed costs)		3,300,000	4,400,000	11,600,000	7,800,000
Less depreciation on factory		-1,000,000	-1,000,000	-1,000,000	-1,000,000
Less cost of demolition		-3,000,000			
Taxable profit		-700,000	3,400,000	10,600,000	6,800,000
Tax		**-175,000**	**850,000**	**2,650,000**	**1,700,000**

Problem 10.2: Debt	
10.2.a Price p/bond (PV at the yield to maturity of 10 years of interest + repayment of face value on the 10th year)	**926.40**
Market value of debt (Price* Number of bonds)	92,640,000
Market value of equity (Price*Number of shares)	160,000,000
Total market value of the firm (market value of debt + market value of equity)	252,640,000
10.2.b Gearing ratio: Debt/(Debt + Equity)	**36.67%**

Problem 10.3: Equity	%
Cost of equity using the Dividend Growth Model: Cost of equity = $(Div_0*(1+g)/Price)+g$	14
Cost of equity using CAPM: Cost of equity = Risk free + Beta*Market Risk Premium	16
Average cost of equity	**15**

Problem 10.4.a: WACC

	Weight (%)	**After tax cost** (%)	**WACC** (%)
Debt	36.67	4.50	1.65
Equity	63.33	15	9.49
			11.14

Problem 10.4.b: Present value as of year 4 of the net cashflows from year 5 to year 10:	
Use Annuity Table to get an approximate factor, or in Excel® use the formula: = PV(rate, nper, pmt). Using the data we have: = (11.14%, 6, −6,000,000)	**25,278,822**

Problem 10.4.c: Calculating the NPV of the project

Year	0	1	2	3	4
Net cashflows, years 0–4	−15,000,000	3,275,000	2,290,000	9,360,000	6,100,000
PV as of year 4 of cashflows for years 5–10					25,278,822
Total net cashflows	−15,000,000	3,275,000	2,290,000	9,360,000	31,378,822
Discount rate	1.000	0.900	0.810	0.728	0.655
Present value	−15,000,000	2,946,648	1,853,827	6,817,522	20,563,843
NPV	**17,181,840**				
IRR	**40%**				

Index

R. Manos et al., *Corporate Finance for Business*,
https://doi.org/10.1007/978-3-030-92419-5

The manufacturer's authorised representative in the EU is Springer Nature Customer Service Centre GmbH, Europaplatz 3, 69115 Heidelberg, Germany. If you have any concerns regarding our products, please contact ProductSafety@springernature.com

Printed and bound by CPI Group (UK) Ltd, Croydon, CR0 4YY
30/09/2026
02225495-0009